Managing to improve public services

How are public service organizations governed? How is performance in such organizations measured, managed and improved?

Public services play a central role in the well-being, sustainability and growth of communities, cities and nations. *Managing to Improve Public Services* shows how management can be harnessed to improve a range of public services (e.g. policing, health, local government) by examining them through different theoretical lenses (e.g. governance, innovation and change, performance metrics and management). It advances both theory and practice, beyond traditional public administration and 'new public management', by considering the inter-relationships between governance and public management. The book is written by a group of leading social science and management specialists, who were awarded the prestigious ESRC/EPSRC Public Service Fellow awards as part of the Advanced Institute of Management Research initiative. It will be of interest to graduate students, academics and policy-makers involved in public service management and performance measurement.

Jean Hartley is Professor of Organizational Analysis at the Institute of Governance and Public Management, Warwick Business School, University of Warwick.

Cam Donaldson is the Health Foundation Chair in Health Economics and Director of the Institute of Health and Society, Newcastle University Business School.

Chris Skelcher is Director of Research for the School of Public Policy and Professor of Public Governance at the Institute of Local Government Studies, University of Birmingham.

Mike Wallace is Professor of Public Management at Cardiff Business School, Cardiff University.

Managing to improve public services

Edited by

Jean Hartley,

Cam Donaldson,

Chris Skelcher

and

Mike Wallace

CAMBRIDGE UNIVERSITY PRESS
Cambridge, New York, Melbourne, Madrid, Cape Town, Singapore, São Paulo, Delhi

Cambridge University Press
The Edinburgh Building, Cambridge CB2 8RU, UK

Published in the United States of America by Cambridge University Press, New York

www.cambridge.org
Information on this title: www.cambridge.org/9780521708272

First published 2008

Printed in the United Kingdom at the University Press, Cambridge

A catalogue record for this publication is available from the British Library

Library of Congress Cataloguing in Publication data
Managing to improve public services / edited by Jean Hartley ... [et al.].
    p.   cm.
ISBN 978-0-521-86641-5 (hdbk) – ISBN 978-0-521-70827-2 (pbk)
1. Public administration – Management.   2. Public administration – Management – Evaluation.
I. Hartley, Jean, 1953–
JF1351.M352   2008
351–dc22

                                                                                    2008026926

ISBN-13 978-0-521-86641-5 hardback
ISBN-13 978-0-521-70827-2 paperback

Contents

List of figures   *page* viii
List of tables   ix
List of contributors   x
Preface
Robin Wensley   xiii
List of abbreviations   xv

Introduction   1

1   The agenda for public service improvement
     Jean Hartley and Chris Skelcher   3

Part I: Governance and accountability   25

2   Does governance perform? Concepts, evidence, causalities
     and research strategies
     Chris Skelcher   27

3   Performativity, management and governance
     Paul M. Collier   46

4   A critical assessment of performance measurement for policy
     making
     Michael Pidd   65

5   Priority setting in the public sector: turning economics into a
     management process
     Cam Donaldson, Angela Bate, Craig Mitton, Stuart Peacock and Danny Ruta   88

Part II: Performance metrics   113

6   Public service productivity: new approaches to performance
    measurement in health sectors
    Mary O'Mahony, Philip Stevens and Lucy Stokes   115

7   Performance measurement systems and the criminal justice
    system: rationales and rationalities
    Barbara Townley   134

8   Valuing public sector outputs
    Rachel Baker, Helen Mason, Cam Donaldson and Michael Jones-Lee   153

9   The use of geodemographics to improve public service
    delivery
    Paul A. Longley and Michael F. Goodchild   176

Part III: Managing innovation and change   195

10 The innovation landscape for public service
    organizations
    Jean Hartley   197

11 Innovation type and organizational performance: an empirical
    exploration
    Richard M. Walker and Fariborz Damanpour   217

12 Public service failure and turnaround: towards a contingency
    model
    George Boyne   236

13 Orchestrating complex and programmatic change in the public
    services
    Mike Wallace and Michael Fertig   257

Postcript

279

14   Conclusions: current themes and future directions
      for research
      Cam Donaldson, Jean Hartley, Chris Skelcher and Mike Wallace   281

      Index   289

Figures

4.1   Feedback control – a cybernetic metaphor   *page* 76
4.2   Grid : group classification   79
4.3   Professionalism and public service workers   81
5.1   The public sector scorecard (Moulin 2004)   102
5.2   Model of PBMA process   105
6.1   Public and private per-capita health expenditure in the EU and US,
      2000   121
6.2   Life expectancy at 65 years and expenditure on health, in $PPP per
      capita and as a percentage of GDP   124
6.3   Age-standardized death rates (SDR) for major illnesses and
      expenditure on health   124
9.1   Visual labelling of the 'City Adventurers' type of the 2001 Mosaic
      UK classification (© Experian Ltd)   179
10.1 Relationships between innovation and improvement (Hartley
      2005)   206
11.1 Governance, management, policy and performance   218
13.1 Three aspects of complex and programmatic change   270

Tables

2.1	Governance concepts: analytical distinctions	*page* 28
2.2	Performance domains: analytical distinctions	29
2.3	Theoretical relationships between modes of governance and performance domains	32
4.1	Hofsted (1981) on control	77
5.1	Five questions about resource use	94
5.2	Seven stages in a PBMA priority setting exercise	96
5.3	Broad review criteria for Best Value	104
6.1	Health systems: the EU and the US	119
6.2	Life expectancy in the EU and US	123
6.3	Ratio of WHO attainment and health levels to health expenditure	126
9.1	Results of geodemographic profiling local policing strategies, using the Mosaic geodemographic classification. (source: Ashby 2005)	186
11.1	Descriptive data of measures used in multiple regression models	225
11.2	Innovation measures, descriptive data and Cronbach alphas	226
11.3	Relationships between organizational innovation and internal and external measures of organizational performance	228
11.4	Relationships between process and service innovations with internal and external measures of organizational performance	229
11.5	Relationships between process and service innovations with internal and external measures of organizational performance, controlling for prior performance	230
12.1	Failing English public services 2002–4	238
13.1	Tentative characteristics of complexity of single and programmatic change	266

Contributors

Rachel Baker
Institute of Health and Society
Newcastle University

Angela Bate
Institute of Health and Society
Newcastle University

George Boyne*
Cardiff Business School
Cardiff University

Paul M. Collier*
Monash University, Melbourne Australia

Fariborz Damanpour
Rutgers University, New Jersey

Cam Donaldson*
Institute of Health and Society,
Newcastle University and Newcastle
University Business School

Michael Fertig
University of Bath

Michael Goodchild
University College London

Jean Hartley*
Institute of Governance and Public
Management, Warwick Business School
University of Warwick

Michael Jones-Lee
Newcastle University Business School

Paul A. Longley*
University College London

Helen Mason
Institute of Health and Society
Newcastle University

Craig Mitton
Faculty of Health and Social
Development, University of British
Columbia (Okanagan)

Mary O'Mahony*
Birmingham Business School, University
of Birmingham and National Institute of
Economic and Social Research

Stuart Peacock
British Columbia Cancer Research
Centre, British Columbia Cancer Agency
Vancouver

Michael Pidd*
Lancaster University Management
School

Danny Ruta
Director of Public Health, Newcastle
Primary Care Trust and Newcastle City
Council

Chris Skelcher*
INLOGOV, Birmingham University

Philip Stevens
Medium Term Strategy Group, Ministry of Economic Development, New Zealand

Lucy Stokes
National Institute of Economic and Social Research

Barbara Townley*
University of St Andrews

Richard M. Walker*
Cardiff Business School and Hong Kong University

Mike Wallace*
Cardiff Business School, Cardiff University

Robin Wensley
Director, ESRC/EPSRC Advanced Institute of Management Research (AIM), and Institute of Governance and Public Management, Warwick Business School, University of Warwick

* Denotes this person is an AIM Public Service Fellow.

Preface

Robin Wensley

The AIM Public Service Fellows initiative

This book arises from the bold experiment of the ESRC, supported by the EPSRC, in setting up the Advanced Institute of Management (AIM) research initiative and in particular the funding of 11 Public Service Fellowships. AIM is an innovatory approach to creating conditions for synergy amongst management researchers through their collaborative efforts to inform research investment in high-priority areas of national policy. AIM was established in order to increase significantly the contribution of, and future capacity for, world-class UK management research. In specific terms this means supporting research that will identify actions to enhance the UK's international competitiveness (with the public services having a key role in this as explained later); to raise the quality and international standing of UK research on management, to expand the size and capacity of the active UK research base on management; and to engage with practitioners and other users of research within and beyond the UK as co-producers of knowledge about management. AIM, within the UK, consists of 289 Fellows, of whom 11 are Public Service Fellows, 41 Research Fellows and 62 Scholars. There are also 74 International Visiting Fellows attached to the AIM network.

The AIM Public Service Fellowships were developmental in that Fellows were appointed, for a period of a year (for between 60 and 100 per cent of their time), not for a specific project but to develop theory and research in their personal stream of activities and associated outputs in key areas of national priority. Thus, the Public Service Fellows initiative was not an ESRC programme (where projects are generally selected to cover a field or to complement each other). Each Fellow undertook demonstration projects, case studies, quantitative analysis of large databases, systematic reviews of evidence, and the development of new techniques. They worked on a wide range of public services where there are large disbursements from the public purse (e.g. education, health, local government, criminal justice).

While each Fellow had his or her own speciality to pursue, the work was enhanced by interdisciplinary collaborative work through a series of working group seminars. Each Fellow presented work at least once at these seminars and this work was subjected to constructive scrutiny from the other Fellows, from a range of disciplinary, epistemological and methodological perspectives. Management research is inevitably an interdisciplinary field, and the seminars enhanced the process and hopefully the outputs of this dialogic enquiry for each of the Fellows. International Visiting Fellows, from the USA, Canada, the Netherlands, South Africa and Australia, helped to broaden the scope of individual Fellows' work, either in comparative research (not all of which is reported here) or in exploring the opportunities and limitations on generalizing from UK research.

AIM Public Service Fellows' work has been explored in a range of workshops and seminars with central government departments and agencies, and a range of local public services, consistent with the AIM mission to undertake research which contributes to UK competitiveness. Fellows have produced a number of practitioner reports and academic papers. Copies of the former and detailed references to the latter can be found along with further information about all AIM activities at the AIM website (www.aimresearch.org). AIM Fellows have also shared their skills with other academics in capacity-building conferences and seminars. The work presented in this book reports on some key themes from the Fellowships. We hope that this contributes to the knowledge about, and practice of, public management both through the detailed study of substantive areas and also in the shaping of questions and themes for further research.

Abbreviations

A4R	Accountability for Reasonableness
ACORN	A Classification Of Residential Neighbourhoods
AIM	Advanced Institute of Management
ARD	age-related disease
BV	Best Value
CBA	cost–benefit analysis
CDC	Center for Disease Control (US)
CEA	cost-effectiveness analysis
CHR	Calgary Health Region
CJS	criminal justice system
CPA	Comprehensive Performance Assessment
CPS	Crown Prosecution Service
CSP	core service performance
CUA	cost-utility analysis
CV	contingent valuation
CWOI	cost-weighted output index
DALE	disability-adjusted life expectancy
DCE	discrete choice experiment
DfT	Department for Transport
EQ-5D	five-dimensional health state classification system
GIS	geographical information systems
GP	general practitioner of medicine
IHD	ischaemic heart disease
IPDS	Integrated Personal Development System
IRMP	Integrated Risk Management Plan
K-S4	Kindergarten–Senior Four Agenda
NHS	National Health Service
NICE	National Institute for Health and Clinical Excellence
NIM	National Intelligence Model
NPM	new public management

NSF	National Service Framework
OAC	Output Area Classification
PACE	Police and Criminal Evidence Act
PAR	participatory action research
PBMA	programme budgeting and marginal analysis
PCT	primary care trust
PF	Procurator Fiscal
PI	performance indicator
PM	performance management
PMDU	Prime Minister's Delivery Unit
PPP	purchasing power parity
PSA	Public Service Agreement
QALY	quality-adjusted life year
RAE	Research Assessment Exercise
RSS	Royal Statistical Society
SDR	age-standardized death rates
SG	standard gamble
VOSL	value of statistical life
VPF	value of a prevented fatality
WHO	World Health Organization
WTP	willingness to pay

Introduction

1 The agenda for public service improvement

Jean Hartley and Chris Skelcher

Introduction

The global focus on improving public services reflects a rediscovery of their central role in the well-being, sustainability and growth of communities, cities and nations. This new awareness of the social, economic and cultural contribution of government, public organizations and public services has resulted in a significant period of reform and experimentation. At the heart of these initiatives is the idea that improvements to the ways in which public services can be governed, managed and delivered will produce improved outcomes for citizens. This idea is driving different kinds of reform initiatives in different parts of the world. For example, in the UK, there has been a major process of management reform aimed at enhancing the capacity of public services to deliver improved outcomes for citizens (Newman, 2001; Stoker 2004). In contrast, the post-Soviet states of central and eastern Europe are building democratic governance to guide and steer public services in new ways (Campbell and Coulson 2006).

The field of public service improvement is one in which there are important questions to be answered at the theoretical, conceptual and practical levels. For example, one issue arises from the use of public–private partnerships, co-production with civil society organizations, and other new governance arrangements. These developments open up questions about the extent to which such new organizational forms deliver benefits of innovation, efficiency and responsiveness, as well as their impact on processes of steering and accountability in a democratic context. A second, longer term problem is to understand the conditions under which improvement strategies, and their implementation in complex settings, make a difference to the performance of public services. We need evidence-based theories of the relationships between managerial and political leadership, organizational culture and structure and relevant outputs and outcomes to do so. A third and related question concerns the extent to which metrics can be created and applied such that decisions can be better informed and changes in performance can be tracked and managed. This moves into the politics of performance management as well as the methodology of choice valuation and efficiency measurement. There are, of course, other questions to be addressed. But these give a flavour of the leading-edge public service improvement issues dealt with in this volume and their significance for political, managerial and academic audiences.

The purpose of the book is to build new understandings of managing public service improvement. It does this by using a multi-disciplinary approach to explore the governance, management and performance dimensions of public service improvement and their intersection in various fields of policy. One focus is the contribution of 'public management' as an activity of professionals, managers, and political decision-makers (whether elected or appointed). It is located within the new and growing transatlantic research community who are addressing the question of when, how and why management matters to public service performance (e.g. Lynn *et al.* 2001; Boyne 2003; Lynn 2006). But the book widens the debate by examining the introduction and sustainability of change in large complex systems. There is also a strong focus on the politics and measurement of public service performance, including the application of economic approaches to decision-making and efficiency measurement.

This chapter sets the context. First, we explore the issue of why public services matter. This provides a reference point for the subsequent chapters, grounding them in the reality of public services' contribution to the well-being of societies. Second, we elaborate the governance–management–performance–policy framework which we have developed in this book and show how these dimensions all connect to public service improvement. Third, we use this framework to outline the contribution of the various chapter authors and to show how their work connects with the overall agenda of public service improvement.

Why public services matter

Globally, public services have emerged from a period of considerable criticism and devaluing. This period of challenge to public services and the role of government generally was generated by the rise of neo-liberal ideologies in the 1980s and 1990s. These ideologies promoted market solutions above state provision and led to substantial privatization and disinvestments in public services. Now, in the early years of the twenty-first century, a new settlement between state and society has emerged. This more refined version of neo-liberalism recognizes the role of government and public services in creating stable social and economic conditions, but in a new coalition with business and civil society actors.

Public services are important in a number of ways. First, they matter because of their scale. Public services still consume a major part of GDP. Jackson (2003), using OECD data, notes that the ratio of government spending to GDP across the OECD countries in 2000 was 37 per cent, just over a third of GDP. He also notes that the relative size of the public sector in most OECD countries was greater in 2000 than it had been in 1980, despite the attempts to 'roll back the frontiers of the state' under the Thatcher and Reagan administrations in the UK and USA. Indeed, the UK was slightly above the OECD average, with the public sector consuming 38 per cent of GDP in 2000. In recent years there has been a substantial increase in UK public expenditure, particularly for health and school education services and consequently, by 2005, 45 per cent of GDP was consumed by the public sector (Pettigrew 2005).

Public services are therefore 'big business' when it comes to expenditure, employment, organization size, investment, and the production of goods and services. In employment terms, for example, over 5.8 million employees, or 20.2 per cent of total employment in the UK, worked in some part of the public sector in 2006. Of these, 2.9 million worked in local government (National Statistics 2006). The National Health Service is also a substantial employer, with over 1 million employees across the UK. While the civil service was 'downsized' in the early 1980s, there still remain 558,000 direct employees (National Statistics 2006). The criminal justice system, the armed services and other parts of the public service also employ substantial numbers.

This analysis of employment is based on direct employees. However it is also necessary to include the workforce providing public services in contracted-out services, such as some street cleaning and prisons, in privatized services such as water, electricity and railways and in hybrid organizations which are a mixture of public support and private services, such as universities and some museums and art galleries. Ferlie *et al.* (2005) and Benington (2000) amongst others have pointed to the increasing inter-relationships between the public, private and voluntary sectors in the design and provision of public services. Public sector and public services are no longer co-terminous.

Public services are critical to the competitiveness of a nation. The welfare state is an important part of the public services; but so too is the role they play in building the conditions and infrastructure for an entrepreneurial and prosperous private sector, and for the integrity of the nation state. At a local level, public sector organizations (such as the health service and the local authority) may be the largest employers and have a significant impact on the local economy and on regeneration (Geddes 2001). On a larger, national scale, governments provide 'positive freedom goods' such as education, health, pensions and unemployment benefits which enable a country to develop economically (Jackson 2003). Governments also provide other infrastructure to support manufacturing and commercial development such as roads and transport, business development, labour market training, trading regulations and inspections and so forth. It is not surprising that global institutions such as the World Bank and the United Nations Development Programme see 'good governance' as central to effective economic and social progress in developing countries (UNDP 2002). Marquand (2004) also notes the crucial role of the public sphere in producing collective rules by which a society agrees to be governed (including the rules that govern markets, trading and aspects of international relations).

The above maps out the scale and range of functions of the public service sector, but different societies, different political and economic viewpoints and different ideologies will all affect the normative question about its appropriate role and scope within a fair, prosperous and sustainable society (cf. Pollitt and Bouckaert 2004; Massey and Pyper 2005).

There are, of course, challenges to the perspective on public services as a sizeable and influential part of society and the economy. There are at least two sets of arguments which propose that, academically, an interest in public services is either outdated or else is so straightforward as to warrant little attention. Certain political theories (e.g. the Chicago and Austrian schools of neo-liberal economics), with particular though not exclusive resonance in the USA, maintain that 'big government' is anathema to a free and prosperous society. These theories hold that public services should be limited only to situations of clear market failure (or anticipated failure), and that, where state services do have to exist, clear controls over public servants through, for example, performance targets are essential. This thinking has influenced the New Right (see Denham 1996), which emphasizes the primacy of the market, with smaller and more efficient public services. Neo-liberal economics and public choice theory has been one element of the 'new public management' which has swept many parts of the world, particularly the Anglo-Saxon countries.

The second argument concerns the publicness of public services and also links to 'new public management', though from a different intellectual quarter. There has been a marked export of general management ideas (and fashions) into the particular context of public service organizations in a range of countries over the last two decades (Pollitt and Bouckaert 2004). This has taken place on the grounds that management is underpinned by certain general principles and practices which can be applied across a range of businesses, organizations and sectors. This 'convergence' view of the public and private sectors makes the implementation of management ideas and practices as straightforward (or as problematic) as the use of management ideas and practices in the private sector, and makes the study of the impact of the public sector context on management irrelevant as a consequence.

Both of these perspectives about 'big government' and the ubiquity of general management theory have shaped both rhetoric and practice in the last twenty years and are still influential. But they are now out of kilter with the prevailing approach in the UK, many European countries and around the world. Public services are back on the agenda as a positive feature of a society, but in a new set of relationships with business and civil society groups. The management of public services is recognized as distinct because it must operate in a complex political environment, with due regard to questions of legitimacy, accountability and social outcomes. We now explore this issue in more detail, given the centrality of public management to the agenda of this volume and the importance of sustainable management capacity to the practice of public service improvement.

Distinctive features of public service management

The particular conditions and tasks of government and public services have a direct impact on their management (Ranson and Stewart 1994), but so too does generic management theory. In public service management, we see a distinctive form of general management. Furthermore, as the boundaries between the public, private and not-for-profit organizations become increasingly permeable (Ferlie *et al.* 2005), there will be new kinds of interchange and adaptations between management in the various sectors.

A number of features of public service organizations and their associated governance arrangements make them distinctive from private sector organizations with, therefore, divergent implications for aspects of management and management theory.

Public service organizations do not choose their markets, but are obliged to provide services to anyone who meets the eligibility criteria (e.g. anyone living in a particular locality or anyone with particular needs). Private sector organizations, in contrast, may be under a contractual obligation to public body commissioners to provide services, but they are free to exit from the contract at any time, albeit with penalties if prior to the end of the contract. Furthermore, public organizations may have to provide not only services but also remind people of duties as unwilling 'customers', because they can use state authority to require citizens to submit to obligations, such as criminal prosecutions, planning regulations or environmental health.

Furthermore, public services are under the formal control of politicians (either directly in the case of national or local government, or more indirectly in the case of health organizations and some other public services), and the associated policy context. Politicians themselves are elected representatives of wider constituencies and stakeholders, with a democratic mandate to represent the whole, which includes future generations as well as the current population. This means that public management, operating to take account of the political and policy context, is inextricably linked to governance issues. The fact that services are funded primarily through the public purse means that there is the potential for a high level of debate, accountability and scrutiny – not to mention contested values and priorities – which may all affect the management of public organizations.

Public organizations also operate in arenas of 'market failure' or where the market is thought to be unlikely to operate effectively in the short or longer term. Global warming, other environmental challenges, terrorism and the ageing of the population are examples of such complex and cross-cutting challenges, where government is often expected to play a lead role. Of course, there may be a role for private organizations in addressing part of the challenge, often in partnership with public organizations, e.g. technology companies addressing alternative sources to fossil fuels, but the overall management of the challenges is generally in the hands of government and its agencies and those organizations with a remit to orchestrate the response across a range of stakeholders. The role, or sometimes duty, of public service organizations to address broad social and economic questions means that

There are more stakeholders with a greater variety of interests, and the stakeholders are more present. The boundaries between organizations and the external environment are more permeable . . . Public management is at least as much about managing the external environment as about managing the internal organization (Feldman 2005: 959).

Rainey and Chun (2005) also point to the salience of the external context as predicating certain conditions for the management of public service organizations.

The salience of the external environment is also related to purpose – while private sector organizations have principal aims of profit and market domination and development, public organizations primarily aim to produce not profit or market positioning but 'public value' (Moore 1995; Benington and Moore in press). Public value means what is added to the public sphere and this may be social or economic, or it may be political, environmental or even more broadly about quality of the life. The unit of analysis of benefit may not therefore necessarily be the single organization and its outputs but also extends to consideration of outcomes across an 'institutional field' (Moore 2005). For example, schools may not be just concerned with examination results but with developing broadly educated and informed citizens capable of contributing to society. (Private sector organizations may also contribute to public value, for example, through innovation, philanthropy or service delivery but this is rarely a primary objective.) In addition, a public value perspective requires examining the impact of public services on 'customers' and users but also the impact on them as citizens.

From this brief consideration of public management we may conclude that there are some differences in context that either only exist in public organizations or that exist to a greater degree in public organizations (Ranson and Stewart 1994; Kelman 2005). This suggests that generic management theory may not be universally applied, but rather that there are some issues which require consideration of context and circumstance. Pettigrew (2005) supports this when he states: 'The process of public transformation cannot be explained just by appeals to managerial action and associated drives for efficiency and effectiveness. Context does matter, space and time do matter in accounting for the emergence and fate of public sector reforms' (p. 976).

The application of management theory may therefore be neither solely generic nor solely specific, but contextualized or contingent. There may be some circumstances where the application of management theory and practices is directly relevant to public service organizations. For example, some of the micro-management processes of improving operations management, aspects of quality management, methods to improve efficiency and so forth may be directly applicable (see Longley and Goodchild, chapter 9). In other circumstances, generic management theories and techniques may require modification to fit services which are complex, obligatory or in the public eye. For example, theories about ways to manage turnaround in public organizations may benefit from thinking about private sector analogues, but also require drawing on wider theory, such as institutional theory, to understand the choices facing 'failing' public service organizations (see Boyne, chapter 12). In other circumstances again, the use of private sector theory and practices may be helpful up to a point but could actually be misleading if the particular context is not carefully appraised. For example the concepts of strategy, or leadership, or innovation (see Hartley, chapter 10 on this last) require an understanding of the roles of politicians and the public as well as the internal management processes of the organization. Again, an inter-organizational or institutional, not just organizational, perspective is part of this picture.

This leads to a realist position about management theory in particular contexts, which means examining what works, for whom and in what circumstances (Pawson and Tilley 1997) and an explanation of why this may be the case. And in order to assess whether management theory is generic or specific, we have to pay attention to the governance context and arrangements (how the organization is being steered and how decisions are being made) and to the external environment including the policy context more broadly. These are likely to have an impact on the ways in which problems are conceptualized and framed, and addressed. Townley (chapter 7) explores some of these issues in her analysis of different rationalities governing performance management.

Public services improvement

One approach to defining public service improvement is to measure change in performance against pre-defined standards. While this is how some organizations' improvement is judged, for example, in ministerial speeches and in parts of the media, this is a rather narrow definition. Conformance to a standard ignores both whether the standard is appropriate and also whether achievement of a standard can be sustained over a period of time. Achieving sustainable change, which is likely to involve organizational learning to achieve ongoing responsiveness and potential adaptation to changing circumstances and contexts, may be crucial. Thus, a wider view of improvement includes considerations of sustainability and capacity for future change to meet the dynamic needs of a changing society.

Furthermore, this approach detracts from the complex environment in which public services operate, where definitions of performance, let alone improvement, are contested by multiple groups of stakeholders. Public service organizations are often aiming to address wide challenges in society (for example, the health of the nation, patterns of migration in Europe, minimizing crime and the fear of crime); the degree of improvement cannot be assessed simply by the achievements of an individual organization or service unit, but rather is better assessed through the achievements of the whole institutional field (the set of hospitals or schools, etc.).

Finally, public service organizations are instruments of the state, and their effectiveness is partially dependent on citizens' trust of and engagement with the democratic elements of the state. Public service organizations therefore need to be judged not only in terms of their ability to 'deliver' services but also their contribution to creating a fair and just society.

There has been any number of prescriptions for public service improvement, not only within the UK but around the world, with policy and practice proposals from central government departments, think-tanks, public service peak organizations and from management consultancies and political parties. New structures have been established to 'drive' reform, such as, in the UK, the Prime Minister's Delivery Unit. Pollitt and Bouckaert (2004), taking an international view, note that reforms, transformations and restructuring have been endemic in public services but that the most recent phase is distinctive in being explicitly international with an international vocabulary, giving the impression of a unitary approach to 'modernization' of public services, but in fact concealing a hereterogeneity of activities and consequences. They also note that the approaches have 'a degree of political salience that mark them out from the more parochial or technical changes of the preceding quarter century' (p. 24). In the UK, politicians have staked their reputation on improving public services, across all political parties, and improvement continues to be a high priority. This is likely to be so for the foreseeable future.

The reasons for the continuing emphasis on public service improvement are multiple and varied. Globalization and the pressures of remaining competitive in a global market-place are analysed by some academics (Benington and Moore, in press), along with continuing fiscal pressures. Socio-demographic and geodemographic changes, including an ageing population and changes in the composition of the family, are important in many different national settings and at a range of spatial scales (Longley and Goodchild, chapter 9). Changing expectations from the public themselves, with more disposable income and with experience of some customer-responsive and post-Fordist commercial services, and with changing attitudes to authority, have also shifted the standards by which public services are judged by both the public and the media.

Governments have adopted a number of distinct approaches to public service improvement. In the UK, an early period of blame, name and shame by politicians and policy advisors (the semtex in Benington's (2000) phrase 'carrot and semtex') had a limited shelf-life as an improvement strategy both because it did not directly tackle improvement and also because in the longer term it was counter-productive for the finger-pointers (Pollitt and Bouckaert, 2004). A Cabinet Office document (2006) outlines four main approaches to improvement and examines their strengths and weaknesses. These are: the use of competition; the use of performance measurement and management; citizen/user engagement; and organization development and capacity-building. Each of these domains has a number of mechanisms designed to 'drive' improvement and each also has a strong management component, which will be examined in more detail below. In the following section, we provide a conceptual framework to help make sense of the range, utility and applicability of the initiatives on offer.

A framework for understanding public service improvement

The chapters in this book are conceptualized within a larger framework, which sees public service improvement arising from the interplay of governance, management and performance in particular policy contexts.

Governance provides the source of legitimacy and authority for public services. It concerns the arrangements for establishing values, identifying needs, establishing the public purpose, and overseeing and monitoring performance and improvement through management action. Management is a system for harnessing and using organizational resources for public purposes, and for producing performance outcomes and improvements, some of which can be assessed through performance metrics. Outcomes include those for citizens and users of services as well as the procedures of management and organization. These management processes take place in distinctive policy contexts. Such policy contexts may be highly professionally defined (as in the police and health fields) or more complex and less well structured, as in urban regeneration and poverty reduction.

Each of the chapters in this book addresses management as a central theme, but also examines the inter-relationships between the themes of governance, context and performance. We turn to examine the contested concepts of management, governance, performance metrics and policy contexts in the following sections, outlining some key research questions and avenues for further exploration, both in this book and in the longer term.

The irreducible management component of improvement

The centrality of management as a means to achieve improvement is indicated by the review of sources of public service improvement analysed by Boyne (2003). He examined evidence from sixty-five quantitative empirical studies in key international journals, grouping findings on the basis of five theoretical perspectives on improvement: resources, regulation (e.g. legislation, audit and inspection), markets (the role of competition), organization (e.g. size and the mixed economy of provision) and management. Only management and resources showed a significant relationship with public service improvement. Qualitative analysis (e.g. Rainey 1997; Rainey and Steinbauer 1999) also points to the value added by management in effective public service organizations. It appears, then, that management matters (Lynn *et al.* 2001).

Yet, what is meant by 'management'? This is a word with a variety of meanings. For some, public management has introduced an emphasis on discretion, proactive decision-making and resource allocation by officials that was not part of the traditional concept of 'public administration' (Bovaird and Löffler 2003; Hughes 2003; Pollitt and Bouckaert 2004; Massey and Pyper 2005). Hughes (2003) argues that 'there is more involved than merely a change of name. Once the conception of management is adopted, a series of changes follows, including: changes to accountability, external relations, internal systems and the conception of government itself' (p. 7). Public administration, with its semantic roots in ministration, or service, has been seen to be about 'how governments make decisions and apply or enforce those decisions' (Massey and Pyper 2005; 4), with a focus particularly on the large departments and bureaucracies of state. It is seen as particularly concerned with the implementation of policies made in the legislative arm of government through established policies and procedures. Public management came to be associated with activities of leadership and particularly activities and systems with a focus on results. Clarke and Newman (1997) argue that the phrase 'public management' tends to be associated with a different set of symbols and meanings from public administration, signalling ideological as well as technical debates.

For other writers (Hughes 2003; Massey and Pyper 2005), public management is seen as synonymous with 'new public management' (NPM). New public management is an ideologically rooted cluster of activities, techniques and aims adopted in the UK public service reforms of the 1980s and 1990s

(Hood 1991), and subsequently found in a number of variants around the world (Batley and Larbi 2004; Pollitt and Bouckaert 2004). Any number of academics have now analysed the goals, activities and processes of 'new public management' (Pollitt 2000; McLaughlin *et al.* 2001; Newman 2001; Ferlie *et al.* 2005; Massey and Pyper 2005) and have broadly characterized this as the application of particular private sector management techniques to the public service sector, often underpinned by a neo-liberal and public choice theoretical framework. In NPM, there is a strong emphasis on markets and market-like mechanisms (such as contracting out services, market testing of service delivery and private finance initiatives); decentralization and the development of semi-autonomous agencies; a greater emphasis on performance management, more devolved financial management, and an emphasis on making the public services more efficient through a host of generic management techniques and activities.

While NPM is sometimes used as a shorthand for the means to achieve 'modernization' and public service reform, Pollitt (2000) has argued that the overall core features vary somewhat between different analysts and that the evidence for the success of NPM in terms of the claimed benefits is ambiguous or deficient. Pollitt and Bouckaert (2004) also note that there is no single prescription which is relevant to all the countries that have undertaken public service reform or improvement, and they therefore argue for the significance of the particular context and history in understanding 'what works, for whom and in what circumstances', to adopt a realist perspective (Pawson and Tilley 1997).

Recently, a number of writers have argued that as governments have now moved beyond NPM to experiment with other approaches to public management, further theorizing is needed in order to understand the changing relationships between state, market and civil society that have an influence on management ideas and practices (e.g. Benington 2000; Newman 2001; Stoker 2006). There is a growing awareness of the importance of societal outcomes, the recognition of the limitations of government in addressing complex, long-term social and economic issues on its own, and the need to address declining engagement in democracy and trust in government. This has led policy-makers and managers to place a greater emphasis on partnerships between the private and public sectors (along with the voluntary sector) as a means to plan, design and deliver services, and sometimes to fund services as well. The UK has been a particularly fruitful area for these ideas (Sullivan and Skelcher 2002). Some governments have also placed greater emphasis on citizen or user engagement in service planning and there is a greater interest in the co-production of services (e.g. Alford, in press). These developments are being theorized in terms of 'networked governance' (Benington 2006; Klijn and Skelcher 2007).

Four chapters in this volume explore the role of management in more detail. They give a particular emphasis to leading and managing organizational change and innovation, examining how managers and other stakeholders perceive and act in relation to these elements of the organization and its environment.

Wallace (chapter 13) explores the complex changes entailed in large-scale high-profile government initiatives with local consequences, and argues for the importance not only of management in its traditional conception of planning and control, but in a wider role of orchestration of the goals, interests, plans and activities of a wide range of stakeholders (both managers and others) across a variety of organizations. In this situation, change may be emergent as much as planned and shaping innovation becomes important. The concept of orchestration is a theme relevant to a number of the chapters in this book and particularly in the context of 'networked governance', where many organizations may interact in complex ways to achieve services.

The wider institutional context is also examined in Boyne's analysis of the variety of management strategies and tactics used to achieve turnaround of those organizations that are deemed to be failing by central government and its agencies (chapter 12). This chapter shows that managing the turnaround process requires managers to pay attention to external institutional relations (particularly but not exclusively with central government) and also shows the limits of the impact of managerial action on the achievement of planned outcomes. The management of influence and managing with political awareness become key skills in complex change with uncertain outcomes. This is also true of innovation, as one particular type of change.

Two chapters on innovation and its varied links to improvement are provided by Hartley (chapter 10) and Walker and Damanpour (chapter 11). Both chapters draw from but go beyond the private sector literature, showing the need to take context into account in considering the management of innovation. They highlight the need for research that is focused on the public services, of which there is still a serious shortage. Each chapter shows that there is a variety of strategies for, and catalysts of, innovation, and that there is a clear need to consider not just product but also process (e.g. service, organizational, governance, inter-organizational) innovations. While innovation ideas and development may emanate from managers and staff inside the organization, others are initiated by policy-makers, while others still are shaped by normative and mimetic institutional forces between organizations. The diffusion of innovation is particularly important for public service organizations in order to spread good practice in the public sphere. Not only is the immediate impact of innovation on performance nuanced but also there are important research questions about how the benefits and risks of innovation are weighed up, given that the benefits may be long term, contested by different stakeholders, and may be realized by organizations other than the originator.

These chapters all challenge the assumptions of change as rational, formal and without risk. They examine ways in which improvement can be managed to be deep and sustainable, not just superficial and transient, to meet external expectations.

Governance and accountability for improvement

It is difficult to consider public management without paying attention to governance issues, as several chapters show, because the concepts are so related. Kooiman (2003) has defined governing as

The totality of interactions, in which public as well as private actors participate, aimed at solving societal problems or creating societal opportunities; attending to the institutions as contexts for these governing interactions; and establishing a normative foundation for all these activities (p. 4).

Keohane and Nye (2000) formulate governance as 'the processes and institutions, both formal and informal, that guide and restrain the collective activities of a group' (p. 37). Governance is therefore a means of social coordination but gives rise to further questions about the modes of governance across a society and also the corporate structures and cultures in organizations that are responsible for making and implementing public policy (Skelcher, chapter 2).

Forms of public service governance have expanded significantly in the last decade, with appointed boards, multi-organizational partnerships, public interest companies, and various other corporate forms found alongside more traditional elected bodies (Skelcher 2005). Hill and Lynn (2005) have argued that 'the focus of administrative practice is shifting from hierarchical government towards greater reliance on horizontal, hybridized and associational forms of governance'. These shifts, in line with other changes associated with 'networked governance' (see earlier) have implications for management, both in terms of processes and also potentially in terms of the performance of the organization. Hierarchical government has been able to harness the use of state authority as well as resources to achieve outcomes, sometimes coercively (e.g. through legislation about taxation and military service powers) and sometimes through its claim to have a democratic mandate to proceed. But the shift towards achieving societal goals through partnerships with the private, voluntary and community sectors means that influence becomes a significant strategy (Hartley and Allison 2000) as well as (sometimes instead of) formal hierarchical authority. This has implications for the ways in which managers undertake their tasks and the organizations and partnerships within which they do this. In Moore's (1995) terms, the authorizing environment which gives consent to action is dynamic not static. Hill and Lynn (2005) have raised some key questions about governance research, including questions about how governance factors influence the practice of public management (administrative structures, managerial tools, or values and strategies). There is considerable work to be undertaken to explore the inter-relationships between governance and public management.

Skelcher, in chapter 2, examines how governance impacts on performance, and vice versa. He highlights the implicit assumption in public service reforms that changes to governance arrangements will impact positively on performance outcomes. His analysis finds limited empirical support for this assumption, and proposes a number of alternative relationships between these two variables. Collier examines a related issue in chapter 3. He shows how police professionals mandated to manage performance are caught in a series of tensions between upward accountability to governance structures and the downward discretion of frontline operational activity. Pidd, in chapter 4, develops this theme by examining the variety of paradoxical functions that performance data are expected to play in governing and managing public service organizations, revealing both the links and tensions that this creates in the relationship between governance and management. These chapters also implicitly problematize the notion of 'strong leadership' which has informed some of the public service improvement debates in the UK.

Performance metrics

The UK is a particularly rich source of theory and data about performance and improvement, though other countries also have valuable data for comparative analysis. In policy terms, there has been a strong emphasis on performance targets, indicators and measures, as part of the approach by central government to 'drive' improvement across a wide range of public services. Performance measures and indicators have been used to construct league tables, measures of comprehensive performance assessment, and they form the basis of the extensive audit and inspection regimes which have burgeoned over the last two decades, and especially since the late 1990s (Power 2003; Downe and Martin 2007). In a society such as the UK, with a strongly centralized governmental system, performance is relevant not only for resources but also for the reputation and influence of individual organizations and services.

Much previous research on performance has examined the relationship between policy and management without examining impacts, or else has focused on management processes (for example, strategy, leadership, management of staff) but without necessarily linking these to performance (Boyne 2003). This is also an issue for generic management research, where the links between management processes and outcomes are still insufficiently investigated (Hartley 2002; Wall *et al.* 2004). A number of the chapters in this book contribute to remedying the gap by examining both the concept of performance and also the ways in which performance is measured, managed and reported. There is, as a number of chapters show here, a need to problematize the data as well as its interpretation. Longley and Goodchild (chapter 9) illustrate those activities that are required to build data pertaining to the needs, aspirations and behaviours of citizens and consumers into public service decision support systems in a wide range of international settings.

Data derived from indicators and measures may be neither reliable nor valid in relation to actual service performance. O'Mahony *et al.* (chapter 6) show both the constraints on, and also opportunities for, constructing measures of efficiency and effectiveness from data of variable quality, suggesting that this is a perennial problem for policy-makers and managers and is not restricted to the public service sector. Their work at the national and European level, and that of Donaldson *et al.* (chapters 5 and 8) in their analysis of priority-setting and valuation in health organizations, both show that policy and managerial implications about value, and hence efficiency and effectiveness, do not arise in an automatic, rational fashion from the data but require understanding and interpretation. Townley (chapter 7) provides additional insights by showing that a variety of rationalities may be applied to the same set of data, leading to potentially quite divergent conclusions. Different stakeholders may have different (and multiple) purposes in wishing to use, promote or conceal performance measures, illustrated vividly by Collier (chapter 3) in his analysis of police services, police authorities and the Home Office. Performance reporting, particularly to central government with its close grasp on resources, may also influence which data are gathered and the ways in which such data are interpreted.

Far from being a 'magic bullet', performance measurement has both strengths and weaknesses in terms of improving services, as the chapters in this book show. Indeed, the UK central government emphasis on performance measurement has not resulted in the scope, scale or sustainability of change that had been anticipated by policy-makers (Cabinet Office, 2006). In particular, there may be a danger that performance targets emphasize conformance to standards at the expense of organizational learning, thereby reducing the capacity of the organization to address future challenges or to innovate. For Pidd, in chapter 4, government has a 'Pandora's box' and not a 'magic bullet' as performance measurement considered as a system has conflicting aims and impacts. He explores the paradox that part of the rationale for publishing performance data is to provide information to the public at large and to reassure the public about the quality of (or improvement in) public services but that the publication may often have unintended and perverse consequences for public reassurance.

Policy contexts

We have already made an argument for context in the earlier discussion about the linkages between generic management and public management, as context has an impact on the constraints and opportunities available to public service managers. However, context is neither totally immutable nor solely a causal force on management behaviour. Research on leadership has shown that a key leadership skill is being able to 'read' the context and to be able to articulate opportunities, mobilize support and shape longer term interests (Leach *et al.* 2005; Morrell and Hartley 2006). Contexts can sometimes be shaped as well as given. This is seen clearly in some of the chapters in this book, for example, in Boyne (chapter 12), in Collier (chapter 3) and in Townley (chapter 7).

The full range of national and international contexts is particularly difficult to classify or use conceptually in a predictive way, but a range of social scientists recognize the importance of context in contributing to explanations of behaviour and variations in behaviour over time and space. In this consideration of public management, we suggest three levels of analysis. First is the context of the external environment, whether this is globalization, changing demographics or new technologies. We have already seen how these have shaped the salience and urgency of governmental calls for 'public service reform'. Second, a particular element of the external context is the 'institutional field' (Scott 2001), which consists of those other organizations that have inter-dependence with the activities and performance of the focal organization. Particularly important here is the policy context created by central government (though some policies may emanate locally), especially in the UK, given the strong role that central government plays in determining legislation and providing the overwhelming proportion of resources for local public service organizations. 'Managing upwards' to influence resources and reputation is critical for many public service organizations (see also Boyne, chapter 12). Finally, the third part of the context is the internal context, which includes local policy, history and existing cultures and practices (Hartley 2002).

Methods and methodologies for public management research

This agenda for research into the policy and practice of improving public services through management would not be complete without some reflections on research methodologies. As well as being multi-disciplinary, the chapters in this book draw on and develop concepts and empirical data using a wide range of investigative methods, including literature reviews, case studies, statistical analysis of large datasets and demonstration projects.

A number of academics, such as Ferlie *et al.* (2003), have commented on the dominance of qualitative approaches, particularly the case study, within public management research and have tried to urge a wider range of methodologies on researchers. There is a clear place for case studies in social science and management research, for they provide the contextual richness and embeddedness that is so critical for understanding the historical, political, policy, economic and social circumstances at play. It was noted earlier how public service organizations, to a greater degree than private sector organizations, have to take into account the external context and that they have more permeable boundaries. Context is therefore critical to their analysis, and reinforces the need to examine management not in isolation but in its policy and governance context, as shown in this book's overarching framework. This is illustrated in a number of the chapters here, which use single or multiple case studies to examine ambiguity, uncertainty and complexity in ways that are not achievable in quantitative analyses.

Nevertheless, the value of the case study approach will be undermined unless other methodologies are also used in complementary ways. Quantitative methodologies have been insufficiently in evidence until fairly recently (Boyne *et al.* 2006). There is a clear need for theory-driven quantitative studies, which are able to examine the broader picture of change and performance improvement, subjecting data to tight statistical analyses and enabling comparisons over time, over jurisdictions and over different contexts. The increase in availability of data about public service organizations' processes and performance notably in the UK (both in aggregate and at the level of the four constituent countries or provinces) but also internationally has aided the argument for, and feasibility of, quantitative studies. Yet the data available are insufficient for good research on their own. Also required are theory-based research questions and research frameworks to use to interrogate the data. Some chapters in this book illustrate how quantitative analysis needs to be theory-led. The second requirement is for researchers with the quantitative skills to interrogate, rather than be overwhelmed or misled by, the quantitative data. Walker (2005) notes that 'It is clear from the literature review work ... and the empirical analysis, that quantitative skills still need to be enhanced in the academic community' (p. 21). The quantitative chapters in this book lay some important foundations for further, systematic quantitative analysis and they make the argument for the establishment and use of large, longitudinal and – as far as possible – reliable and valid datasets from the UK Government's collection of policy, process and performance data. There is also a need for insights from quantitative analysis to be tested and explored for their meanings and contextual influences by undertaking case studies, and for case studies to generate propositions to be tested with large datasets. In this interwoven way, understanding about the contribution of management to the improvement of public services will be enhanced.

REFERENCES

Alford, J. (in press) Public value from co-production by clients, in Benington J. and Moore, M. (eds.) *Debating and Delivering Public Value*. Basingstoke: Palgrave.

Batley, R. and Larbi, G. (2004) *The Changing Role of Government: The Reform of Public Services in Developing Countries*. Basingstoke: Palgrave Macmillan

Benington, J. (2000) The modernization and improvement of government and public services. *Public Money and Management* 20(2): 3–8.

    (2006) *Reforming Public Services*. London, National School of Government and Stationery Office.

Benington, J. and Moore, M. (eds.) (In press) *Debating and Delivering Public Value*. Basingstoke: Palgrave.

Bovaird, T. and Löffler, E. (2003) *Public Management and Governance*. London: Routledge.

Boyne, G. (2003) What is public service improvement? *Public Administration* **81**(2): 211–7.

Boyne, G., Meier, K., O'Toole, L. and Walker, R. (2006) *Public Service Performance: Perspectives on Measurement and Management* Cambridge: Cambridge University Press.

Cabinet Office (2006) *The UK Government's Approach to Public Service Reform: A Discussion Paper*. London, Cabinet Office.

Campbell, A. and Coulson, A. (2006) Into the mainstream: local democracy in central and eastern Europe. *Local Government Studies* **32**(5): 543–61.

Clarke, J. and Newman, J. (1997) *The Managerial State: Power, Politics and Ideology in the Remaking of Social Welfare*. London: Sage.

Denham, A. (1996) *Think Tanks of the New Right* Aldershot: Ashgate.

Downe, J. and Martin, S. J. (2007) Regulation inside government: processes and impacts of inspection of local public services. *Policy and Politics* **35**(2): 215–32.

Feldman, M. (2005) Management and public management. *Academy of Management Journal* **48**(6): 958–60.

Ferlie, E., Hartley, J. and Martin S. (2003) Changing public service organizations: current perspectives and future prospects. *British Journal of Management* **14**: S1–S14.

Ferlie, E., Lynn, L. and Pollitt, C. (2005) (eds.) *Oxford Handbook of Public Management*. Oxford: Oxford University Press.

Geddes, M. (2001) What about the workers? Best Value, employment and work in local public services. *Policy and Politics*, **29**(4): 497–508.

Hartley, J. (2002) Organizational change and development, in Warr, P. (ed.) *Psychology at Work* 5th edn. Harmondsworth: Penguin pp. 399–425.

Hartley, J. and Allison, M. (2000) The role of leadership in modernisation and improvement of public services. *Public Money and Management* April: 35–40.

Hill, C. and Lynn, L. (2005) Is hierarchical governance in decline? Evidence from empirical research. *Journal of Public Administration Research and Theory* **15**(2): 173–95.

Hood, C. (1991) A public management for all seasons. *Public Administration* **69**(1): 3–19.

Hughes, O. (2003) *Public Management and Administration* 3rd edn. Basingstoke: Palgrave.

Jackson, P. (2003) The size and scope of the public sector: an international comparison, in Bovaird, T. and Löffler, E. (eds.) *Public Management and Governance*. London: Routledge, pp. 25–39.

Kelman, S. (2005) Public management needs help! *Academy of Management Journal* **48**(6): 967–9.

Keohane, R. and Nye, J. (2000) Introduction, in Nye, J. and Donahue, J. (eds.) *Governance in a globalization world*. Washington, DC: Brookings Institution.

Klijn, E.-H. and Skelcher, C. (2007) Democracy and network governance:compatible or not? *Public Administration* **85**(3): 587–608.

Kooiman, J. (2003) *Governing as Governance*. London: Sage.

Leach, S., Hartley, J., Lowndes, V., Wilson, D. and Downe, J. (2005) *Local Political Leadership in the UK*. York: Joseph Rowntree Foundation.

Lynn, L. (2006) *Public Management: Old and New*. London: Routledge.

Lynn, L., Heinrich, C. and Hill, C. (2001) *Improving Governance: A New Logic for Empirical Research*, Washington, DC: Georgetown University Press.

McLaughlin, K., Osborne, S. and Ferlie, E. (2001) *The New Public Management: Current Trends and Future Prospects*. London: Routledge.

Marquand, D. (2004) *Decline of the Public*. Cambridge: Polity.

Massey, A. and Pyper, R. (2005) *Public Management and Modernisation in Britain*. Basingstoke: Palgrave Macmillan.

Moore, M. H. (1995) *Creating Public Value*. Cambridge, MA: Harvard University Press.
  (2005) Break-through innovations and continuous improvement: two different models of innovative processes in the public sector. *Public Money and Management* **25** (January): 43–50.

Morrell, K. and Hartley, J. (2006) A model of political leadership. *Human Relations* **59**(4): 483–504.

National Statistics (2006) www.statistics.gov.uk/pdfdir/pse1206.pdf accessed February 2007.

Newman, J. (2001) *Modernising Governance: New Labour, Policy and Society*. London: Sage.

Pawson, R. and Tilley, N. (1997) *Realistic Evaluation*. London: Sage.

Pettigrew, A. (2005) The character and significance of management research on the public services. *Academy of Management Journal* **48**: 973–77.

Pollitt, C. (2000) Is the emperor in his underwear? An analysis of the impacts of public management reform. *Public Management Review* **2**(2): 181–99.

Pollitt, C. and Bouckaert, G. (2004) *Public Management Reform: A Comparative Analysis*. Oxford: Oxford University Press.

Power, M. (2003) Evaluating the audit explosion. *Law and Policy* **25**(3): 185–202.

Rainey, H. (1997) *Understanding and Managing Public Organizations*. San Francisco: Jossey Bass.

Rainey, H. and Chun, Y. (2005) Public and private management compared, in Ferlie, E., Lynn, L. and Pollitt, C. (eds.) *Oxford Handbook of Public Management*. Oxford: Oxford University Press, pp. 72–102.

Rainey, H. and Steinbauer, P. (1999) Galloping elephants: developing elements of a theory of effective government organizations. *Journal of Public Administration Research and Theory* **9**: 1–32.

Ranson, S. and Stewart, J. (1994) *Management for the Public Domain: Enabling the Learning Society*. London: Macmillan.

Scott, W. R. (2001) *Institutions and Organizations*, 3rd edn. Thousand Oaks: Sage.

Skelcher, C. (2005) Public–private partnerships and hybridity in Ferlie, E., Lynn, L. and Pollitt, C. (eds.) *Oxford Handbook of Public Management*, Oxford: Oxford University Press, pp. 347–70.

Stoker, G. (2004) *Transforming Local Governance: From Thatcherism to New Labour*. Basingstoke: Palgrave Macmillan.
  (2006) Public value management: a new narrative for networked governance? *American Review of Public Administration*, **36**(1): 41–7.

Sullivan, H. and Skelcher C, 2002. *Working Across Boundaries: Collaboration in Public Services*. Basingstoke: Palgrave Macmillan.

United Nations Development Programme (UNDP) (2002) *Deepening Democracy in a Fragmented World*. New York: Oxford University Press.

Walker, R. (2005) End of ESRC/EPSRC AIM end of award report. Swindon: ESRC.

Wall, T. D., Michie, J., Patterson, M. G., *et al.* (2004) On the validity of subjective measures of company performance. *Personnel Psychology* **57**: 95–118.

Part I

Governance and accountability

2 Does governance perform? Concepts, evidence, causalities and research strategies

Chris Skelcher

Introduction

Public service reform programmes have created a greater diversity in the governance arrangements for making and delivering public policy. The traditional archetype for public service organizations – the politically headed bureau – has lost its monopoly in the face of experimentation with a range of corporate forms. It is now common to find such governance forms as arm's length executive agencies (Pollitt *et al.* 2001), multi-organizational collaboratives (Sullivan and Skelcher 2002), public–private partnerships (Skelcher 2005b), quasi-governmental hybrids (Koppell 2003), and public interest companies (Prabhakar 2004). These governance changes are closely related to debates about public service performance. For example, one rationale for moving away from the politically headed bureau and towards other forms of governance is that it enables greater discretion to be exercised by managers within an incentive-based performance framework (Boyne *et al.* 2003). Managers freed from the constraints of day-to-day political supervision are assumed to be able to apply a technical rationality that will enhance the organization's performance (Clark and Newman 1997). The new governance forms also potentially offer gains in democratic performance by opening additional pathways into the public policy process. For example, neighbourhood regeneration boards often include local residents and community organizations as well as civic officials and business leaders.

However there are arguments that change to governance arrangements leads to undesirable consequences. First, the quasi-governmental status of new governance forms introduces concerns about confused and weak

An earlier version of this paper, co-authored with Dr Navdep Mathur, was published as 'Governance Arrangements and Public Service Performance: Reviewing and Reformulating the Research Agenda', AIM Research Working Paper Series 11, 2004.

accountability (Rhodes 1997). Second, the fragmentation of large bureaux into congeries of smaller quasi-autonomous bodies potentially degrades the performance of the public policy system as a whole. Significant transaction costs and institutional barriers create problems of reaching agreement between multiple semi-autonomous jurisdictions in relation to over-arching public policy goals (Skelcher 2005a).

The purpose of this chapter is to explore the relationship between the new forms of public governance and public service performance, and provide an agenda for research. To date, there has been little systematic research on the relationship between governance and performance. Debate is driven by theoretical propositions and individual case examples rather than an integrated corpus of empirically based knowledge. Consequently academics do not have a strong basis from which to inform policy design by governments. This chapter starts with a discussion of the two key concepts – governance and performance – and then explores the theoretical relationship between them. In the next section, the focus turns to the empirical evidence on the impact of governance forms on organizational performance. The chapter then explores two ways forward for research. One approach is to examine the multiple possible causalities between governance and performance. The other is to adopt an interpretivist approach to the critical examination of the sets of governance design solutions embedded in prevailing discourses. I argue that this offers practical benefits for those engaged in designing governance arrangements that are intended to enhance performance.

The central concepts: governance and performance

Governance

At its most abstract level, 'governance' is a way of conceptualizing the means of social coordination (Mayntz 1993; Kooiman 2003) (table 2.1). Within the public

Table 2.1: Governance concepts: analytical distinctions

Concept	Definition
Governance	A means of social coordination
Mode of governance	Coordination through hierarchy, market or network
Public governance	The corporate structures applied to organizations that make and manage public policy

management field, however, the discussion typically revolves around the question of 'modes' of governance. This is normally formulated in terms of the triptych of hierarchy, market and network, and debate hinges on the relative impact of each in terms of public service performance, a point discussed in more detail below. The concept of governance therefore takes on normative as well as descriptive/analytical connotations, especially in the context of the powerful theoretical and political motivations to moderate public service hierarchies with a strong dose of market forces. Finally, it is important to be aware that govern*ance* is frequently employed in an oppositional pairing with govern*ment*, to describe the network arrangements for steering and coordinating public, private and not-for-profit activity that have replaced hierarchical, state-centred policy-making and delivery (Rhodes 1997). This relationship has recently been subject to some critical analysis (e.g. Davies 2000).

'Public' governance refers to the different corporate arrangements applied to the organizations through which public policy is shaped, made and executed. Public governance includes the formal constitutional design and legal status of these bodies. For example, it includes the rules that set out how a legislature and executive are to operate, or how a public–private partnership is to be held accountable. A similar usage is found in the 'governance and performance' literature in the US, where Lynn, Heinrich and Hill (2001: 7) talk about governance in terms of 'the regime of laws, rules, judicial decision, and administrative practices that constrain, prescribe, and enable the provision of publicly supported goods and services'.

Performance

Performance is conceptualized in three ways (table 2.2). The *organizational performance* of public service bodies is typically constructed with reference to the metrics of effective implementation, productivity, service outcomes and client satisfaction (de Bruijn 2002). The basis on which judgements about performance are made draws principally on measures of efficiency,

Table 2.2: Performance domains: analytical distinctions

Concept	Definition
Organizational performance	The substantive outputs and outcomes of a public organization
Democratic performance	The extent to which a public organization is able to demonstrate mechanisms for legitimacy, consent and accountability
System performance	The extent to which a system of public organizations is integrated

effectiveness, service quality, and compliance with normative standards. The UK, with its extensive array of performance indicators and targets for all public services, is a particular example of this model. The logic of this emphasis on transparent data on organizational performance can be constructed in public choice terms. Theoretically it should incentivize top-level decision-makers to take corrective action to address less than satisfactory performance, with the added impetus that failure so to do may have undesirable results at the ballot box or in terms of external intervention by higher levels of government.

However this argument has an important flaw, since changes in governance arrangements in the UK and a number of other countries have relocated areas of public service outside of direct control by elected politicians. The relationships between organizations delivering public policy and the democratic system that defines the goals to be achieved vary from those that are tightly coupled (the minister heading a central government department) to others that have an arm's-length relationship to elected politicians (public interest companies and multi-organizational collaborations). This observation introduces a requirement to consider the democratic performance of public service organizations.

Democratic performance refers to the extent to which the governance arrangements of an organization enable the exercise of legitimacy, consent and accountability (Mathur and Skelcher 2007). Legitimacy refers to the political validation of institutional authority, consent concerns the capacity of citizens and other relevant actors to agree courses of organizational action, and accountability involves the explanation of action linked to renewal or revocation of mandate by the principal.

Finally, performance needs to be conceptualized in terms of the overall functioning of the governmental system and its capacity to coordinate activities and resolve collective action problems across jurisdictions. This is termed *system performance*. Questions of system performance are inherent in governance design. Where there are large politically headed bureaucracies, system performance is potentially sub-optimal due to the rigidities of organizational domains. In situations of decentralization and flexible governance, problems of coordination across multiple jurisdictions arise.

Relationships between mode of governance and public service performance

The discussion thus far has begun to indicate some theoretical relationships between the governance modes of hierarchy, market and network, and the organizational, democratic and system dimensions of public service performance (table 2.1). Hierarchical modes of governance appear to offer a means of high organizational performance through bureaucratic control, with a clear link to political principles, thus assuring democratic performance. System performance is high due to the limited number of public service organizations. However these benefits need to be set against the potential for rigidity and proceduralism, and the inter-departmental and intra-departmental political contest (Peters 2000). In contrast, market modes of governance offer enhanced organizational performance as central regulation decreases, but with increased transaction costs. Democratic performance is reconfigured away from detailed delivery issues and towards goal definition and outcome accountability, while system performance is potentially reduced due to contract lock-in and increases in self-interested behaviour in the absence of central control. Finally, network modes of governance suggest gains in organizational performance due to flexibility of forms in a collaborative environment, and with a transformation of the means of democratic performance from a top-down representative system to more interactive modes of decision-making (Edelenbos and Klijn 2006). Network governance may be a coordinative instrument better suited to the complex, distributed authority of 'hollowing-out' and contemporary global society. This normative conception of network governance draws from theoretical positions that emphasize the generative power of cooperation and resource sharing by public and other actors to achieve social goals, in contrast to the command and coercive power of government (Pierre and Peters 2000).

The empirical evidence on these hypothesized relationships is limited and to date has not been systematically codified and examined. Most progress in this task is being made in a major series of studies in the US, associated with the 'governance and performance' project (e.g. Heinrich and Lynn 2000; Lynn *et al.* 2001). This project is a systematic empirical (predominantly quantitative) examination of the relationships between forms of governance, methods of management and public service performance. A recent meta-analysis of the literature in the field has concluded that the majority of evidence thus far is on the relationships between management and performance, and that there is a key gap in terms of the impact of governance (Hill and Lynn 2005). However there are extant research designs to further empirical work in this field (Skelcher 2007), and some initial work is being undertaken in respect of the performance effects of network modes of governance (e.g. O'Toole and Meier 2004). For the purposes of this chapter, however, we now turn from the broader issue of modes of governance to a consideration of the specific issue of the corporate structure of public organizations (see table 2.3).

Table 2.3: Theoretical relationships between modes of governance and performance domains

Mode of governance	Performance domains		
	Organizational	Democratic	System
Hierarchy	Bureaucracy provides means for efficient organization of work, leading to effective outcomes; however proceduralism, rational choice, etc., pose constraints on this organizational form.	Strong democratic performance in theory due to politically headed public service bureaucracy; but constrained by power of professionals and managers. Strong procedures for democratic performance may limit responsiveness and flexibility.	High system performance in theory, although this will be limited by frictional and structural conflicts between politically headed bureaucracies, and gaps in service provision between them.
Market	Potential to increase organizational performance due to efficiency gains implicit in contracting and innovation arising from market context, although these need to be compensated by increased transaction costs.	Increases focus by politicians on the definition of service, thus enhancing accountability. Reduces democratic accountability of service provision due to inflexibility in contracts and market orientation.	Reduces potential for alignment and change at the level of service delivery, due to the contractually defined nature of service provision.
Network	Potential to increase organizational performance due to loose coupling to formal representative democratic institutions, flexibility in constitutional arrangements, incorporation of key stakeholders and managerial discretion.	Weakening of traditional forms of democratic performance through representative democracy; potential strengthening through emergence of deliberative democratic forms.	Possible reduction of system-wide coherence and problems of coordination and collective action on overarching public policy goals; however potential for institutional creation to meet more specific needs, leading to more responsive system overall.

Empirical perspectives on governace and performance

The form of public governance can be understood as embodying assumptions about the 'right' or 'best' way to constitute an entity in order to deliver a desired level of organizational performance. The public service reform movement associated with new public management and its variants reflects a change in these normative assumptions when compared with traditional public administration. For example, the new discourse privileges arm's-length public bodies over politically controlled departments on the theoretical grounds that their non-partisan boards will facilitate efficient decision-making and effective managed service delivery. The democratic accountabilities of politically headed bureaux are regarded as less preferable on the theoretical grounds that their organizational performance will be sub-optimal (Skelcher 1998).

These positions lead to the question of whether there is a discernable difference in the performance of different forms of public governance. For example, is a multi-agency collaboration structured as a company limited by guarantee likely to lead to better or worse performance than one constituted as an unincorporated association? If evidence on the relationship between forms of governance and performance can be adduced, this would offer the possibility for advances in both theory and policy design. The issues involved in such research are conceptually and methodologically complex (Skelcher 2007). Here, some of the key evidence is explored, as a basis for reconsidering the nature of the governance–performance relationship.

Public governance and organizational performance

The first set of studies relates to the institutional economics-inspired theory that underlies much recent public management reform. This predicts improvements in organizational performance where an entity gains greater autonomy from politicians and greater engagement with market forces. Dunsire, Parker and colleagues examined these propositions in a study of ten UK public service organizations that had changed their governance arrangements (Dunsire et al. 1991). Some had been privatized while others changed status within the public sector, for example from government department to public corporation or trading fund to executive agency. Dunsire et al.'s hypotheses were that improvements in performance (defined as productivity, employment and financial ratios) would be positively associated with three changes:

(a) Movement in corporate status away from government department and towards privatization, by way of intermediate levels of autonomy. The argument here is that this increases the exposure of the entity to the policing role of the capital market, hence placing a greater premium on the productive use of resources.

(b) Movement towards operating in an increasingly competitive market, and

(c) Movement in management structure from command to results orientation, leading to greater incentives for managerial performance.

The study failed to find clear evidence to support these hypotheses, although in four or five of the cases these was some association between change in status and improved performance. However, the causality is by no means clear. For example, the decision to sell a public enterprise can lead government to initiate measures to boost its pre-sale performance, hence making it attractive to investors and maximizing the returns to government.

Parker (1995) subsequently sought an explanation for the mechanism that might link change in corporate status to change in organizational performance. He undertook a further analysis of the qualitative data from the perspective of strategic contingency theory. The hypothesis was that change in corporate status would unlock the capacity of the organization's management better to respond to adjust to the external environment. Such change, Parker argued, might occur in six spheres: developing managerial leadership, establishing commercially oriented goals, creating divisionalized structures with greater managerial autonomy, introducing performance management, greater flexibility in the nature and location of the business, and greater flexibility in human resource policies and systems. Parker found supporting evidence in six of the ten cases. However he also noted that such changes might have occurred without altering corporate status because of the broader cultural shifts arising from the adoption of the managerial ethos in the public sector. The research did not test for differences between organizations that had and had not changed status.

Considine's (2000) analysis of Australian employment services begins to fill this gap. He compared an employment assistance system that contained both private and public sector operators. His conclusion was that the best private operators outperformed those in the public sector. However the standard of performance by public agencies was more consistent. Considine accounts for these findings in terms of the differential impact of results-based funding on public and private agencies, rather than the corporate form of governance, and thus reinforces Parker's contingency explanation.

Public governance and democratic performance

The second issue concerns the relationship between forms of public governance and democratic performance. A small group of studies (e.g. Weir and Hall 1994;

Wälti *et al.* 2004; Skelcher *et al.* 2005) have used criteria-based methods derived from the 'quality of democracy' literature to assess the democratic performance of national and local quangos, and multi-organizational collaborations in the UK. They find that these bodies have lower levels of democratic performance than elected bodies. Multi-organizational collaborations in particular tend to have a wide variation in the extent of their democratic performance.

However, it can be argued from a managerialist perspective that reduced public transparency and accountability requirements can have a positive impact on organizational performance by allowing managers discretion in designing strategies to resolve public policy problems, and especially those with a significant technical component or where public views are sharply divided. This is not to say that such decisions are somehow 'outside' politics. However policy deliberation could conceivably be aided by locating it in an arena in which competitive partisan politics is not the norm. This view has two somewhat conflicting justifications. One is the empiricist technocratic position that the application of 'value-free' knowledge and expertise holds out the promise of the wider public interest being served. The other is the populist democratic view that participation by all actors involved in a public policy issue offers the prospect of initial positions being transformed through informed dialogue such that a collective agreement is reached (Barber 1984; Reich 1990).

Some support comes from van Thiel's (2001) study of two Dutch ZBOs (quangos). Her initial conclusion, like that of Dunsire *et al.*, is that change in organizational status does not necessarily lead to more efficient and effective policy implementation. However she conjectures that the political efficiency produced by quangos may be more important than their economic efficiency. This takes us in the direction of the theory of credible commitment (Miller 2000; Elgie and McMenamin 2005; Bertelli 2006), in which the arm's-length status of a public function insulates it from political contest and enables relatively uninterrupted policy implementation to proceed. Thus Moe's (2001) view is that, paradoxically, the lower level of accountability of US quasi-governmental bodies has an important benefit for the elected government.

Public governance and system performance

The third area of investigation concerns the relationship between public governance and system performance. Foster's (1997) study of special purpose governments in the US examines the proposition that single purpose public bodies have a capacity for focus that is more difficult to achieve where services are bundled together in a multi-purpose organization, and that this is likely to be translated into stronger organizational performance. Foster uses the extensive US Census of Government dataset to undertake a quantitative comparison between areas where single purpose districts are widespread and those where multi-functional government is the norm. She demonstrates that single purpose governments have three main effects. First, there is upward spending bias, even after controlling for service demand factors. Special purpose governments spend more on capital projects, operations, and administrative expenditures. Foster explains this as a function of the economic and political effects of organizational specialization. The economic advantages of scale are reduced, the costs of coordination are increased, and limited political visibility reduces the opportunity for scrutiny and accountability. Second, special districts cause policy-shaping effects. Areas with a high proportion of special districts tend to give greater emphasis to development and 'housekeeping' functions (i.e. collective consumption services such as libraries and parks), and less priority to social welfare services. She comments:

Given an opportunity to make discrete, rather than bundled, choices in a public services marketplace, middle- and upper-income residents are apt to pass over social welfare services, from which they derive little direct benefit, in favour of development and housekeeping services, which offer more direct payoffs to individual utility. (1997: 223)

Finally, Foster turns to the question of system performance. She finds that areas with a high proportion of special districts impact on the institutional capacity of system-wide governance. They aggravate coordination problems in areas that are politically fragmented (i.e. where policies and interests diverge) but conversely provide a means of accommodating diversity in politically uniform areas (for example, by enabling a public service to be governed by and delivered to an ethnic or religious minority). This reflects the issues examined some time earlier by Ostrom *et al.* (1962), and which have continued to limit the possibilities for integrated governance across metropolitan areas in many parts of the US.

Initial conclusions

The main conclusions from these empirical studies are:
1. Change in governance arrangements *per se* do not cause changes in organizational performance. But where they involve greater organizational autonomy, they do motivate changes in management that can have a positive effect on organizational performance.

2. Changes in governance arrangements towards arm's-length status are associated with lower levels of democratic performance, over and above the loss of electoral competence.

3. Areas where governance arrangements are polycentric and specialized exhibit upward spending bias, oriented towards development and collective consumption services and away from social welfare services.

4. Single purpose entities increase coordination problems but offer the potential for local communities to meet their distinctive service needs.

This analysis has four implications. First, the theoretical connections between forms of public governance and organizational performance are poorly supported by empirical evidence, a conclusion also drawn by Pollitt (2003) in his review of the research on agencies and quangos. This gap is not for want of methodological sophistication and analytical energy. The studies reviewed above are carefully designed and professionally executed pieces of work. But the number of potential causal relationships involved is too great to capture, reflecting the range of theoretical positions available on the issue and the complexity of the reality that researchers are trying to investigate.

Second, it is easier to establish the implications of governance arrangements for democratic and system performance than for organizational performance. This is because democratic performance is integral to the governance arrangement.

Third, a number of governance forms are organizational hybrids (Borys and Jemison 1989). This accentuates the problem of modelling and drawing meaningful conclusions about the relationship between governance and organizational performance since it may not be clear how the constituent elements of the hybrid form will interact. For example, Cornford and Edwards (1999) show how the boards of non-profit organizations employ a variety of different roles and approaches. A classic tension for nominees from public service organizations who hold positions as directors on companies created to deliver non-profit activity is between the strict view of the legal obligation on them to 'put the interests of the company first' and a more relaxed interpretation, since they hold their directorships precisely to represent the interests of their nominating organization.

Fourth, the studies show that positivist social science can take us so far in understanding the relationships between governance forms and organizational performance, but to date has not provided more than contingent findings. Even research that sets out to test the parsimonious hypotheses of public choice theory has difficulty in attributing changes in organizational performance to the policy prescriptions arising from this school of thought, as Boyne *et al.* (2003) show in their careful analysis of three areas of UK public policy. Consequently there is a question about whether it is possible to uncover or validate scientific associations between governance arrangements to public service performance. Yet despite this, we see no signs that policy-makers are lessening their willingness to engage in institutional design of new governance arrangements. If social science is to contribute to this process, it needs a new entry point.

Developing the research agenda on governance and performance

The development of the research agenda contains at least two elements. The first element is to critically examine the implied causality in predominant models of public service reform that particular changes in public service governance design will lead to improvements in performance. This section sets out a number of alternative causalities, illustrated with small-scale case studies undertaken in Denmark, the UK, the US and the Netherlands during 2004. The focus of the discussion is specifically on the organizational dimension of performance; space does not permit the analysis to be extended into democratic or system dimensions of performance. The second element in a research agenda should be to consider the methodological approaches to be used by researchers in the field. The literature to date has largely used quantitative hypothesis testing operating from a positivist epistemology. However there are significant opportunities for knowledge development by adopting interpretivist approaches.

Exploring patterns of causality

The core hypothesis (H1) informing the policy of creating new forms of public governance, and the positivist assessment of their relationship to performance, is that the arrow of causality runs from 'governance' (G) to 'performance' (P) thus:

$$H1 : G \rightarrow P$$

In other words, performance is dependent on governance (for the sake of explication, intervening variables are ignored). For example, in the late 1990s politicians in England were concerned that a significant proportion of young people who left the compulsory education system were neither going into the labour market nor into further education. The policy response was to create an integrated occupational advice and personal support service delivered through local agencies. The creation of these agencies as independently constituted companies was specifically intended to create a distinct identity and organizational coherence, and to demonstrate their independence from the agencies that had previously delivered these services. This focus was considered to be essential if performance in delivering the policy goal was to improve relative to the previous organizationally fragmented system.

H1 is only one of a number of possible hypotheses. The converse to H1 is that governance arises because of performance (H2).

$$H2: G \leftarrow P$$

Here, the design of the corporate form is motivated by the need to offer a framework to legitimate existing performance. For example, a small town in England had a very active but informal community network. The organization was able to mobilize community efforts to deliver outcomes for the area, but was marginalized in its work because it lacked a formal corporate status. It decided to transform itself into a community-controlled company limited by guarantee in order to give its activities higher status with other organizations operating in the area. The form of public governance provided a wrap-around structure to legitimize the organization in the eyes of key stakeholders, and to provide assurance for its performance in the future. However the ethos of the informal network was retained as far as possible. For example, the design of the board's accountability arrangements included considerable opportunity for citizen involvement.

A further variant is that the form of public governance undermines performance (H3).

$$H3: G \nrightarrow P$$

For example, a museum and educational centre was established in Denmark. Its board was composed initially of professional scientists and distinguished supporters. The museum became highly significant to the life of the town in which it was located. As a result, local politicians pressed for membership on the board, a request that was eventually granted. This change in governance inserted a 'political' culture into a board that had a tradition of scientific professional debate. This produced tensions. The scientists felt that their contribution was being undervalued. The politicians thought that the museum was not sufficiently in touch with local people. Until they were resolved, these issues reduced the capacity of the board to focus on improving the service performance of the museum.

The fourth hypothesis (H4) is that performance undermines the form of governance. This can be seen as the precursor of H1.

$$H4: G \nleftarrow P$$

There are numerous instances where a concern that a public service is not performing at a sufficient level results in a change of governance form. For example, the widespread introduction of quasi-governmental organizations (quangos) of various forms in the UK and the US was motivated by a view that the public bureau form of governance had contributed to underperformance (Skelcher 1998; Koppell 2003). Conversely, high levels of service performance by units within a public service bureaucracy may lead to a bid for greater autonomy, thus undermining the prevailing form of governance.

The fifth hypothesis is that governance forms are the symbols used in a political struggle between different actors to capture the current or future performance of an organization (H5). In other words, what is important is not performance *per se*, but the ability of different interests to attribute or explain that performance in terms of the form of public governance preferred by each (G^1, $G^2 \dots G^n$). Thus, if we assume that there are two contesting actors A^1 (favouring governance form G^1) and A^2 (favouring governance form G^2), A^1 will present the argument that G^1 will produce the desired performance and that G^2 will not:

H5: $G^1 \rightarrow P$; $G^2 \nrightarrow P$

For example, bodies established as trading concerns but operating within a regulatory framework can explain their good (or poor) performance in two ways. It could be due to the organization's board being able to operate in ways that are close to conventional business practice (or else, why adopt this model?). Or it could be due to the regulatory framework operated by government (or else, why create one?). Commercial orientation and governmental regulation are a compromise between market freedoms and government values. And because they are a compromise, there will always be a tension reflected in actors' attempts to negotiate the boundary to their advantage. Wettenhall (1998) illustrates this with reference to the changing design of government-owned companies in Australia. The governance form (enterprise model or public interest regulation) thus becomes a symbol to be deployed in this process of negotiation.

The final and sixth hypothesis is that governance and performance are unrelated (H6).

H6: $G \nleftrightarrow P$

In this case, performance is a function of other variables including tradition, management, the nature of the community served, or the level of resources. Governance is there to provide an assurance of accountability and control, but operates at one remove from concerns about service performance.

Overall, therefore, the governance–performance causality is complex. The search by political actors for an institutional design that will deliver policy goals to a desired level of performance assumes that the causality runs in the direction indicated in H1. But there are a number of other possibilities, especially as one moves the analysis away from an apolitical environment and into the contestation found in governmental environments. Here, forms of governance are aligned with different discourses associated with competing sets of actors (Skelcher *et al.* 2005).

Reformulating the research design

This leads to the question of how researchers should respond to the problem of exploring the governance–performance relationship. At the level of generalizable, empirically supported causal statements, social science research has been able to contribute little to the normative project of designing governance institutions. There is certainly theory, and this has informed the design of public policy initiatives. But the empirical evidence on the relationship between governance arrangements and organizational performance is weak. We simply do not know whether outcomes are achieved more effectively through an agency, a multi-organizational collaboration, or a politically headed bureau. What are the options, then, for policy-oriented social science research? There are two courses that could be followed.

The first possibility is to redouble the analytical effort within the largely positivist approach adopted thus far. This is the position advocated by Pollitt (2003) in his critical appraisal of the state of knowledge on the causes and consequences of autonomous bodies. He observes that research has given relatively little attention to explaining whether agencies and quangos are more economic, efficient or effective than any alternative governance arrangement, nor to identifying what conditions influence their capacity to achieve these gains. He argues that these, and other, research gaps might be met in three ways. The first is by undertaking work that utilizes different theoretical perspectives in order to provide a more rounded picture of agency performance. The second is to develop middle-range theory that will help to explain variations between superficially similar organizational forms. And the third is to undertake comparative research in order to explain the impact of contextual factors.

This option could certainly be applied to the case of research on forms of public governance. However there are two reservations. The first is that the earlier discussion of several carefully designed and implemented studies shows that inconclusive results are not uncommon, reflecting the complexity of the measurement and modelling problems involved. The second limitation is that the nearer a theoretical formulation approaches to an empirical reality, the less generalizable and hence the more trivial it becomes. The specifics of context ('the creation of the agency was enhanced by a major allocation of resources') and individual behaviour ('the new director was well-connected politically') squeeze out more generalizable and policy-relevant explanations of how public service performance is associated with the particular design of the organization's governance.

This takes us to an alternative path for social science research into the performance dimension of different corporate forms for governmental action. By adopting an interpretivist position, explanation proceeds from an understanding that the context comprises different sets of logically inter-related ideas, theories and concepts ('discourses') that supply meanings to actors and offer a guide to practice (Fischer 2003). The discourses validate particular forms of governance in terms of their performance, and thus guide the practices of actors. In the current environment in the UK, for example, the discourse of 'partnership' validates collaborative forms of governance in which authority is shared between groups of 'stakeholders' (a term that is also associated with particular meaning systems) (Newman 2001).

From this perspective, governance and performance are understood as being enacted in a specific context, rather than being formal attributes of a system. For example, the way in which actors in the UK understand the discourse of 'partnership' leads to certain day-to-day practices that produce a particular pattern of organizational, democratic and system performance. Partnership may be understood as a managerial technique for working across organizational boundaries, or as a means of including citizens in deliberative policy making. These understandings are generative of practices that produce particular forms of performance, a point discussed in more detail elsewhere (Skelcher *et al.* 2005).

The task of applied social science research, then, is to uncover, illuminate and critically appraise the policy discourses and institutions that shape meanings and generate action in relation to particular policy questions (Yanow 2000). The purpose of this approach is to increase the public interest component of the governance design process by exposing underlying taken-for-granted assumptions, causal theories and meanings. This approach is more considered than Pollitt (2003) suggests in his critique of interpretive and constructivist theories. It has a place to play alongside research from a positivist tradition in advancing effective public policy solutions, but uses a different strategy to achieve this goal.

Conclusions

The contemporary environment is one in which there is considerable experimentation with forms of public governance. At the same time, the organizational performance of public services is under pressure for improvement. It is tempting to conclude that forms of governance impact on the performance of public services. The theory to support this is available. Hierarchy, market and network modes of governance each have potential gains in terms of organizational, democratic and system performance. And at a more detailed level, there are strong arguments as to why particular corporate forms might be expected to have benefits in terms of outcomes for citizens and users. However the empirical evidence to support this is problematic. The picture is more complex. And there are a number of other possible causal relationships between governance and performance.

So what is the 'best' form of governance? This is a question that can only be answered by understanding the predominant discourse applying in a particular context. Ideas change and evolve, and as they do so our understandings about preferred solutions change (Blyth 2002). The artefacts that are created by politicians and managers – boards, organizational types, performance systems, and so on – have a symbolic as well as a substantive reality. At the symbolic level, they are imbued with meanings arising from the predominant discourse. For example, 'board' could mean 'progressive' and 'modernized', or 'traditional' and 'outdated', depending on the terms of the debate. The meanings are used to interpret the performance of the organization.

The interpretivist approach outlined above offers practical contributions to the real-world dilemmas of policy-makers. It does this by exposing the taken-for-granted and providing a critical insight into the institutional design solutions that are embedded in the prevailing discourse. In this way the analytical contribution of this social science method offers insights to the deliberative process through which public policy and governance arrangements are now more commonly designed. Its value is in helping to clarify the choices facing policy-makers, and in so doing it contributes to a more informed debate in a complex world.

REFERENCES

Barber, B. R. (1984) *Strong Democracy*. Berkeley: University of California Press.

Bertelli, A. (2006) The role of political ideology in the structural design of new governance agencies. *Public Administration Review* **66**(4): 583–95.

Blyth, M. (2002) *Great Transformations: Economic Ideas and Institutional Change in the Twentieth Century*. Cambridge: Cambridge University Press.

Borys, B. and Jemison D. B. (1989) Hybrid arrangements as strategic alliances: theoretical issues in organizational combinations. *Academy of Management Review* 14(2): 234–49.

Boyne, G., Farrell, C., Law, J., Powell, M. and Walker, R. M. (2003) *Evaluating Public Management Reforms: Principles and Practice*. Buckingham: Open University Press.

de Bruijn, H. (2002) *Managing Performance in the Public Sector*. London: Routledge.

Clarke, J. and Newman J. (1997) *The Managerial State*. London: Sage.

Considine, M. (2000) Selling the unemployed: the performance of bureaucracies, firms and non-profits in the new Australian 'market' for unemployment assistance. *Social Policy and Administration* 34(3): 274–95.

Cornforth, C. and Edwards, C. (1999) Board roles and the strategic management of non-profit organizations: theory and practice. *Corporate Governance* 7(4): 346–62.

Davies, J. S. (2000) The hollowing out of local democracy and the 'fatal conceit' of governing without government. *British Journal of Politics and International Relations* 2(3): 414–28.

Dunsire, A., Hartley, K. and Parker, D. (1991) Organizational status and performance: summary of the findings. *Public Administration* 69(1): 21–40.

Edelenbos, J. and Klijn, E.-H. (2006) Managing stakeholder involvement in decision-making: a comparative analysis of six interactive processes in the Netherlands. *Journal of Public Administration Research and Theory* 16(3): 417–46.

Elgie, R. and McMenamin, I. (2005) Credible commitment, political uncertainty or policy complexity? Explaining variations in the independence of non-majoritarian institutions in France. *British Journal of Political Science* 35: 531–48.

Fischer, F. (2003) *Reframing Public Policy: Discursive Politics and Deliberative Practices*. Oxford: Oxford University Press.

Foster, K. A. (1997) *The Political Economy of Special-Purpose Government*. Washington, DC: Georgetown University Press.

Heinrich, C. J. and Lynn, L. E. (2000) *Governance and Performance: New Perspectives*. Washington, DC: Georgetown University Press.

Hill, C. J. and Lynn, L. E. (2005) Is hierarchical governance in decline? Evidence from empirical research. *Journal of Public Administration Research and Theory* 15(2): 173–95.

Kooiman, J. (2003) *Governing as Governance*. London: Sage.

Koppell, J. (2003) *The Politics of Quasi-government: Hybrid Organizations and the Dynamics of Bureaucratic Control*. Cambridge: Cambridge University Press.

Lynn, L. E. Heinrich, C. J. and Hill, C. J. (2001) *Improving Governance: A New Logic for Empirical Research*. Washington, DC: Georgetown University Press.

Mathur, N. and Skelcher, C. (2007) Evaluating democratic performance: Methodologies for assessing the relationship between network governance and citizens. *Public Administration Review* 67(2): 228–37.

Mayntz, R. (1993) Governing failures and the problems of governability: some comments on a theoretical paradigm, in Kooiman, J. (ed.) *Managing Public Organizations: Lessons from Contemporary European Experience*. London: Sage, pp. 9–20.

Miller, G. (2000) Above politics: credible commitment and efficiency in the design of public agencies. *Journal of Public Administration Research and Theory* 10(2): 289–328.

Moe, R. C. (2001) The emerging federal quasi-government: issues of management and accountability. *Public Administration Review* **61**(3): 290–312.

Newman, J. (2001) *Modernising Governance: New Labour, Policy and Society*. London: Sage.

O'Toole, L. J. Jr. and Meier, K. J. (2004) Public management in intergovernmental networks: Matching structural networks and managerial networking. *Journal of Public Administration Research and Theory* **14**(4): 469–94.

Ostrom, V., Tiebout, C. M. and Warren, R. (1962) The organization of government in metropolitan areas: a theoretical inquiry. *American Political Science Review* **55**: 831–42.

Parker, D. (1995) Privatization and agency status: identifying the critical factors for performance improvement. *British Journal of Management* **6**: 29–43.

Peters, B. G. (2000) *The Politics of Bureaucracy*. 5th edn. London: Routledge.

Pierre, J. and Peters, B. G. (2000) *Governance, Politics and the State*. Basingstoke: Macmillan.

Pollitt, C. (2003) Theoretical overview, in Pollitt, C. and Talbot, C. (eds.) *Unbundled Government: A Critical Analysis of the Global Trend to Agencies, Quangos and Contractualisation*. London: Routledge, pp. 319–41.

Pollitt, C., Bathgate, K., Caulfield, J., Smullen, A. and Talbot, C. (2001) Agency fever? Analysis of an international policy fashion. *Journal of Comparative Policy Analysis: Research and Practice* **3**: 271–90.

Prabhakar, R. (2004) Do public interest companies form a Third Way within public services? *British Journal of Politics and International Relations* **6**: 353–69.

Reich, R. B. (1990) *Public Management in a Democratic Society*. Englewood Cliffs, NJ: Prentice Hall.

Rhodes, R. (1997) *Understanding Governance: Policy Networks, Governance, Reflexivity and Accountability*. Buckingham: Open University Press.

Skelcher, C. (1998) *The Appointed State: Quasi-governmental Organisations and Democracy*. Buckingham: Open University Press.

(2005a) Jurisdictional integrity, polycentrism and the design of democratic governance. *Governance* **18**(1): 89–110.

(2005b) Public–private partnerships and hybridity, in Ferlie, E., Lynn, L. E., and Pollitt, C. (eds.) *Oxford Handbook of Public Management*, Oxford: Oxford University Press, pp. 347–70.

(2007) Does democracy matter? A transatlantic research design on democratic performance and special purpose governments. *Journal of Public Administration Research and Theory* **17**(1): 61–76.

Skelcher, C., Mathur, M. and Smith, M. (2005) The public governance of collaborative spaces: Discourse, design and democracy. *Public Administration* **83**(3): 573–96.

Sullivan, H. and Skelcher, C. (2002) *Working across Boundaries: Collaboration in Public Services*. Basingstoke: Palgrave.

van Thiel, S. (2001) *Quangos: Trends, Causes and Consequences*. Aldershot: Ashgate.

Wälti, S., Kübler, D. and Papadopoulos, Y. (2004) How democratic is 'Governance'? Lessons from Swiss drug policy. *Governance* **17**(1): 83–113.

Weir, S. and Hall, W. (1994) *EGO-Trip: Extra-governmental Organisations in the United Kingdom and their Accountability*. London: Charter 88.

Wettenhall, R. (1998) The rising popularity of the government-owned company in Australia: problems and issues. *Public Administration and Development* **18**(3): 243–55.

Yanow, D. (2000) *Conducting Interpretive Policy Analysis*. London: Sage.

3 Performativity, management and governance

Paul M. Collier

Introduction

The notion of performativity, according to Lyotard (1979/1984), is that knowledge and action are not based on abstract principles such as logic or theorizing, but on how effective actions are in achieving desired results. Notions of professionalism and public service that historically separated the public from the private sector have been pushed aside in the relentless pursuit of public sector performance improvement. This paradigm has been constituted by knowledge that is based on quantitative assessments of the results of actions taken by public sector managers and professionals. A consequence of performativity is that some aspects of performance (defined below) are highlighted, while other elements are downplayed. This narrow perspective raises important issues for policy-makers, governance bodies and management in relation to their respective roles and the need to separate these roles. The use of performativity as a construct also questions the public sector privileging of a single (accounting) dimension of performance.

In this chapter I am primarily concerned with how performativity is connected with management and governance using research illustrative evidence from a study of performativity in English police forces. In doing so, limitations of historical approaches to performativity are drawn out and a new approach to performativity is presented. In particular, I consider:

1. Performance as the object of accountability;
2. Management as the subject of accountability;
3. Governance as the focus of accountability.

Academic and policy issues

There has been a global movement towards the measurement of public sector performance (Organization for Economic Cooperation and Development

1997) much of which emanates from the notion that government needed to be reinvented into a more entrepreneurial form (Osborne and Gaebler 1992). The demands of political economy for better outcomes in return for limited funding have institutionalized a rhetoric of economy, efficiency, effectiveness, 'value for money' and 'Best Value' in the delivery of public services in the UK. However, given that the inception of the new public management was rooted in adopting private sector management practices into the public sector (Rhodes 1994; Gray and Jenkins 1995; Hood 1995), it is of concern that government has increasingly moved beyond dictating what performance should be delivered (a role for governance, and perhaps of policy), to the manner in which that performance should be produced (a role for management).

Tensions have emerged between the exogenous, policy- and politics-driven approach to improving performance that is the focus of government, and the endogenous, professional- and experience-driven approach that is the ambit of manager-practitioners. Governance mechanisms in public sector organizations can sit uneasily between these managerial and professional extremes. The issue of importance is, therefore, how to separate and distinguish the respective roles of policy, governance and management in relation to performance.

But such a separation raises questions of accountability: Who is accountable? To whom are they accountable? And for what are they accountable (Collier 2005)? This chapter considers the last of these questions first, seeing performance as the object of accountability. The chapter then considers management as the subject of accountability mechanisms. Finally, the chapter considers governance as the focus of accountability, both in terms of being accountable to various publics, and of simultaneously holding managers accountable. The chapter also considers the overlap between policy and governance roles of government.

Each of these issues presents dilemmas. The historic approach to performativity in public services is considered and illustrated with the example of police performance and its impact on management and governance. Through this illustration, the tensions inherent in different notions of performativity are drawn out.

The historic approach to performativity in public services – and its limitations

The new public management (NPM) in the UK shifted the emphasis from process accountability towards a greater element of accountability in terms of results (Hood 1995; Brereton and Temple 1999), often through decentralization of responsibility (Gray and Jenkins 1995).

The literature on public sector performance measurement tends to be critical, emphasizing the dysfunctional or unintended consequences of measuring performance in an environment in which public sector values have traditionally been dominant (Humphrey *et al.* 1993; Jackson 1993; Likierman 1993; Gray and Jenkins 1995; Smith 1995a; 1995b). The five strategic responses to external pressure identified by Oliver (1991) all have negative connotations and there is little suggestion that external pressure may be 'correct' not only economically and politically but professionally, morally and ethically. Dysfunctional or unintended consequences tend to overshadow any real consideration of the potential benefits of performance management.

Research in the public sector has also focused on resistance and absorbing groups (Preston *et al.* 1992; Covaleski *et al.* 1993; Broadbent and Laughlin 1998) in which resistance in the creation of 'absorption' processes counteracts and mutes any changes imposed by government (Broadbent and Laughlin 1998: 404–5). A contrast with this literature was the study by Collier (2001c), who found that a shift in power accompanying delegated budgets overcame resistance, largely due to the interests of different actors coinciding rather than competing.

We need first to consider performance as the object of accountability.

Problematics of performance

Understanding 'performance' is problematic on a number of dimensions. First, performance may be a discrete event, as in performance in diagnosing an illness, educating a child, or detecting a crime. This can only really be assessed qualitatively in terms of whether the illness was correctly diagnosed, whether the child learned anything of value and whether a criminal was successfully prosecuted. This process approach is likely to involve interventions in methods of diagnosis, education and detection by those who seek to improve performance – generally government through its various inspection and quality assurance agencies.

Within broad policy and regulatory parameters that establish boundaries of what is acceptable behaviour, the methods by which results are achieved are more clearly the focus of management and professionals, rather than of policy-makers or governance. However, the focus of public, press and political attention often encroaches on the professionalism of public sector workers, as though those outside the profession – without the education, ethics or experience of that profession – somehow have a better understanding of what is necessary to achieve results.

Second, performance may be seen as a continuous process which culminates in some more measurable results. This assessment is largely a quantitative one, as in the improving overall health of the community, improving educational attainment of children, and decreasing levels of crime. The problem here is one of summation: how do we (if we can at all) apply weightings to different illnesses (quality-adjusted life years (QALYs) is one way), or to the special educational needs of children, or to different crimes (for example, a violent crime is more serious than theft from a vehicle, yet crimes are added together without weighting as to their relative severity).

A third view of performance is as theatre, a drama or ritual acted out for the public stage, to satisfy politicians, the public, and the press by legitimizing public institutions with the actors in their institutional environment. Certain behaviours are required and certain results expected as part of this process of legitimization. To some extent this is similar to the notion of 'being seen to be doing something' articulated by Pidd in chapter 4 in this volume.

In simple terms, therefore, performance may be what is done and how it is done; the results of what is done; or a mere presentational device.

Problematics of performance applied to policing

Prior to the 1990s, police performance was considered largely in terms of process issues (the 'how' of policing), exemplified in the behaviour of the police. A Royal Commission on Criminal Procedure in 1981 led to the Police and Criminal Evidence Act (PACE) of 1984, which continues to be the single most important regulator of police powers and responsibilities (Reiner 1992). The Scarman inquiry (Scarman 1982) following the Brixton riots, the Hillsborough stadium disaster (Taylor 1989), the miners' strikes during the late 1980s, and the anti-poll tax demonstrations of the early 1990s impacted on how the police behaved in relation to public disorder, while miscarriage-of-justice scandals led to the Runciman Royal Commission on Criminal Justice in 1991. Subsequent legislation has built on PACE and sought to increasingly prescribe police behaviour, such as the requirement to disclose evidence to the defence under the Criminal Procedure and Investigation Act, 1996, and the control of covert surveillance through the Regulation of Investigatory Powers Act, 2000.

Police behaviour has continued to face extensive scrutiny. High-profile examples include deaths in police custody (Police Complaints Authority

1999) and findings of institutional racism against the police in the Stephen Lawrence murder enquiry (Cm. 4262 1999). The review of a major murder enquiry in England (the 'Soham murders') resulted in serious criticism of police practices, in terms of the resilience of one force and its 'lack of grip' at strategic command level (Flanagan 2004) and the 'very serious failings' by senior management in two forces in relation to intelligence sharing, as well as criticism of government for the absence of national information systems for recording intelligence (Bichard 2004: 5).

Politicians, the press and the public are rightly concerned with excesses of police practice and adherence to human rights. However, the concern with how performance has been achieved has become confused with the results of police performance, resulting in tensions between performance measurement and ethical responsibilities (Collier 2001a; 2001b; Neyroud and Beckley 2001).

For over a decade there has been a concern to improve the performance of the forty-three police forces in England and Wales (the 'Home Office' forces) in terms of the results of what the police do. Political and press concern focuses on crime and the relative performance of police forces (Audit Commission 1998a; 1998b; 1999; Public Services Productivity Panel 2000). This concern has been addressed in part by a performance management regime which has resulted in changes to police practices. For example, the demand gap between recorded crime and available resources led to changes in the grading of police response (Collier 1998). Local financial management aimed to devolve resources down to operational levels (Collier 2001c) while the costing of police services made certain aspects of what the police do more visible (Collier 2006a). Performance indicators (and the measurement, monitoring, and management of performance) aim to improve performance trends, achieve targets and raise the standard of relative performance by benchmarking between comparable police forces (Collier 2006b).

Collier (2006b) showed that despite the ascendancy (at the time of writing) of Public Service Agreements, National Policing Plans, the Police Performance Assessment Framework and Statutory Performance Indicators, the life cycle of earlier initiatives was short and the changes made through each successive initiative were not incremental, unidirectional or unambiguous. Police performance measurement changed over the twelve years between 1992 and 2004 to reflect changing political priorities and a shift in focus of what was important, first from output and outcome measures in the 1990s to input indicators, although process measures remained important over both periods. This shift was reversed after 2000 away from process indicators towards outputs (detections) and outcomes (public satisfaction). However, problems of finding suitable measures meant that outcome measures were less important in the early years after 2000 until they were resurrected some four years later.

Of particular importance in this performance regime is the emphasis on continually improving performance trends and comparisons of performance between police forces, especially in relation to levels of volume crime (violent crime, burglary, theft, vehicle crime, etc.) and detections. Of less importance has been the achievement of targets, principally because of the admitted difficulty experienced by local police authorities in setting objective targets grounded in any verifiable evidence base.

Simultaneous with the emphasis on performance measurement, there has been a shift from a reactive, response-led to a proactive, intelligence-led style of policing. The Audit Commission (1993) recommended the targeting of criminals through strategies such as surveillance and crime pattern analysis, rather than merely responding to reported incidents. The *Streetwise* report (Audit Commission 1996) identified the need for targeting of prolific offenders and crime patterns, and a problem-solving approach, using intelligence information. In the UK, the intelligence-led approach to policing (Her Majesty's Inspectorate of Constabulary 1997) has been developed into a systematic approach through the *National Intelligence Model* (NIM: National Criminal Intelligence Service 2000).

NIM uses crime and incident analysis to identify crime series, geographic hotspots and prolific offenders in order to task activity and focus investigative efforts to address emerging crime trends. Tasking is largely concerned with resource allocation decisions such as: the creation of specialist teams to address particular areas of volume crime; named operations that focus resources on particular locations or offenders; the allocation of budgets, particularly overtime; and patrol strategies (Collier 2006c).

This brief overview of police performance reveals a shift from attention to financial performance through local financial management and activity costing and measures of performance emphasizing inputs to one emphasizing improving trends and benchmark comparisons in non-financial performance measures. However, there has been a continual attention to processes in which police behaviour is routinely scrutinized, partly through measurement but also through reviews of individual cases of performance, such as those previously mentioned.

This leads us to a consideration of management as the subject of accountability for performance.

The management of performance

Collier (2006b) reveals that performance in police forces commenced its journey as a set of 'indicators'. Although this term is still used, 'performance' is variously linked with 'measurement', 'monitoring' and 'management' in government publications. These terms are most commonly used interchangeably, as though the distinction in meaning between the terms has become lost. What is implicit in the combinations of 'performance' with indicator, measure, monitor, management and improvement is the notion of control, typically seen as part of a feedback or feed forward cycle in a goal-oriented organization.

Management control is a taken-for-granted element of public management. Managers are accountable for the performance of the public organizations they manage. In the private sector, performance is unambiguous and readily measurable by profit and cash flow measures, reflected in the increasing or falling price of a company's shares. However, public sector performance is more ambiguous.

Public sector organizations typically have a cash-limited budget within which public demands for service need to be satisfied, a process of allocating and rationing resources to try to balance competing demands. While demands for quantitative performance emanate from government, demands for qualitative performance emanate from society at large.

The underlying principle behind 'accountable management' is the accountability of managers for the use of delegated resources in the pursuit of designated objectives (Gray and Jenkins 1986: 181). The development of performance management in the UK has been primarily top-down with a dominant concern for enhancing control and upwards accountability rather than promoting learning and improvement (Sanderson 2001).

The thrust of the reform agenda has also been hostile to the values of traditional public sector professionals (Gray and Jenkins 1995: 81). Professionalism tends to be associated with a diminished need for administrative rules, largely because the behaviour of professionals is controlled through social and self-control mechanisms (Dirsmith *et al.* 2000). A 'clash of cultures' can eventuate between the professional and administrative modes of control, although conflicts between professional and administrative norms and values are reduced when those with a high professional orientation do not operate in a control environment where output controls dominate (Abernathy and Stoelwinder 1995).

The management of performance applied to policing

Policing is unique in public services in that management is dominated by police officers rather than administrators. While police support staff represent one third of the establishment of police forces nationally, the divide between physicians and managers evident in the health service does not exist in policing. While schools are quite small, police forces are large organizations, typically with several thousand staff. The roles played by finance directors, human resource directors and performance managers in policing are always subservient to those of Chief Constables and the rank hierarchy of 'operational' officers. These support roles can be effectively marginalized in terms of any impact they may have on policing. In this way, there is no tension between administrators and professionals within police forces, although there can be between 'street cops' and 'management cops' (Reuss-Ianni and Ianni 1983).

Chief Constables are clearly accountable to their local police authorities (see below) for the budget and for meeting local targets but are also accountable to government (the Home Office) for meeting national targets and for satisfactory performance compared with benchmark forces. They are, perhaps more importantly, answerable primarily to the law for their operational role under the notion of 'constabulary independence' which has been reinforced by case law.

Performance is managed by police through an institutionalized attention to reporting and monitoring performance through regular performance reviews that take place within each force. Performance is collated and reported nationally by the Home Office, which maintains the national data base (*iQuanta*) from which police performance is judged. It is also managed through attention to the National Intelligence Model (NIM, see above) process that consists of a parallel set of meetings that review intelligence and allocate resources in line with tasking priorities. Although both are inter-related, the performance regime has a more administrative and centralized focus with more appeal to the management cop, while NIM is more professionally focused and has more appeal to the street cop.

The particular tension here is in relation to where the police focus their attention. Policing is a complex area of public service because of the diversity of activities the police undertake. Crime represents only about 27 per cent of what the police do (CIPFA 2003) yet it dominates political, press and public concern about police performance. Crime dominates the national policing priorities but at the local level, the fear of crime (which is often unrelated to actual levels of crime) and anti-social behaviour typically concern the public most.

Resource allocations within police forces must balance the competing priorities of being response-led (answering calls from the public), reassurance-led (being visible to the public in order to reduce the fear of crime) and intelligence-led (using knowledge to proactively allocate resources). The result of these tensions can be seen in the increase in the public's fear of crime, despite overall crime reductions as measured quantitatively, itself a likely consequence of removing resources from reactive roles and allocating those resources to proactive units. This tension can only be resolved through governance mechanisms. We now turn to governance as the focus of accountability, both in terms of being accountable itself and simultaneously holding managers accountable.

The governance of performance

Since the inception of the new public management, there has been a shift from public administration to public management to governance (Dunsire 1995). Corporate governance has been defined as the processes by which organizations are directed, controlled and held to account. All bodies need to have at their head a group that is responsible for giving leadership and strategic direction, defining control mechanisms and supervising the overall management of the entity's activities, and reporting on stewardship and performance (International Federation of Accountants 2001: 3) with a need for a clearly defined division of responsibilities to ensure a balance of power and authority (p. 16).

The presumption of managerial authority and unitary purpose evident in the private sector can be contrasted with a pluralistic governance model comprising four elements: leadership through management; citizenship via stakeholders; institutionalized formal and informal patterns of relating; and ideologies or beliefs. These constitute multiple rationalities, in which fit 'implies an accommodation among interest groups as well as the matching of organization to environment advocated by contingency theory' (Dermer 1988: 31).

A feature of the public sector is the existence of multiple publics: at national level represented by central government; at local level represented by local government; and sometimes, at regional level, further complicated by a variety of special interest groups and regulatory bodies. The press purport to represent these diverse publics, seemingly ignorant of both the diverse preferences of publics in each of these forms, and oblivious to the norms and values embodied in professional behaviour.

A significant responsibility of governance is to ensure that systems of management control are adequate. These management controls comprise budgets, non-financial performance measures, personnel and other administrative controls, as well as cultural norms. The relative importance of these controls in the overall control package constitutes the control mix. The control mix is a function of an organization's institutional environment, with pressure being exerted through government funding, together with the mimicking by public sector managers of private sector practices and professional norms. These pressures can lead to a concentration on changing the governance structure, the promotion of a resource management culture, increased budgetary control and cost consciousness (Abernathy and Chua 1996).

Governance applied to policing

The Police Act, 1996, regulates the governance of policing through a tripartite structure. The Chief Constable has operational control, and case law supports constabulary independence from political interference in operational decisions. The police authority for each force has budgetary responsibility, sets local priorities in the form of a local Policing Plan, and holds the Chief Constable accountable for his or her performance. The Home Secretary has responsibility for the efficiency and effectiveness of the police service nationally and sets national priorities for policing through the National Policing Plan.

Chief Constables are in a dual role, being both chief executives of their police forces and one of the members of the tripartite governance structure, effectively being both superior and subordinate in a self-reporting relationship. Chief Constables also have a dual accountability: nationally to the Home Secretary, and locally to the Police Authority. Although there is little doubt that the Home Secretary is the more powerful of the two, national and local priorities may diverge. This is particularly evident in the relative importance of crime and anti-social behaviour. Local issues also extend to the level of public satisfaction with the service provided by the police.

Police authorities are bodies accountable to their local public for the delivery of police services to meet local priorities, while being expected to stand aside while their Chief Constables are held accountable by government for satisfying national expectations. Police authorities are themselves inspected by regulators in relation to their own efficiency; simultaneously holding Chief Constables accountable for their performance.

These competing power relations with the Home Secretary, together with a lack of knowledge, skill and aptitude of many members, has led to the criticism of the effectiveness of police authorities, which have not, on the whole, held Chief Constables sufficiently to account for their performance. The need to strengthen police authorities to ensure the effective delivery of policing has been recognized (Home Office 2004a) and has resulted in the Home Office taking the more dominant role.

One of the difficulties of governance in policing is the need to reconcile the disparate demands of a diverse stakeholder group. Research by Collier *et al.* (2004) identified the different expectations of multiple external stakeholder groups and the difficulty of communicating to the 'general public' through those stakeholder groups. Eighty-six different stakeholder groups were identified, clustered around 'communities' of stakeholders encompassing different demographic and socioeconomic groups, special interest groups, the business community, offenders, victims, the vulnerable, and government agencies responsible for health, social services and education, etc., although it was recognized that individuals could be members of multiple communities.

Collier *et al.* (2004) also found that the knowledge expected by stakeholders, whether in relation to their interest groups or as members of the public, was quite different to the knowledge about performance reported publicly. This highlighted the need to communicate effectively with multiple stakeholder groups, which was likely to be impeded by the publication of performance data by government in set ways.

Public management cannot be divorced from politics (Gray and Jenkins 1995) and performance indicators can play a central role in informing the electorate about the activities undertaken by the public sector (Smith 1995c). However, a significant complexity for governance is that of the role of the citizen as both taxpayer and consumer. While the public as taxpayer legitimates the pursuit of economy and efficiency, the public as consumer legitimates the pursuit of improvement in standards of service (Clarke and Varma 1999: 40). For this reason, it is important that issues of policy are considered.

Policy and police performance

Government, in the form of the Home Secretary in the case of policing, has confused its governance role (as one of the members of the tripartite structure) with its policy-making role and has partially taken over some of the functions of management. For example, national targets established for police priorities have been politically generated rather than evidence based.

In relation to performance, the Home Office agrees Public Service Agreement (PSA) targets for policing with the Treasury (Home Office 2003), establishes national priorities for policing (Home Office 2004b), determines what is measured and how it is measured, and collects and reports on that performance information (Home Office 2002; 2005). The Home Office also interprets performance and, where deemed necessary, intervenes in police forces through the Police Standards Unit in order to direct the steps necessary to improve performance.

Establishing PSA targets and national policing priorities can be understood as a valid policy-making role. However, it seems that within that broad context, it is a matter for governance, in conjunction with management, to define the performance measurement and management process. The interpretation of performance is similarly a matter for management and governance, with reference to policy (e.g. intervention) only when governance and/or management fails to satisfy the national priorities and targets.

The problem for the Home Office is that it sets policy and is dominant amongst the tripartite governing bodies, largely through failures of police authorities to hold chief constables accountable, but also because Chief Constables are at the same time the operational chief executive and a prescribed tripartite player. Police authorities, through their relative independence, ought to take the dominant role, but they have largely been unable or unwilling to do so. The Home Office has stepped into the vacuum, even invading the space of management in its prescriptive approach to performance.

Much of this seems to have been driven by Treasury's demand for an improved cost : performance ratio, but without regard for professionalism, as though the whole of police services could be reduced to a simple input–output equation. This seemingly also disregards the fact that only 27 per cent of police activity is concerned with crime.

Performance measurement is necessary but not sufficient for improved management practice. The concentration on technical efficiency has shifted accountability from politicians to managers; and insufficient attention has been directed at analysing cause–effect relationships between different means of policy intervention and outcomes (Jackson 1993; Smith 1995c). This is an important role for policy-makers, but one that has been abandoned in favour of more direct involvement in governance and management. We return to this later in this chapter.

A new approach to performativity

At the beginning of this chapter, the notion of performativity was introduced. Under performativity, knowledge is defined in terms of how effective actions are in achieving desired results (Lyotard 1979/1984).

Performance is a policy-governance construct in policing, a response to demands for Treasury-driven accountability at a national level. It is aimed at legitimizing the government to the electorate by collecting and reporting historic knowledge about crime and showing that government is active in combating crime. It is also aimed at legitimizing policing to the public through the power of the press. It further legitimizes policing by ensuring that police behaviour is reviewed whenever complaints about process emerge.

By contrast, the intelligence-led approach exemplified by the National Intelligence Model (NIM) is a professional-managerial construct, aimed at using local and current knowledge and skills to address emerging operational issues. NIM is concerned with crime, but also with a variety of local rather than national issues, including anti-social behaviour and other non-crime incidents, quality of life and public reassurance. While there are overlapping issues such as violent crime and burglary, national concerns are not universally shared by local communities, such as vehicle crime. Similarly, local concerns such as prostitution and business crime are not necessarily national issues.

Both performance measurement and the intelligence-led approach are modes of control that are inter-dependent in their influence, together comprising the control mix (Abernathy and Chua 1996). They occupy the space between the need for institutional legitimation and satisfying the demands of the technical environment (Thompson 1967) – in this case, public demand for police services. Tensions between being performance-driven and being intelligence-led can result in a clash of cultures, not between professionals and administrators (Abernathy and Stoelwinder 1995) but between administrative and professional modes of control.

These modes of control or narratives of policing have a different language and appeal to different sub-cultures within police forces, broadly distinguishing the appeal of intelligence-led policing to the 'street cop' while performance measurement appeals to the 'management cop' (Reuss-Ianni and Ianni 1983). These are evident sub-cultures within policing (Collier 2001c).

Both performance-driven and intelligence-led approaches are performative in that they legitimate knowledge and action, albeit different knowledge which leads to different action. Each achieves results, albeit in different ways, despite overlaps (i.e. performance and intelligence may both lead to the same action and result, although this will not always be the case). This is an example of performativity, where narratives located in sub-cultures legitimize different forms of knowledge and different actions to achieve results.

The legitimating principles behind each narrative and form of knowledge are different. The performance-driven approach is top-down, emphasizing accountability to government through the pursuit of improved performance and efficiency in terms of political economy. It is largely reactive to historic trends and benchmarks. This translates into government's accountability to the national public, often made vocal through the power of the press, and through the electoral process. This ensures that taxes are being spent effectively to purchase police services and that the police are performing efficiently by reducing crime.

The intelligence-led approach is accountability to the local public, to not only address crime, but also issues of local concern based on a local knowledge and the expressed concerns of the local community, such as the fear of crime and anti-social behaviour. This approach is largely proactive by addressing emerging issues before they are reflected in historic performance knowledge.

Thus different performances, allied to each sub-culture, and each deemed effective in its own right, construct different knowledges. These knowledges may overlap or compete, but they reinforce action within their own paradigm. The pluralistic approach of Lyotard (1979/1984) towards performativity is reflected in both the overlaps and tensions between the narratives and knowledges of the performance-driven and intelligence-led approaches. Achievement of results in both approaches legitimizes the knowledge, actions and approaches within those domains. But legitimation of knowledge through performativity is anathema to Lyotard. However, the need to legitimate what the police do by demonstrating performativity – through either approach – militates against Lyotard's 'paralogy', the movement against an established way of reasoning, the production of new ideas by acting contrary to established norms.

A consequence of performativity is that some aspects of performance are highlighted, while other elements are downplayed. In policing, it is the norms of managerial behaviour explicit in performance measurement and professional behaviour explicit in the National Intelligence Model that compete. The power of government privileges the former, yet professionalism dictates a real and continuing concern with the latter. While legitimation is a powerful device, in a complex stakeholder environment the source of legitimation can be ambiguous. The Home Office is a powerful actor in the institutional realm, yet it is only one of the tripartite actors in the governance of policing. The pursuit of performativity is undoubtedly implicated in tensions between policy, governance and management, at least in the case of policing.

Conclusions and implications

This chapter brings to the forefront some important impacts for policy-makers, governance bodies and management. First, governance structures need to be strengthened. Second, policy, governance and management need to be clearly separated into functions that do not overlap. Third, performance needs to be recognized as a multi-dimensional construct. Whilst the first two of these are structural solutions driven by differential power relations, the third is based on a shared recognition of the sometimes competing values held by professionals and administrators.

Governance needs to be strengthened. Local governing bodies are rarely acknowledged for their expertise or ability. Governing bodies of schools are subordinate to local education authorities, housing associations to the Housing Corporation as industry regulator, and National Health Service (NHS) trusts to various national bodies regulating aspects of health. Weaknesses in local governance arrangements are sometimes cited as a reason for increased government interference, exemplified in the creation of regional Government Offices and their impact on local government.

The weaknesses in governance are particularly evident in policing. It is important to recognize that Chief Constables cannot, for accountability reasons, be both chief executive and an equal partner in their own governance. The tripartite structure should perhaps be replaced by a bipartite one, where the Chief Constable as chief executive of a police force is responsible to both Home Secretary and police authority. More important is the apparent failure of police authorities to be effective governance partners. This has led to the overly dominating role of the Home Office and its encroachment into areas of governance and management. To its credit, the Home Office has recognized the need to strengthen police authorities (Home Office 2004a).

Avoiding overlapping functions is particularly important for government and the confusion between its policy and governance roles. The pluralistic governance model requires recognition of the importance of actors other than central government. In education, housing and the NHS, government is entitled to establish policy (hopefully based on evidence) and to play *a* governance (rather than *the* governance) role, unless it wishes to be more honest about what is often seen as the fiction of local governance.

Government needs to consider issues of allocative efficiency and cause–effect relations (Jackson 1993; Smith 1995c), holistic issues which have largely been ignored as policy-makers have been subsumed in their concern with micro-management. This involves encouraging a balance between national and local priorities. Techniques such as programme budgeting and marginal analysis (PBMA, described by Donaldson *et al.* in chapter 5 in this volume) present the ability to compare, at the margin, the impact of increased (or reduced) resource allocations to programmes, as a means of improved allocative efficiency.

Continuing the example of policing, the Home Office needs to stand back from its dominance of governance once it strengthens the role of police authorities as an equal partner in governance. However, it needs to go further by reducing its overly active role in defining *how* things are done by management. Allocative efficiency can be considered at national and local levels through adopting techniques such as PBMA.

The use of performativity as a construct helps to understand tensions between policy, governance and management. All forms of knowledge and the resulting actions need to be valued, and not just by practitioner-managers. Performance needs to be understood as a multi-dimensional construct rather than a unidimensional one, addressing discrete events, a continuous process culminating in results and legitimation-through-theatre. More attention needs to be focused on discrete events – both what is achieved and how it is achieved – a management function at the local level. This is likely to be of more importance to the local public as consumers of public services. Quantitative results are of course also important, and management and governance have roles to play in demonstrating performance improvement to policy-makers. However, the relative importance of measurable results should be seen in the context of its limitations, widely accepted in the academic and practitioner literatures. The political need for legitimation means that elements of theatre are likely to continue, and even be valuable as a demonstration of accountability.

In policing, statistics reveal that overall crime levels have fallen over recent years in England. This knowledge legitimates the performance-driven regime and the role undertaken by the Home Office, reinforcing its power base. However, that same crime reduction legitimates the intelligence-led approach, which is similarly credited with achieving success. Knowledge and action on both administrative and professional dimensions are therefore institutionalized. What is not institutionalized, what is not part of knowledge, is that which fails the test of performativity: the immeasurable, qualitative aspects of police performance. The failure of performativity is its inability to look beyond results to discrete events, and the processes that are carried out in pursuit of results (unless they are the subject of a public enquiry due to some significant failure). This is an accounting mindset, not compatible with professional public service values and ethos.

The research into policing described in this chapter shows how performativity privileges an emphasis on a single (accounting) dimension of performance, and how the pursuit of quantitative results can impact on the relationship between policy, governance and management, resulting in unclear and ambiguous accountabilities, in which the visibility of control via performance legitimizes while important aspects of policy and governance become invisible.

Finally, there are implications for future research. The need for further research into professionals in organizations has been recognized (Dirsmith *et al.* 2000: 535) as has the need for a greater understanding of the control mix (Abernathy and Chua 1996) and tensions within organizations between administrative and professional modes of control. Performativity is a useful device to explicate the tensions between professional and administrative controls. While this can be demonstrated in policing, the conclusions drawn in this chapter need testing more broadly across the public sector.

REFERENCES

Abernathy, M. A. and Chua, W. F. (1996) A field study of control system 'redesign': the impact of institutional processes on strategic choice. *Contemporary Accounting Research* **13**: 569–81.

Abernathy, M. A. and Stoelwinder, J. U. (1995) The role of professional control in the management of complex organizations. *Accounting, Organizations and Society* **20**: 1–17.

Audit Commission. (1993) *Helping with Enquiries: Tackling Crime Effectively*. Rep. Paper No. 12.

(1996) *Streetwise: Effective Police Patrol*. London: HMSO.

(1998a) *Local Authority Performance Indicators 1996/97: Police Services*, London: HMSO.

(1998b) *The Publication of Information Direction '98: Performance Indicators for the Financial Year 1999/2000*. London: Audit Commission.

(1999) *Local Authority Performance Indicators 1997/98: Police Services*. London: HMSO.

Bichard, S. M. (2004) *The Bichard Inquiry Report*. London: HMSO.

Brereton, S. M., and Temple, M. (1999) The new public service ethos: an ethical environment for governance. *Public Administration* **77**: 455–74.

Broadbent, J. and Laughlin, R. (1998) Resisting the 'new public management': absorption and absorbing groups in schools and GP practices in the UK. *Accounting Auditing and Accountability Journal* **11**: 403–35.

CIPFA (2003) *Police Statistics: 2002–03 Actuals*. London: Statistical Information Service.

Clarke, C. J. and Varma, S. (1999). Strategic risk management: the new competitive edge. *Long Range Planning* **32**: 414–24.

Cm. 4262 (1999) *The Stephen Lawrence Inquiry: Report of an Inquiry by Sir William Macpherson of Cluny*. London: Audit Commission.

Collier, P. M. (1998) Operations and accountability: the role of performance indicators, financial devolution and strategy in the management of a police force. *International Journal of Police Science and Management* **1**: 81–93.

(2001a) Police performance management – an ethical dilemma? in Neyroud, P. and Beckley, A. (eds.) *Policing, Ethics and Human rights*, Cullompton: Willand, pp. 94–123.

(2001b) Police performance measurement and human rights. *Public Money and Management* **21**: 35–9.

(2001c) The power of accounting: a field study of local financial management in a police force. *Management Accounting Research* **12**: 465–86.

(2005) Governance and the quasi-public organization: a case study of social housing. *Critical Perspectives on Accounting* **16**: 929–49.

(2006a) Costing police services: the politicization of accounting. *Critical Perspectives on Accounting* **17**: 57–86.

(2006b) In search of purpose and priorities: police performance indicators in England and Wales, 1992–2004. *Public Money and Management* **26**(3): 165–72.

(2006c) Policing and the intelligent application of knowledge. *Public Money and Management* **26**(2): 109–11.

Collier, P. M., Edwards, J. S. and Shaw, D. (2004) Communicating knowledge about police performance. *International Journal of Productivity and Performance Management* **53**: 458–67.

Covaleski, M. A., Dirsmith, M. W. and Michelman, J. E. (1993) An institutional theory perspective on the DRG framework, case-mix accounting systems and health-care organizations. *Accounting, Organizations and Society* **18**: 65–80.

Dermer, J. (1988) Control and organizational order. *Accounting, Organizations and Society* **13**: 25–36.

Dirsmith, M. W., Fogarty, T. J. and Gupta, P. (2000) Institutional pressures and symbolic displays in a GAO context. *Organization Studies* **21**: 515–37.

Dunsire, A. (1995) Administrative theory in the 1980s: a viewpoint. *Public Administration* **73**: 17–40.

Flanagan, S. R. (2004) *A Report on the Investigation by Cambridgeshire Constabulary into the murders of Jessica Chapman and Holly Wells at Soham on 4 August 2002: Summary of Conclusions and Recommendations.* London: HM Inspectorate of Constabulary.

Gray, A. and Jenkins, B. (1995) From public administration to public management: reassessing a revolution? *Public Administration* **73**: 75–99.

Gray, A. and Jenkins, W. I. (1986) Accountable management in British central government: some reflections on the financial management initiative. *Financial Accountability and Management* **2**: 171–86.

Her Majesty's Inspectorate of Constabulary. (1997) *Policing with Intelligence: Criminal Intelligence – A Thematic Inspection on Good Practice.* London: HM Inspectorate of Constabulary.

Home Office (2002) *Police Performance Assessment Framework.* London: Home Office.

(2003) *SR2002 Public Service Agreement Technical Notes.* London: Home Office.

(2004a) *Building Communities, Beating Crime: A Better Police Service for the 21st Century,* London: HMSO.

(2004b) *National policing plan 2005–08: safer, stronger communities.* London: Home Office.

(2005) *Police Performance Assessments 2004/05.* London: Home Office.

Hood, C. (1995) The 'new public management' in the 1980s: variations on a theme. *Accounting, Organizations and Society* **20**: 93–109.

Humphrey, C., Miller, P. and Scapens, R. W. (1993) Accountability and accountable management in the UK public sector. *Accounting Auditing and Accountability Journal* **6**: 7–29.

International Federation of Accountants (2001) *Governance in the Public Sector: A Governing Body Perspective. Rep. Study 13*, New York: IFAC.

Jackson, P. M. (1993) Public service performance evaluation: a strategic perspective. *Public Money and Management.* **13**(4) 19–26.

Likierman, A. (1993) Performance indicators: 20 early lessons from managerial use. *Public Money and Management* **13**(4), 15–22.

Lyotard, J.-F. (1979/1984) *The Postmodern Condition: A Report on Knowledge.* Manchester: Manchester University Press.

National Criminal Intelligence Service (2000) *The National Intelligence Model.* London: NCIS.

Neyroud, P. and Beckley, A. (2001) *Policing, Ethics and Human Rights.* Cullompton: Willan.

Oliver, C. (1991) Strategic responses to institutional processes. *Academy of Management Review* **16**: 145–79.

Organization for Economic Cooperation and Development. (1997) *In Search of Results: Performance Management Practices*, Paris: OECD.

Osborne, D. and Gaebler, T. (1992). *Reinventing Government: How the Entrepreneurial Spirit is Transforming the Public Sector.* Harmondsworth, Middlesex: Plume Books.

Police Complaints Authority (1999) *Deaths in Police Custody: Reducing the risks.* London: Police Complaints Authority.

Preston, A. M., Cooper, D. J. and Coombs, R. W. (1992) Fabricating budgets: a study of the production of management budgeting in the National Health Service. *Accounting, Organizations and Society* **17**: 561–93.

Public Services Productivity Panel (2000) *Improving Police Performance: A New Approach to Measuring Police Efficiency*, London: HM Treasury.

Reiner, R. ed. (1992) *Police Research in the United Kingdom: A Critical Review.* Chicago: University of Chicago Press.

Reuss-Ianni, E. and Ianni, F. A. J. (1983) Street cops and management cops: the two cultures of policing, in (ed.) Punch, M., *Legality and Workmanship: Introduction to Control in the Police Organization.* Cambridge, MA: MIT Press, pp. 251–74.

Rhodes, R. A. W. (1994) The hollowing out of the state: the changing nature of the public service in Britain. *Political Quarterly* **65**: 138–51.

Sanderson, I. (2001) Performance management, evaluation and learning in 'modern' local government. *Public Administration* **79**: 297–313.

Scarman, L. (1982) *The Scarman Report.* Harmondsworth: Penguin.

Smith, P. (1995a) On the unintended consequences of publishing performance data in the public sector. *International Journal of Public Administration* **18**: 277–310.

(1995b) Performance indicators and control in the public sector, in Berry, A. J., Broadbent, J. and Otley, D. (eds.) *Management Control: Theories, Issues and Practices*, Basingstoke: Macmillan, pp. 163–78.

(1995c) Performance indicators and outcome in the public sector. *Public Money and Management* Oct.–Dec.: 13–6.

Taylor, L. J. (1989) *Interim Report into the Hillsborough Stadium Disaster.*

Thompson, J. (1967) *Organizations in Action: Social Science Bases of Administrative Theory.* New York: McGraw-Hill.

A critical assessment of performance measurement for policy making

Michael Pidd

Why performance measurement matters

UK public expenditure in 2008 will amount to about £530 billion and consume about 40 per cent of GDP. Though the political parties make different noises about the role of the public sector, there is a consensus that public services should be comprehensive and not just limited to defence and public order. In the UK, as in many countries, the largest chunks of expenditure are on health, education and defence. However, though the political consensus supports the broad provision of public services, there is a widespread perception that these services are inefficient and, when compared to private sector counterparts, ineffective. Whether this perception is correct is another matter; however it does exist. As we shall see later, this perception provides several rationales for performance measurement in the provision of public services. If service performance is measured then it can be assessed against private sector comparators or against public services in other localities. The measurement should also allow service managers to assess whether their performance is improving and enable them to spot instances of good practice. Presented properly, performance data can be used to demonstrate how well (or badly) a provider of a public service is performing. Hence, there is a very strong case for taking performance measurement seriously.

In chapter 12, Boyne distinguishes between results and legitimacy as two types of performance that may lead policy-makers and others to conclude that a public service body is performing well or poorly. The concept of results, close to Skelcher's notion of organizational performance in chapter 2, relates to the outputs and outcomes from the public service. In most cases, these are summarized in performance indicators (PIs) that are weighted aggregations of different aspects of performance. The concept of legitimacy refers to processes and structures adopted by the service provider and the degree to which they fit central prescriptions on how things should be done. In this chapter, we are concerned with the PIs used to summarize the performance of a public service organization in terms of its outputs and outcomes; that is, with results.

If we are to take performance measurement seriously then we must recognize that it can be dysfunctional if not done properly. Done really badly, its negative effects may outweigh the positives. It is wise to face up to some of these dysfunctionalities and to consider why they occur and what can be done to avoid them. When considering the possible benefits of introducing a measurement scheme it is important to consider potential problems when trying to assess the likely costs and benefits of the scheme. Things can go wrong and things do go wrong, but better planning and an understanding of possible problems should help to reduce the risks.

Measurement, then, is important but can be dysfunctional if not done properly. This chapter considers some of the evidence for that dysfunctionality and examines its causes. It marshals insights from a range of theory in an attempt to improve understanding as a contribution to a debate on the improvement of performance measurement. It presents an argument based on four legs. First, performance measurement systems can change the way in which people regard their work – meeting targets can become a dismal substitute for real performance improvement. Hence, it is important to understand how those whose performance is being measured will perceive the measurement and how this will affect what they do. Second, inappropriate notions of control are often called into play when designing and justifying performance measurement. Third, ambiguity and uncertainty play an important role in the management and provision of public services and ignoring this can lead to significant problems. Finally, I point out some technical issues that need to be addressed in any form of performance measurement.

It would be hopelessly unrealistic to assume that this analysis will, overnight, improve performance management; however, it seems reasonable to hope that better theory will provide the basis for more appropriate debate and, ultimately, to better regimes.

Performance measurement in the provision of public services

Performance measurement is often taken to be fundamental to the delivery of improved public services as part of the new public management (NPM). Manning (2000) defines NPM as

a management culture that emphasizes the centrality of the citizen or customer, as well as accountability for results. It also suggests structural or organizational choices that promote decentralized control through a wide variety of alternative service delivery mechanisms, including quasi-markets with public and private service providers competing for resources from policymakers and donors.

Since NPM employs a range of service delivery mechanisms, it is hardly surprising that control mechanisms, decentralized or not, and accountability are fundamental to its implementation. Control, as we shall see later, is impossible without some form of measurement. Hence, performance measurement is fundamental when monitoring and attempting to improve public services.

The UK is often regarded as a leader in NPM and its government places great stress on performance measurement in public service delivery. This has been the subject of parliamentary enquiry, as recorded in the Public Administration Select Committee's 5th report (Stationery Office 2003). In this, Michael Barber, then head of the Prime Minister's Delivery Unit (PMDU), describes a six-stage approach to performance measurement and management, which can be summarized thus:

1. National standards are set out in Public Service Agreements (PSAs).
2. Devolved funding and flexibility are given to delivery units that must organize and plan so as to achieve those targets and report this in Delivery Plans.
3. Regular benchmarking and monitoring of progress using performance indicators occurs during the period covered by the PSAs.
4. Transfer of best practice is encouraged so as to allow units to learn how best to operate.
5. Delivery units are held to account against the PSA targets, using inspection regimes and published data.
6. Services, units and managers that meet their targets are rewarded for doing so and those that do not may suffer.

The targets and measures may be initially rather crude, but there is an expectation that the performance of this performance management system will itself improve after several iterations.

This list may be taken as typical of performance measurement and management as employed in the delivery of public services under NPM. Details may differ in other countries, but the overall approach is unlikely to be much different – in aspiration, at least. Targets (National Standards) are set and carrots and sticks are used to encourage the achievement of these targets. It is well known that, though powerful, such approaches have severe limitations and that alternative approaches may be required in some circumstances.

There is, though, more to performance measurement than this. Because its members were concerned about the misuse and possible abuse of performance indicators, the Royal Statistical Society (RSS) commissioned a report (Bird *et al.* 2003) to encourage best practice. This report suggests three reasons why performance should be measured in the provision of public services:

1. To find out what works. That is, it is important to base policy on evidence and some of this evidence may be based on properly constructed performance indicators. This seems very sensible and such measurement can be done after the event, as a form of *post hoc* evaluation, or before the event by some form of modelling.

2. To identify functional competences. This seems to be based on a view that it is important to establish which service providers or individuals achieve the best performance, as well as establishing what works. Excellent performance can be rewarded and poor performance investigated: praise and blame. Clearly, it is important to know how well service providers are performing, however there is a risk that, once published, such performance data may be used to create league tables. The section of this chapter on handling statistical uncertainty discusses how this can lead to misunderstanding by the public and by policy-makers.

3. To support democratic accountability. Since the public sector is supported through taxation it seems reasonable to argue, at least in a democracy, that the public have a right to know about the performance of public services. The main problem is that it is difficult to get the public much interested in these measures.

However, a moment's reflection on this chapter's argument so far reveals that this RSS list is incomplete. There are least two other common reasons why performance is measured in public services. The first reason, already discussed here but strangely omitted from the RSS Report, is that performance is very commonly measured as part of a control regime. Hood (1991: 4–5) argues that this is fundamental to NPM, in which public services may be provided through decentralized organizations. The second additional reason why performance may be measured in public service delivery is that politicians have to be seen to do something. That is, they engage in symbolic action and this can be very effective if the symbolic action chimes with the zeitgeist. Performance measurement is often used in this way.

Basics of performance measurement

Some form of performance assessment is found in even the smallest organization, which makes it pointless to argue whether such assessment is desirable or not. All humans make judgements and these judgements rest on measurement of some kind. Much of this assessment is informal, as people note the effects of their actions and keep records, possibly for their own benefit.

All assessment and measurement is based on classification. At its simplest, this rests on nominal scales, which consist of categories (such as black, white, red, green, etc; male, female; married, never married, divorced, etc.). As humans, we apply nominal scales all the time as we categorize our experiences. However, nominal scales only allow limited comparison, in the sense of saying whether an item is one thing or another. In mathematical terms, nominal scales support only two operators (=, $\neq$). If we wish to do more than discriminate between objects, we need ordinal scales, which consist of a set of categories in some ordered sequence. An example might be a Likert scale (such as very poor, poor, OK, good, very good) or hospital star ratings. Using an ordinal scale enables us to say that something is better/longer/bigger than something else, but the intervals between the points on the scale have no consistent meaning. In mathematical terms, an ordinal scale supports (=, $\neq$, <, >).

If we wish to say how much better/longer/bigger one thing is than another, then we need an interval scale in which the intervals between values on the scale are equal. Fahrenheit and Celsius temperatures are measured on interval scales. In mathematical terms, interval scales support the (=, $\neq$, <, >, $-$, $+$) operations. Finally, if we wish these measures to relate to a true zero, allowing us to say that something is 'n' times better than another, then we need a ratio scale. The Kelvin or absolute temperature scale is an example, as are length and monetary values. A ratio scale supports the full set of mathematical operators (=, $\neq$, <, >, $-$, $+$, $/$, $\times$). Note, though, that different people may differently value the same monetary amount: for example, £1,000 is a small amount to a billionaire, but may be a large sum to someone on the poverty line. Hence, even though monetary values are expressed on an interval scale it can be dangerous to use them to compare interpersonal preferences.

When people refer to performance measurement they usually mean something rather more complex than simple categorization using nominal scales. Performance measurement is usually based on interval or ratio scales that permit formal comparison and allow quantification. For presentation purposes they may be simplified onto ordinal scales (e.g. in star ratings) and it is important to understand the difference. Most people working in organizations take measurement for granted and it forms an unquestioned part of their working lives. That is, the use of measurement in managing organizations, whether based on nominal, ordinal, interval or ratio scales, is non-controversial. However, this does not mean that it is always done well.

Balanced Scorecards

In the private sector, financial measures predominate, as the focus is on the bottom line. Kaplan and Norton (1996), recognizing the limits of purely financial measures, proposed the Balanced Scorecard as a supplement to conventional accounts. In its original form, this required the statement of objectives, measures, targets and initiatives from each of four perspectives:
1. Learning and growth: how well does the business develop its people for the future?
2. Business processes: how well does the business operate internally?
3. Customers: how does the business appear to its customers?
4. Financial: how well does the business perform in financial terms?

These four perspectives cover much of what a business organization does and some could include almost anything, so how should someone choose which factors to measure within each perspective? Though such scorecards are supposedly balanced, when push comes to shove the usual advice is to focus on those aspects of the four perspectives that are leading indicators of future financial success. That is, the bottom line has the strongest pull in the private sector, even when Balanced Scorecards are in use.

Various forms of Balanced Scorecard have become popular in the public sector in recent years and it is probably true that they are ubiquitous in UK government departments. However, using Scorecards in the public sector is much more complicated than in the for-profit sector, since there is rarely a single measure of success. Moore (2003), for example, criticizes the use of conventional Balanced Scorecards in the public and not-for-profit sectors and proposes, instead, a public value scorecard based on the notion of a public value chain. Public value is an elusive concept, but refers to the need for public and non-profit bodies to measure how well they are performing against their declared social mission. Unlike in the for-profit sector, financial measures should be regarded as intermediate measurements and as subsidiary not dominant.

Baskets of measures: combining measures into performance indicators

The use of Balanced Scorecards highlights an important feature of most performance measurement in the provision of public services: any measurement that focuses solely on a single performance criterion is likely to lead to distortion. Thus, measuring only patient waiting times in the health sector may lead to a stress on throughput but also to a reduction in quality. The goals of public service organizations are rarely one-dimensional and this means that any measurement must embody multiple criteria. However, measures based on multiple criteria are hard to understand. Hence, multiple measures are often reduced to one-dimensional summary measures that allow the formation of league tables. That is, a single performance indicator (PI) P is often formed from the combination of performance measures p such that

$$P = w_1 p_1 + w_2 p_2 + \ldots + w_n p_n$$

where P is the overall, summary performance measure, $p_1, p_2 \ldots p_n$ are the performance scores on the n different measures, and $w_1, w_2 \ldots w_n$ are the weights applied to the individual performance measures.

There are two important issues to face when developing such a summary PI. The first, which is obvious, is that the relative values given to the ws determine how much of an effect they have on the overall performance measure. The greater the comparative weight given to each performance score, the greater its effect on the overall measure. Changing the weights can radically affect the summary score, an issue investigated in Jacobs *et al.* (2005; 2006). When establishing such a summary measure, the important questions are: who determines these weights; and what values should they take? Sadly, the weights and the processes by which they were determined are not always revealed. As ever, information is power.

The second issue is more subtle: the individual ps may be correlated with one another – either negatively or positively. This can make it very difficult to interpret the summary PI without access to the individual p scores. These are not simple issues to understand and some skill is needed to present the summary PI so as to minimize possible misunderstandings. Needless to say, when journalists construct league tables they show little interest in these problems with composite PIs and often ignore them.

Macro level performance measurement

Measurement of public sector output and outcomes is notoriously difficult, but is attempted at all levels. At the top level, the UK Government's concern about an apparent productivity gap led to the creation of the Atkinson Review. Its final and interim reports (Atkinson 2004; 2005) argue that relatively simple performance measures are needed, appropriately adjusted for quality and inflation. In chapter 6, O'Mahony *et al.* discuss the different approaches to assessing the effects of health care on morbidity and mortality at a national level. This chapter is not concerned with the assessment of output at the macro level of the economy, but addresses the ways that performance measurement is used in attempts to monitor and improve public services. It is probably true to say that the measures employed at the top level (e.g. an entire government department) are actually simpler than those used at the bottom level (e.g. one of its offices), which may be contrary to expectations.

Virtualism, performativity and perverse effects

Perverse effects and unintended consequences

It is well known that the use of performance measures and indicators can have perverse effects and unintended consequences. Ridgway (1956), writing over fifty years ago, discusses this in the very first volume of the *Administrative Science Quarterly*. More recently, Smith (1990) discusses the types of performance indicators used in the public sector and highlights some of the problems that can occur. Smith (1995) extends this by focusing on the unintended consequences of their publication when used in the internal management of UK public sector organizations, particularly the NHS. Eight such unintended consequences are listed, together with suggestions about how such problems can be avoided or minimized. These unintended consequences range from *tunnel vision*, which is an 'emphasis by management on phenomena that are quantified at the expense of unquantified aspects of performance'. They end with *ossification*, in which fear of failure or 'an obsessively rigid system of performance evaluation' causes managers not to innovate, but rather to seek a conservative and easy life.

Hence, like performance measurement itself, the existence of such perverse effects is uncontroversial and seems to be an accepted part of organizational life in both public and private sectors. However, these perverse and dysfunctional effects do have costs; some direct and some indirect. These are often ignored when planning a measurement system: presumably in the optimistic belief that the system in question will not produce them; only other people make mistakes. It should surely be obvious that those planning a performance measurement system ought to ensure that its benefits outweigh the costs, and there are two main sets of costs:

1. The costs of establishing and maintaining the measurement system itself – which will involve staff time, computer resources and other tangible elements. These are relatively straightforward to estimate.
2. The performance lowering effects of the dysfunctionalities, which may lead to undesirable outcomes or poorer performance than anticipated. These

costs are usually hidden, are rather harder to estimate and are often ignored. Interesting though it may be to attempt to produce accurate estimates of these costs of dysfunctionalities, it makes more sense to try to understand why these perverse effects occur so as to reduce their occurrence. This should lead to reductions in these costs.

To summarize the argument so far, performance measurement in some form or other is probably present in all organizations and it is pointless to argue about whether or not this is desirable. It is also well known that this measurement can lead to side effects, unintended consequences and dysfunctionalities. Some of these may be inevitable, some a consequence of poorly designed measurement systems and some may result from deliberate abuse of the measures in place. As noted earlier, measurement in public service organizations is typically complicated because the organization is seeking to perform against a range of criteria that may be incommensurate. This latter point makes it more likely that dysfunctionalities will occur, since public service managers will constantly need to balance one criterion against another unless they have unlimited resources available, which is very unlikely.

Virtualism and performativity

Perverse effects often occur despite the best efforts and good intentions of those developing the measurement systems and, usually, despite the similar intentions of those whose performance is being managed. Why should this be? Miller (2003) describes an anthropological study of UK local authorities under inspection by the Audit Commission as part of the Government's Best Value (BV) programme. BV is an improvement regime that has performance measurement and comparison as two of its cornerstones. To describe what he observed, Miller (2003) uses the concept of 'virtualism' – when an intended aspect or agent is subtly replaced by another.

Miller (2003: 72) lists four ways in which virtualism is evident in BV, two of which are relevant to this discussion. First, some unintended consequences occur because the pursuit of high scores on PIs may displace efforts to improve the actual outcomes. That is, 'there is an exaggerated respect for hard quantitative over soft qualitative data' (Miller 2003: 72) Though an individual or organization may achieve high scores on a PI, this good performance may be virtual rather than real when considered against what the organization has been established to achieve – similar to 'tunnel vision' as discussed in Smith (1995). In addition, organizations will, if subject to such regimes, employ staff charged to ensure that performance data and reports are presented in ways that place the organization in the best possible light. Performance presentation becomes a profession.

As an illustration of this first aspect of virtualism, consider the star ratings that have been used to summarize the performance of NHS Trusts in England. Until 2006, each Trust was awarded three, two, one or no stars depending on its performance on a basket of measures that emphasize political priorities such as patient waiting times for treatment. It was originally intended that Trusts awarded three stars would be eligible for Foundation Status, which gives them greater autonomy in decision-making and investment. Trusts awarded zero stars were labelled as failing and their Chief Executives and other directors were unlikely to remain in post for long. This highly focused regime put enormous pressure on Trusts to meet specific targets so as to achieve as high a star rating as possible. In the early days of star rating, one target related to the time that a patient must wait before an initial assessment in Accident and Emergency. It is said that some Trusts were quick to employ people to serve as 'Hello Nurses', whose job was to meet and greet the patients and to take limited information. The fact that the patient must then wait a long time for proper assessment did not matter – the target for initial assessment was met. In this, and other ways, a form of virtualism appeared in which the meeting of specific targets replaced a need to provide better patient care. This also led to another, subtle, form of virtualism in which most Trusts employ Performance Directors who are tasked with ensuring that their Trust displays itself in the best way possible for star rating – performance presentation becomes a profession.

The second relevant aspect of virtualism identified in Miller (2003) occurs when one agent is subtly replaced by another. An oft-cited justification for the publication of performance data is that it enables the public to choose between different public service offerings, which will lead to quality improvement as people flock to the better quality providers and spurn the poorer ones. Hence, public consultation and the publication of performance data to the public are fundamental to BV. However as Miller points out, it is very difficult to organize proper public consultation, and there is little evidence that the public is hungry for performance information (Marshall *et al.* 2000). However, if no general or representative public can be mobilized to deliberate over this feedback then closing the public loop is problematic. Most local authorities do their best to organize some form of public consultation, but this is often unsatisfactory and unrepresentative. Hence Miller reports that the BV auditors slipped into a role in which they acted as a virtual public. That is, they attempted to assess likely public reactions, because the public itself is uninterested in the performance data.

Performativity, which is also discussed by Collier in chapter 3, is a term that often crops up when discussing the effects of performance measurement. It is closely related to the idea of virtualism discussed above. The term *performative* seems to have arisen within linguistics (Austin 1962) and was then picked up in the field of gender relations. Perhaps implicitly drawing on these origins, researchers studying public sector performance measurement use the term *performativity* in two ways. First, people whose performance is being measured find ways to operate that will maximize the chance of a high score in the indicators being used. As Miller (2003) describes, this high score may, however, be virtual. That is, it may not lead to improved performance in the terms of the intended outcome of the system whose performance is being assessed. Nevertheless, the actions taken are performative in that they lead to a high score on the performance indicators and this is taken as a measure of success. This in turn, may lead to a second form of performativity – a subtle change through which the performance, as measured, comes to define the reality.

As an example of the second case, consider again the UK's periodic Research Assessment Exercises (RAEs). These were introduced in the early 1990s as a way to justify differential funding awarded to universities for their research activities. Until 2008, the RAE awarded a numeric grade to each university department that submitted its research for assessment. The higher the numeric grade awarded, the more funding was given to the department in question. However, as is so often the case, this rather simple performance indicator was used in very different ways by the institutions themselves. Departments that did well were quick to use the declared grade in their promotional literature and those that did badly were often threatened with closure. In effect, the RAE grades became badges of honour to indicate success in research or blemishes on a department's record. Implicit in this, and often explicit in discussion and decision-making, is that a good research department is one with a high RAE score, preferably one rated as 5∗. Thus the role of the institution is redefined by the performance assessment system as the RAE score comes to constitute the reality, that is, it leads to performativity.

The RAE is a form of non-financial audit and it should be no surprise that astute commentators on the spread of auditing have made the same point: 'Accounting information systems do not simply describe a pre-existing economic domain but ... serve to constitute a realm of facts' (Power 1997: 94). That is, if an auditing regime focuses on certain elements of performance, then these elements may take on the role of facts that define the essence of that performance. The same applies to any system of performance measurement: it starts to define how people see the world.

Performance measurement in the new public management

The simple cybernetic metaphor

Since control is a common reason for measuring performance it is worth examining what is often meant by control. Cybernetic ideas of control are widely used, sometimes just as metaphors (Morgan 1997) but sometimes in approaches such as the Viable System Model (Beer 1985) are presented as basic principles claimed to be of value in any organization. Cybernetic control is based on an assumption that control is exercised through information feedback. Much has been written on this theme, so a short summary will suffice here, using the basic idea of feedback control as shown in Figure 4.1. The role of a manager, in this metaphor, is to monitor what is happening at the output, to compare this performance with a given target and to use this information so as to move towards the target. This is done by modifying the resources used and organizing the process itself, as seems appropriate.

Hofsted (1981) uses four dimensions to assess the degree to which cybernetic control is a good fit for different types of activity. As shown in table 4.1, the four dimensions are concerned with the nature of the objectives, the degree to which performance is measurable, the state of knowledge about the activity and its effects and, finally, the degree to which this activity is continually repeated. Using these four dimensions, Hofsted (1981) considers six approaches to control, starting with routine control and ending with political control. Routine control is the term preferred by Hofsted for

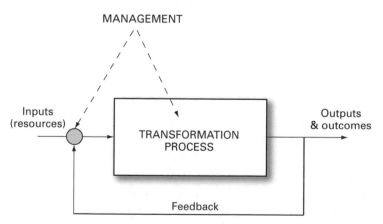

Figure 4.1 Feedback control – a cybernetic metaphor

Table 4.1: Hofsted (1981) on control

Type of control	Objectives	Measurability	Knowledge	Repetition
Routine	Unambiguous	Total	Complete	Frequent
Expert	Unambiguous	Total	Complete	Never or rare
Trial and error	Unambiguous	Total	Limited or none	Frequent
Intuitive	Unambiguous	Total	Limited or none	Never or rare
Judgemental	Unambiguous	Limited or none	Doesn't matter	Doesn't matter
Political	Ambiguous	Doesn't matter	Doesn't matter	Doesn't matter

approaches that are closest to simple cybernetic control. Essentially, this is a mechanistic approach in which a system is tuned by repetitive action so that it achieves a particular target state. At the opposite end of the spectrum is political control in which the job of a manager is to create and manage coalitions between different interest groups.

Thus, routine control (which is closest to the mechanistic cybernetic metaphor) works well when the objectives are unambiguous and agreed, the outputs and outcomes from the process can be meaningfully quantified, when there is complete knowledge of how to intervene and what the effects of the intervention will be, and when the activity is repetitive.

Moving towards the opposite end of the spectrum, there is increasing ambiguity about what the object is and it becomes much harder to measure things and increasingly unimportant whether knowledge is complete or whether the activity is continually repeated. Once we reach the political end of the spectrum, Hofsted argues that the ambiguity about objectives means that it matters little whether we can measure, have reasonable amounts of knowledge or whether the activity is repeated frequently. Hence, Hofsted argues that there are some situations in which mechanistic cybernetic control is appropriate, but there are many situations in which it is not.

Culture and control

Ouchi (1979; 1980) argues that, from the point of transaction costs, there are three distinct forms of organizational mediation and control. First, there are situations in which interdependent individuals cooperate and base this possibly brief cooperation on a price mechanism. This in turn is supported by a labour market against which the price and other terms of exchange may be tested. In Ouchi's terms, this is control exercised through a *market*. Ouchi's second form of organizational mediation and control is the *bureaucracy* in which 'each party contributes labor to a corporate body, which mediates the relationship by placing a value on each contribution and then compensating it fairly' (Ouchi 1980: 130). Whereas a market can be based on very short-term commitments, a bureaucracy requires a much longer term view. In addition, Ouchi suggests a third form of mediation and control, the *clan*, in which members of an organization are socialized into it and internalize its values. This is intrinsic control based on intrinsic motivation. Forms one and two come easily to mind when considering the classical notions of organization, compensation and control.

These three approaches involve three different control mechanisms, which shifts the argument away from simple cybernetic metaphors. In *market control*, the worker is controlled by the agreement of a suitable price for the job to be done. This brings with it the notion of agency costs, to be borne by the principal in securing the labour of the agent, or worker. Payment, in market control, is based on performance, which may be specified via an explicit contract in which as much ambiguity as possible is removed. Workers are free to take their labour elsewhere and may even break the contract if the benefits to themselves of doing so outweigh the costs. Thus, securing long-term commitment is problematic if market control is exercised.

In *bureaucratic control*, the worker receives payment in exchange for accepting day-to-day supervision in a hierarchy in which each person's work is supervised by his or her superior. This implies the existence of standards against which performance can be measured, which may not work well when there is a high degree of ambiguity and uncertainty. It does, however, form the basis of a long-term relationship and is rather like a stable marriage that may be less exciting than a series of affairs, but has other compensations. Curiously, most for-profit organizations seem to prefer market control for their senior executives, bureaucratic control for their long-term staff and market control for non-core activities.

Control by clan, however, is very different, and is based on internalized control, which may reflect values shared with the organization or from membership of an external professional group. Members of a clan share common values and beliefs – if these are the result of socialization in the organization, they will be congruent with the organization's goals. If they come from an external professionalism, then this cannot be guaranteed, since the allegiance may be to the profession rather than to the organization.

In a similar vein, Hood (1998) develops a classification scheme based on Mary Douglas's grid : group theory. The original version of this theory (Douglas 1973) came from anthropological study of the role of religion in

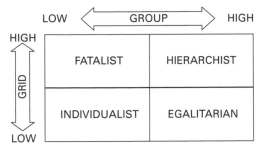
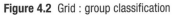

Figure 4.2 Grid : group classification

disparate communities and was a device to explain how individuals within the same group related to one another. The later version (Douglas 1982) is more general and aims to provide a way of understanding and classifying communities as a whole. Hood (1998) uses the later version, as in figure 4.2, which shows a 2 × 2 matrix with axes defined as:

- *Grid*: the degree to which people are controlled by reference to an externally imposed system of rules. The more heavily structured and dominant the set of rules, the higher will be the score on the grid dimension.
- *Group*: the degree to which people abide by the norms of the group into which they have been socialized.

As an oversimplification, grid represents externally imposed control rules (which need not mean that an individual will find them disagreeable) and group represents internally absorbed control rules.

The resulting 2 × 2 matrix contains the following four positions:

- *Hierarchist*: a group, organization or society in which both grid and group scores are high. Members of these are highly socialized into the group and abide by externally imposed norms and rules. This is similar, if not identical, to Ouchi's notion of an organization in which control is bureaucratic.
- *Individualist*: in which both the grid and group scores are low, with relationships that may be short-lived and based on mutual convenience rather than group or external norms. This is close to Ouchi's notion of a market.
- *Egalitarian*: in which the group score is high but the grid effect is low. This is similar to Ouchi's notion of an organization in which control is by clan.
- *Fatalist*: in which the grid effect is high, but the group score is low. Thus individual behaviour is governed by external rules and there is minimal cooperation between individuals. This has no counterpart in Ouchi, and Hood also regards this as a rare beast even on the public service landscape.

To recap the argument so far: some form of performance measurement is found in most, possibly all, organizations and can be well or poorly executed.

Its use in public services is essential to NPM where it forms part of a drive to ensure control over services whose provision may be decentralized and sub-contracted. However, there is a danger that the control and measurement systems may be based on highly dubious, unspoken assumptions about measurement and about control.

Ambiguity and uncertainty

Quantitative performance measurement should rest on properly designed measurement scales. Hence, it might be thought that increased measurement precision will lead to better measurement – that is, uncertainty should be reduced or, preferably, removed entirely. Such a view accords with the normal principles of the cybernetic model criticized by Hofsted (1981). However, based on public sector experience, Noordegraaf and Abma (2003) present a counter-view that some attempts to reduce uncertainty and ambiguity may be mistaken. This conclusion stems from a categorization of public management practices into three groups:

1. *Canonical practices*: those in which all the important issues are known, the necessary standards are uncontested and it is clear how to address the issues. Hence, it is sensible to use quantitative PIs to manage the performance of such practices, since ambiguity and uncertainty have, as far as possible, been reduced. It should be obvious that these canonical practices fit the criteria suggested by Hofsted for situations in which cybernetic control may be appropriate.

2. *Practices in transition*: these apply in two situations. First, they occur when facing complex issues that are difficult to address even though they are known and understood and even when values and standards are uncontested. For example, the necessary action may be just too disruptive. Second, they occur when issues are known and understood, but standards are contested – which leads to a debate about values and a need to mobilize support. In these practices in transition, quantitative PIs are of limited value and assessment is best done by expert opinion based on negotiated professional agreement.

3. *Non-canonical practices*: these apply in processes that are non-routine, fuzzy, innovative and conflictual; that is, in situations considered to be wicked problems (Rittel and Webber 1973). In such situations, the conventional assumptions about measurement systems and control make little sense. This does not mean that measurement has no value, but does mean that great care is needed to avoid virtualism and performativity.

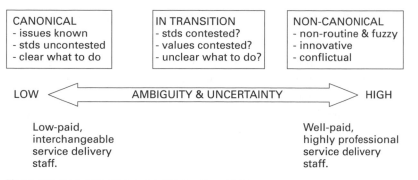

Figure 4.3 Professionalism and public service workers

The mistake, so often, is to apply performance management approaches that are appropriate to canonical practices to those that are not: that is, to practices in transition, and to non-canonical practices. It is clear that all three types of practice are found in the provision of public services and that ambiguity is sometimes necessary if any action is to be taken. Removing this ambiguity may make action impossible.

Measuring professional activity

The delivery of public services is a multi-dimensional task that requires the work and cooperation of different groups with different skills and training. Figure 4.3, based on Noordegraaf and Abma (2003), places types of public service worker on a spectrum that, for simplicity, is labelled as professionalism. At one extreme are highly trained professional groups, such as doctors and lawyers, and at the other are low-paid staff who are effectively interchangeable. The latter might be clerical staff working in an office; relatively unskilled manual workers, or others who might be similarly categorized. Without making any judgement about the value of these different groups, it is instructive to consider the nature of professional work. Though the literature on this is of many years' standing, it rarely seems to permeate discussions on performance measurement.

Schön (1983) discusses the nature of professional practice and argues that as professionals develop, they internalize their own versions of protocols and processes. These ideas, examples and actions form repertoires that become the basis for appropriate responses to new situations. These repertoires are not followed slavishly, rather a form of reflecting-on-action takes place in which the professional sees the similarities and the differences between the current situation and one previously faced.

When a practitioner makes sense of a situation he perceives to be unique, he sees it as something already present in his repertoire. To see this site as that one is not to subsume the first under a familiar category or rule. It is, rather, to see the unfamiliar, unique situation as both similar to and different from the familiar one, without at first being able to say similar or different with respect to what. The familiar situation functions as a precedent, or a metaphor, or . . . an exemplar for the unfamiliar one. (Schön 1983: 138; cited by Smith 2004).

Professionals do not just follow protocols, they develop them and do so to cope with non-canonical practices.

Any control system using narrowly defined performance measures that ignore this thinking in action may cause severe damage to this fundamental aspect of professional practice. Going even further, any measurement system that requires professionals to 'turn off' this aspect of their professionalism deserves to fail. That is, it is sometimes more important to exercise judgements by using nominal categorization than to apply quantification with seemingly accurate interval or ratio scales. This, of course, presents a challenge, since nominal categorization may be subjective. However, in some circumstances, this is preferable to the spurious accuracy of quantified measurement.

Handling statistical uncertainty

Uncertainty and ambiguity are key features of practices that are in transition or are non-canonical. As they become increasingly non-canonical, they are progressively less well suited to simple cybernetic control. So, how should such activities and practices be treated? It is tempting to imagine that they are best handled by pushing them towards the canonical end of the spectrum. That is, it is tempting to try to reduce uncertainty and ambiguity in an effort to bring them under control. This, it should be clear by now, is dangerous, but suppose that this were possible and desirable, how then might performance measurement be properly done?

Goldstein and Spiegelhalter (1996) is a conclusive demonstration of the dangers in using simplified PIs when constructing league tables in which public sector bodies, such as schools and hospitals, are ranked. A main concern of this statistical paper is that such tables rank institutions by using single point values, such as average exam scores. However, if reasonable estimates of the statistical variation of these values are included, then much of the ranking disappears. That is, the difference between the very top and very bottom may be real, but for many others, the difference is an illusion – which is little consolation to those whose careers are wrecked by the publication of these league tables. Because of this and other concerns, the RSS formed a working party that produced the report on performance monitoring in public services (Bird *et al.* 2003).

As discussed earlier, Bird *et al.* (2003) take a rather technocratic approach and argue that performance measurement (PM) and monitoring systems have three broad aims: 'to establish "what works" in promoting stated objectives of the public services; to identify the functional competence of individual practitioners or organizations; and public accountability by Ministers for their stewardship of the public services' (Bird *et al.* 2003: 5). Further, they insist that,

In each role, PM data can be used to promote change, by enabling policy-makers to adopt the most cost-effective technologies, by helping practitioners to identify opportunities for personal or organizational improvement, and by allowing voters to judge the real impact of the government's policies. (Bird *et al.* 2003: 5).

With this in mind, the working party makes a series of recommendations that can be summarized under two headings.

The first set of recommendations seems to be aimed at improving the procedures and practice of performance measurement. The working party proposes that each performance measurement exercise should be based on a detailed protocol that specifies what will be measured, how it will be measured and why it will be measured. Similarly, the RSS suggests that individuals or institutions whose performance is being monitored should have a substantial input to the design of the exercise so that counterproductive behaviour is avoided as far as is possible. The working party is also aware that any performance measurement exercise costs money and they suggest that a realistic estimate of these costs should be made so as to ensure that the benefits outweigh these costs. Finally, possibly seeking a role for the RSS itself, it suggests the independent scrutiny of performance measurement procedures. It is difficult to disagree with any of this first set of recommendations, and it seems reasonable to assume that most are likely to be implemented.

The RSS working party produced other recommendations; in particular they suggest that reported performance indicators should always include measures of uncertainty, so as to enable proper judgement to be made. It seems that, by uncertainty, they mean statistical uncertainty due to sampling schemes. This recommendation seems sensible from a technical perspective, but how such data should be presented will depend, of course, on the audience. Statisticians are very skilled at understanding statistical uncertainty, but this is not true of wider audiences. Hibbard *et al.* (2002) describe experiments in which different approaches were used to present health performance data to the public and conclude that simpler representations, with no indications of uncertainty, are more likely to be recalled sometime later – but, even then, recall is typically very low. This of course presents problems when performance data are published to increase public accountability.

Overall, these proposals seem a sensible approach to tackling the *technical* issues that should underpin sensible performance measurement in UK public services. However, though they rightly suggest that statistical uncertainty be recognized and treated appropriately, they ignore other forms of uncertainty and ambiguity. As suggested by Noordegraaf and Abma (2003), some ambiguity may be a good thing.

Bringing it all together

So what can we learn from all this? It is clear that performance measurement can go wrong and many examples illustrate this. Some conceptual clarity is needed, so that people are clear about what they are trying to do, why they try to do it and how they will do it. To some extent these are the issues addressed by the RSS working party (Bird *et al.* 2003), though its concerns were with technical issues arising from a fairly limited perspective on performance measurement in public service. We have identified five reasons why performance measurement is used in public service delivery, of which the RSS focuses only on the first three:

1. to establish what works
2. to identify functional competences
3. to support public accountability
4. to enable central control
5. for symbolic reasons

So how can this conceptual clarity be developed and implemented? Pidd (2005) uses soft systems methodology (Checkland 1981) to examine these five reasons in systems terms. This is not the place to repeat that analysis, but the main conclusion is worth repeating here – we must be clear about which of the five reasons listed above is intended to dominate in any performance measurement. It will, of course, be true that there are several reasons cited for any such system but it is likely that one will dominate. In one sense, this conclusion is no different from that reached by the RSS working party. However, we have added to other reasons for introducing performance measurement. Of these, the wish to enable central control is surely dominant in much of NPM.

However, if the main reason is to enable central control, then we should be very careful to consider the characteristics of the activities and processes that are to be measured. Hofsted is surely correct to argue that the simple cybernetic metaphor is only appropriate in very straightforward circumstances. These circumstances do occur and are particularly common in activities to the left-hand end of figure 4.3; that is, those that are repetitive and relatively low-level. However it can be tempting to assume that the same methods can be used at the right hand in figure 4.3, where activities include much ambiguity and uncertainty. Though the careful application of technical approaches is a help in coping with uncertainty in measurement, it remains true that some activities are uncertain. In such cases it is surely dangerous to assume that simple measurements and performance indicators can be used.

So what can be used instead? The only way to answer that question is to ensure that we understand something about organizational and professional culture. As we have seen, there is a link between organizational culture and how people can be motivated and controlled. Ouchi's analysis points out that control can be intrinsic, especially in highly professional groups, in which case, the key is to ensure that the goals of the professional group are aligned with the goals of funders. If this can be achieved, intrinsic control and motivation take over. If not, there will always be a battle between those who hold the purse strings and those who carry out the activity. Similar conclusions follow from Hood's use of grid : group theory. That is, it is crucial to recognize that the design and implementation of performance measurement is not just a technical task but must be aligned with the culture of the organization. If that culture needs to be changed, then so be it. However it would surely be a great mistake to assume that performance measurement is the only way of engineering such a change, were it to be desirable.

REFERENCES

Atkinson, T. (2004) *Atkinson Review: Interim Report. Measurement of Government Output and Productivity for the National Accounts.* London: The Stationery Office.
    (2005) *Atkinson Review: Interim Report. Measurement of Government Output and Productivity for the National Accounts.* Basingstoke: Palgrave MacMillan.

Austin, J. L. (1962) *How to Do Things with Words: The William James Lectures Delivered at Harvard University in 1955*. Oxford: Clarendon.

Beer, S. (1985) *Diagnosing the System for Organizations*. Chichester: John Wiley.

Bird, S. M., Cox, D. Goldstein, H., Holt, T. and Smith, P. C. (2003) *Performance Indicators: Good, Bad, and Ugly. Report of the Royal Statistical Society Working Party on Performance Monitoring in the Public Services*. London: Royal Statistical Society.

Checkland, P. (1981) *Systems Thinking, Systems Practice*. Chichester, John Wiley.

Douglas, M. (1973) *Natural Symbols: Explorations in Cosmology* (2nd edn). London: Routledge & Kegan Paul.

(1982) Cultural bias. Occasional paper no. 34, Royal Anthropological Institute of Great Britain and Ireland.

Goldstein, H. and D. Spiegelhalter (1996) League tables and their limitations: statistical issues in comparisons of institutional performance (with Discussion). *Journal of the Royal Statistical Society Series A*, **159**: 385–443.

Hibbard, J., Slovic, P., Peters, E. and Finucane, M. L. (2002) Strategies for reporting health plan performance information to consumers: evidence from controlled studies. *Health Services Research* **37**: 291–313.

Hofsted, G. (1981) Management control of public and not for profit activities. *Accounting, Organizations and Society* **6**(3): 193–211.

Hood, C. (1998) *The Art of the State*. Oxford: Oxford University Press.

(1991) A public management for all seasons? *Public Administration*, **69**(1): 3–19.

Jacobs, R., Goddard, M., and Smith, P. C. (2005), How robust are hospital ranks based on composite performance measures? *Medical Care* **43**(12): 1177–84.

(2006) Public services: are composite measures a robust reflection of performance in the public sector? University of York: Centre for Health Economics. Research Paper 16.

Kaplan, R. & Norton D. P. (1996) *The Balanced Scorecard: Translating Strategy into Action*. Boston, MA: Harvard Business School Press.

Manning, N. (2000) The new public management and its legacy. www1.worldbank.org/publicsector/civilservice/debate1.htm.

Marshall, M. N., Shekelle P. G., Leatherman, S. and Brook, R. H. (2000) The public release of performance data. What do we expect to gain? A review of the evidence. *Journal of the American Medical Association* **283**: 1866–74.

Miller, D. (2003) The virtual moment. *Royal Anthropological Institute* **9**(1): 57–75.

Moore, M. H. (2003) The public value scorecard: a rejoinder and an alternative. Review of strategic performance measurement and management in non-profit organizations, by Robert Kaplan. *HCNO Working Paper Series*, May.

Morgan, G. (1997) *Images of Organization*. Second edn. London: Sage.

Noordegraaf, M. and Abma, T. A. (2003) Management by measurement? Public management practices amidst ambiguity. *Public Administration* **81**(4): 853–73.

Ouchi, W. G. (1979) A conceptual framework for the design of organizational control mechanisms. *Management Science* **25**: 833–48.

(1980) Markets, bureaucracies and clans. *Administrative Science Quarterly* **25**: 129–41.

Pidd, M. (2005) A call for conceptual clarity: a soft systems view of performance measurement in public service delivery. Lancaster University: Management School. Working Paper 2005/24.

Power, M. (1997) *The Audit Society: Rituals of Verification*. Oxford: Oxford University Press.

Ridgway, V. F. (1956) Dysfunctional consequences of performance measurements. *Administrative Science Quarterly* **1**(2): 240–7.

Rittel, H. W. J. and Webber, M. M. (1973). Dilemmas in a general theory of planning. *Policy Sciences* **4**: 155–69.

Schön, D. A. (1983) *The Reflective Practitioner: How Professionals Think in Action*. New York: Basic Books.

Smith, M. K. (2004) D Schon (Schön): Learning, reflection and change. www.infed.org/thinkers/et-schon.htm.

Smith, P. C. (1990) The use of performance indicators in the public sector. *Journal of the Royal Statistical Society*, A **153**(1): 53–72.

  (1995) On the unintended consequences of publishing performance data in the public sector. *International Journal of Public Administration* **18**(2 & 3): 277–310.

Stationery Office (2003) *On Target? Government by Measurement*. London: HMSO.

5 Priority setting in the public sector: turning economics into a management process

Cam Donaldson, Angela Bate, Craig Mitton, Stuart Peacock and Danny Ruta

Introduction

This chapter explores the conundrum that economic frameworks designed to aid resource allocation and priority setting in the presence of scarce resources are rarely implemented by public sector managers. The overarching themes of this chapter are therefore to address why there is a lack of use of economics in priority setting and what contribution it could make, so holding out the prospect of improving accountability and efficiency in the public sector. A case will be made for collaborative research on the development of frameworks to help managers manage scarcity. This is important because, although it might be deduced that the lack of uptake of economics frameworks is due in some way to their irrelevance to management of the public sector resource, surveys of managers have indicated a willingness to work with and adopt such frameworks (Miller 1997; Mitton and Donaldson 2002).

Although the focus here is mainly on health care management, frameworks proposed in other areas of the public sector will also be discussed. The main focus on health is important because it may well represent the most successful area for the application of economics in the public sector (Blaug 1998), yet it still faces a number of major challenges. Priority setting in the health care arena was also the focus of the AIM Fellowship held by the lead author during 2003–4.

First, starting more generally and working towards health care specifically, it is shown that a lack of systematic, defensible frameworks for managing scarce resources represents a gap in the myriad Government health care reforms that have taken place over the past several years. This includes a critique of economics itself, based on the notion that the lack of uptake is as much to do with economists lacking an understanding of management processes as it is to do with managers lacking an understanding of economics. The 'where now?' question is then addressed by highlighting some successes and challenges, based on recent international experience with a framework that has been proposed in the past for health care but which has only recently been adapted in a way that fits better the complexities faced by managers in 'real world' decision-making. This framework, known as programme budgeting and marginal analysis (PBMA), is then compared with two other performance measurement and evaluation tools which are growing in popularity in the public sector more broadly, the Balanced Scorecard and Best Value. Finally, an empirical framework is outlined which can be used to assess 'readiness' of an organization for the use of systematic frameworks as well as for highlighting challenges for future research.

Economic problems in public services

Conceptually, the economic problem in the public sector is that, irrespective of the total resources available, choices amongst claims have to be made. Despite much activity with respect to public sector reform over the past fifteen to twenty years, it could be argued that, ultimately, this fundamental issue has been ignored. In the UK National Health Service (NHS), this situation has persisted for over fifty years of reform. The NHS has recently hailed successes in reduced mortality from heart disease and reduced waiting times for various treatments (Crisp 2004). This might lead one to think that, with such progress, there is now little role for economics in the management of scarcity, or indeed that the dilemma of scarcity no longer exists!

However, it could be argued that such successes have involved major sacrifices – or at least three such sacrifices. First, more resources have been allocated to the total spent on the NHS, the question being whether such investment is actually worthwhile vis-à-vis other uses of the resources. Second, even with more resources, many primary care trusts (PCTs) remain in deficit (Martin 2005). As such, organizations are continuing to add on rather than face the challenge of making difficult choices. This also raises the question of what will happen when funding increases diminish or even stop. Third, it seems that other needs have been sacrificed in order to meet those needs made more visible by the national targets they have associated with them. Local needs, falling outwith national targets, are likely to have been forgone. Current attention given by the UK government to chronic disease in part recognizes that such a 'cost' may have arisen as a consequence of progress elsewhere. Ironically, despite the contention that organizations are not able to face the challenge of making difficult choices, senior managers in the UK and elsewhere recognize a lack of systematization and rigour in their commissioning processes and desire tools to move them towards this (Miller 1997; Mitton and Donaldson 2002). This might, therefore, reflect a lack of confidence to set priorities explicitly, of awareness of tools to assist in this process, or even a fundamental imbalance of power between the managers who are accountable for NHS expenditure, and the clinicians who actually commit those resources. Similar problems have been shown to exist in other major areas of the public sector, such as local government and policing (Preskill and Torres 1999; Sanderson 2001; Collier chapter 3, this volume).

Economics has been successfully taken up in the public sector through some national-level bodies, such as the NHS's National Institute for Health and Clinical Excellence (NICE), but its use has not permeated any further. This is important, because, although NICE makes recommendations to the rest of the NHS about which technologies to adopt, PCTs have fixed budgets. The claims on their resources outstrip what is available and they deal with a much wider range of health care 'goods' than a body like NICE can ever hope to. It is in organizations like PCTs, and no doubt in education and police authorities as examples from other sectors, that scarcity really bites. However, economics is rarely drawn upon to inform the management of such scarcity.

Economics, therefore, seems to be at a stage where it has penetrated national-level bodies, but has not done so at the local level. The NHS is at a stage where some sort of framework is required which allows local commissioners of care to manage scarcity. This is the result of two factors: (i) it is reasonable to assume that the NHS budget will not continue to grow at the same rate once expenditures have come into line with the European average of gross national product spent on health care, as recommended by Wanless (2002); and (ii) existing deficits combined with recommendations of national bodies (such as NICE and National Service Frameworks, or NSFs) are detached from the choices and sacrifices that have to be made.

A mature approach to commissioning would recognize that such local management of scarcity could mean trading off competing national priorities against one another or against local needs, as considerations of the 'local' and the 'national' would be integrated within one accountability framework. Of course, the other side of this coin is that departures from national guidance would have to be justified. But, this could only be done by using a defensible and transparent framework. In principle, such a process would work better, in terms of NHS efficiency and equity, than the suggestion of giving bodies like NICE a budget to pay for the implementation of their recommendations (Maynard *et al.* 2004), not all of which will be suitable for all geographic areas, and which in any case would not address the more insidious problems caused by a lack of financial accountability at the clinical level.

Priority setting in commissioning public services: where are we . . .?

Management of scarcity requires the development of defensible tools and frameworks to help managers and clinicians in this complex task. As economics is the 'science of choice', this discipline should have a central role to play here. However, this has to be about more than developing increasingly technical approaches to cost-effectiveness and cost–benefit analyses (CEAs and CBAs) for bodies like NICE or in simply publishing CEAs and CBAs and expecting the results of such studies to be taken up by managers operating in a different context from that in which the research took place.

So, what are economists to do? It might be that we need to shift to a different research paradigm, such as that provided by qualitative research, to begin to understand the barriers and facilitators to the uptake of economics in public sector management. The discipline may even wish to go further and work with resource managers in thinking about how to take the same basic principles of opportunity cost and marginal analysis (see the relevant sub-section below) on which CEAs and CBAs are based and turning these principles into a management process. This would mean that economists have to think about the stages that managers would have to go through to implement a process of scarcity management in developing local delivery plans and service level agreements and may mean moving from more instrumental forms of rationality, with which economists seem to feel more comfortable, to something more procedural, recognizing behavioural norms and the need for greater pragmatism.

Without such a framework, it is difficult to see a way forward for public sector organizations to achieve (or remain in) financial balance when faced, in the case of the PCTs in the NHS, not only with national targets and guidance, but also with financial demands from Foundation Hospitals and the independent sector, as well as other local needs which have to be met. Development of frameworks to assist in making defensible commissioning choices in the face of such formidable claims on the resources of such organizations would appear to be a missing link in the government's reform agenda across the public sector, recent guidance on practice-based commissioning in the NHS being a case in point (Donaldson *et al.* 2005). Without an explicit, systematic process for priority setting at the local level, commissioners have 'muddled through', relying on a combination of allocating resources to areas historically receiving funding and using the 'squeaky wheel gets the grease' type of politically based decision-making processes (Miller 1997; Mitton and Donaldson 2002).

... and where should we be going?

How do we overcome this? First, it seems that public sector managers receive no formal training in economics and priority setting, which, it could be claimed, is at odds with one of their major day-to-day tasks: the management of a large (but scarce) resource. Interestingly, the lack of ability to implement priority setting initiatives (such as Best Value) in local government has been attributed to aspects such as a lack of capacity for critical reflection and evaluation (Preskill and Torres 1999; Sanderson 2001). To date, in the NHS, no systematic framework for commissioning, which recognizes scarcity and can explicitly address trade-offs, has been implemented. It would seem that the development of such a framework is essential for matching national priorities (and successes) with local needs and to provide local health organizations with a defensible mechanism for (occasionally) justifying a focus on the local as well as the national agenda. An early report on NICE by the House of Commons Health Committee stated that practical systems and structures should be put in place to improve capacity to implement guidance, as implicit prioritization is insufficient, and the government must work towards 'a comprehensive framework for health care prioritisation, underpinned by an explicit set of ethical and rational values to allow the relative costs and benefits of different areas of NHS spending to be comparatively assessed in an informed way' (House of Commons 2002: 50). Publications from NICE itself have also recognized this need (Bate *et al.* 2004).

Second, it is important for managers and economists to work together in order to turn economics into a management process and to work with other disciplines in doing this. For example, another discipline which recognizes scarcity of resources is ethics, and it is possible for ethics to be brought to bear in evaluating priority setting processes in terms of their 'fairness'.

In the next section, the focus is more explicitly on health. An approach to priority setting that has been used in the UK and elsewhere is described, with discussion as to how: (1) it has built on its economic roots; (2) it recognizes complexity, as part of the attempt to entrench it more readily in organizations as part of the management process; and (3) ethics might be drawn into the debate. Subsequent to this section, attempts that have been made to evaluate services in other public sector areas will be compared with that outlined in the next section.

Programme budgeting and marginal analysis: a framework for health care?

PBMA is an approach for setting priorities which has been reported to be used in health organizations mainly in Britain, Australia, New Zealand and Canada.

Basic principles

Programme budgeting and marginal analysis (PBMA) is an economic approach to priority setting that allows for the complexities of health care decision-making, and also adheres to the two key economic concepts of 'opportunity cost' and 'the margin'. When having to make choices within the constraint of limited resources, certain opportunities will be taken up while others must be forgone. Benefits associated with forgone opportunities are opportunity costs. Thus, we need to know the costs and benefits from various health care activities, and this is best addressed 'at the margin', where the focus is on benefit gained from the next unit of resources, or benefit lost from having one unit less. If the marginal benefit per £ spent from programme A is greater than for B, resources should be taken from B and given to A. On the (reasonable) assumption of diminishing marginal benefit, whereby people are treated in order of magnitude of benefits to be gained, other things being equal, cutting back on B will increase the ratio of marginal benefits per £ spent, whilst expanding A will diminish its equivalent ratio as less 'needy' people are treated. This process of reallocation should continue until the ratios of marginal benefit to marginal cost for the programmes are equal, maximizing total patient benefit derived from the combined budgets of the two programmes. The opportunity cost of funding one more hip replacement for example, could be the benefit forgone by not using that resource to fund a renal dialysis intervention. Thus, the application of economics becomes about the balance of such services, not introduction or elimination of a service in totality. Examining changes at the margin is central to attempting to make the most of resources available when deploying them either across or within programmes.

'Five questions' in the PBMA process

The starting point of PBMA is to examine how resources are currently spent before focusing on marginal benefits and marginal costs of changes in that spend (Donaldson and Farrar 1993). Generally, PBMA can be used at a micro

Table 5.1: Five questions about resource use

1. What are the total resources available within a given service area or health organization?
2. On which services are these resources currently spent?
3. What services are candidates for receiving more or new resources (and what are the costs and potential benefits of putting resources into such growth areas)?
4. Can any existing services be provided as effectively, but with fewer resources, so releasing resources to fund items on the growth list?
5. If some growth areas still cannot be funded, are there any services which should receive fewer resources, or even be stopped, because greater benefit per £ spent (or a greater fit with other defined criteria) would be reached by funding the growth option as opposed to the existing service?

level (i.e. within programmes of care) or at a macro level (i.e. across all services and programme areas within a single health organization). At its core, the approach can be operationalized by asking the five questions about resource use listed in table 5.1.

Programme budgeting comprises the first two questions, while the last three pertain to marginal analysis. The underlying premise of programme budgeting is that we cannot know where we are going if we do not know where we are. This fundamental need to understand how resources have been used has led the UK Department of Health to require all PCTs to collect programme budgeting information as part of the 2003/2004 statutory accounts process. After several rounds of returns, results are available on the Department of Health website (www.dh.gov.uk/programmebudgeting).

The focus with marginal analysis, not included in the Department of Health exercise, then moves to examining the costs and benefits of proposed changes in the services provided and using this information to improve benefit overall. This is generally done through the formation of an advisory panel charged with making recommendations in line with better meeting a pre-defined set of criteria.

If the health care budget is fixed, opportunity cost is accounted for by recognizing that the items for service growth (question 3 of table 5.1) can be funded only by taking resources from elsewhere (questions 4 and 5). Resources can be obtained from elsewhere by being more technically efficient (e.g. treating the same conditions differently and achieving the same health outcome at less cost) or more allocatively efficient (e.g. moving resources across conditions to achieve a greater overall health outcome). This can be done 'at the margin' by considering the amounts of different services provided. Although in reality quantitative data on marginal benefits is often lacking in many areas of health care, it is the way of thinking underpinning the PBMA framework that is of importance. Alongside this, criteria can be developed to allow judgement to facilitate the process (see following sub-section).

Of course, governments tend to add real resources incrementally to health organization budgets year on year, and many of these resources will go to the top-priority growth areas. However, given that such increased funds are unlikely to cover all proposed growth areas, the principles of PBMA still apply. In principle, at another extreme, the whole base budget, as opposed to annual increments, is available for consideration for reallocation.

While the application of PBMA is not without challenges (Mitton *et al.* 2004), the framework has been used on well over seventy occasions in over sixty organizations (Mitton and Donaldson 2001). However, one might wonder why even greater use has not occurred, particularly in bodies like NHS PCTs. One explanation might be that the results of traditional economic evaluations generally have a poor track record of adoption within the NHS other than at a national level (McDonald 2002), and PBMA is perceived in a similar light. It is important to stress, however, that PBMA is different to standard economic evaluation. Although based on the same principles, the implementation of PBMA has developed whereby, rather than simply handing over a set of principles and five simple questions to NHS managers, these principles and questions are used to create a *management process*, into which results from standard economic evaluations and other evidence can be incorporated. Thus, even when economic evaluations are not adopted, the principles still can be, and they can be adapted to 'real world' local situations. This requires a more detailed understanding of how health services' planning processes work so that the process can provide more detailed steps for managers to work through. It also requires economists to consider an alternative research paradigm for investigating the use of such a framework and the barriers and facilitators associated with its uptake.

From economic framework to management process

Table 5.2 outlines stages of a PBMA process, serving as a quick reference for such activity. A practical toolkit is available describing the stages in more detail (Mitton and Donaldson 2004).

Scope and programme budget

The first step is to determine the aim and scope of the priority setting activity. This may be to determine optimum investment of resources across all

Table 5.2: Seven stages in a PBMA priority setting exercise

PBMA Stages

(1) Determine the aim and scope of the priority setting exercise
(2) Compile a programme budget (i.e. map of current activity and expenditure)
(3) Form marginal analysis advisory panel and stakeholder advisory groups
(4) Determine locally relevant decision-making criteria
    a. Decision-maker input
    b. Stakeholder input (e.g. service providers, patients, public)
(5) Advisory panel to identify options in terms of:
    a. areas for service growth
    b. areas for resource release through producing same level of output (or outcomes) but with fewer resources
    c. areas for resource release through scaling back or stopping some services
(6) Advisory panel to make recommendations in terms of:
    a. funding growth areas with new resources
    b. decisions to move resources from (5b) into (5a)
    c. trade-off decisions to move resources from (5c) to (5a) if relative value in (5c) is deemed greater than that in (5a)
(7) Validity checks with additional stakeholders and final decisions to inform budget planning process

programmes within a health authority, or alternatively, to determine how best to spend resources within a specific hospital service. Next, a programme budget is developed, mapping current activity and expenditure in the health organization or programme (or set of programmes) under consideration. The programme budget provides a starting point from which resource reallocation and service redesign options can be considered.

Advisory panel

Typically, a PBMA process relies upon an advisory panel which is charged with identifying, for a given budget planning cycle, areas of service growth, and, in order to fund the proposed growth, areas for resource release (Cohen 1994). The balance is in obtaining representativeness but without being overly large, so as to make decision-making manageable. The specific composition will be dependent on the question under consideration and the scope of the exercise but could comprise a mix of clinical personnel and managers, and could include lay membership. For application at a fairly broad level, the core advisory panel might simply be the senior management team of the health organization. For applications within programme areas, programme administrators and relevant clinical staff can be involved. In addition, data and financial personnel are key.

Decision-making criteria

Prior to examining options for change, the panel must determine a set of decision-making criteria on which the activity will be based (stage 4 of table 5.2). These criteria may reflect the values of the given organization, the health care system, or more broadly, society at large. Examples from the literature would include health gain, access, innovation, sustainability, staff retention/ recruitment, and system integration. Criteria can be identified in various ways. One option would be for the decision-makers to do this on their own, which may include a review of relevant business plans and other internal documents. Alternatively, input from other stakeholders, such as the Board of Directors of the health organization can be obtained. The public can also be consulted, through survey work or focus groups. Regardless of the source, it is important that the criteria be specified *a priori*. They may be weighted to reflect their relative importance.

Identifying options for change

Once the advisory panel is set and the criteria have been identified, a prioritized list of service growth options can be developed (stage 5). As well, current expenditure can be examined to determine means of improving operational efficiency, and options for service reduction can be identified. While not without challenges, as discussed below, these processes are perhaps best supported through the use of standardized business cases. In the case of setting priorities across all programmes in the given organization, each senior manager would be required to put forth service growth options from their own programme areas, as well as efficiency opportunities and options for service reduction. If the application is within a specific programme area, the steps are the same conceptually, but potential redesigns will likely be of a smaller scale and middle or frontline managers would be involved (although they are likely to be consulted even in a cross-programme exercise). As outlined above, resource releases can come in the form of operational efficiency gains (achieving the same outcomes at less cost) and service reductions or disinvestments (where a service which is effective, but in only a small way, may be scaled back, at the margin, to release resources for a more effective service development).

Rating options for change

Importantly, each option for growth and reduction should be explicitly rated against the pre-defined criteria, using available supporting evidence. For example, if health gain is a criterion, the business case should contain information on how proposed service growth items will impact health outcomes for the relevant population. A business case template can be designed in a manner which readily facilitates scoring against the selected criteria.

Once the rating of each option against the criteria is completed and relevant supporting information and details are inputted into the business cases, scores can then be vetted by the advisory panel. As per steps (6a–c) in table 5.2, recommendations would be made by the advisory panel to first move resources from operational efficiency gains into growth areas, and then to examine trade-offs between items on the service growth and service reduction lists. For the latter, it is useful to construct a single combined ranking of remaining service growth options and proposed service reduction options based on the business case assessments, according to the pre-defined criteria.

For example, following rating and weighting on each decision-making criterion, all other things being equal, service growth items A, B and C may be assigned scores of 90, 80 and 70 (out of 100) respectively, while proposed service reduction options X, Y and Z may have scores of 85, 75 and 65 respectively. Thus, the combined listing in order of preference, according to the criteria and subsequent scores, would be: A, X, B, Y, C, Z. Ranking in this manner indicates that A is the preferred option, and in order to pursue A, resources could be released from lowest ranked service reduction option(s) currently receiving funding. As option Z is the lowest ranked item, logically, resources should first be freed from this item and put towards A. (Rating can be based on qualitative or quantitative scales.) Weighting of the criteria should be done *a priori*, and may include quite sophisticated methods such as discrete choice experiments. Each criterion weight would be multiplied by the score given to the option under consideration. For example, option A might score 85/100 on health gain and 95/100 on access. With both health gain and access weighted equally (i.e., given a weight of 0.5 each), this would result in option A receiving a total score of 90 out of 100.)

This process of comparing service growth and service reduction options should continue until it is decided that no more gain would be had by switching resources between options. Multi-attribute decision analysis software can be used within the decision-making framework once criteria have been selected and weighted (Mabin *et al.* 2001). Using such software does not alleviate the need for decisions to be made, but can help to organize the options and facilitate the decision-making process.

The notion of freeing resources through improving operational efficiency is commonplace in health organizations. The much more challenging task is to obtain resource releases through actual service reductions and disinvestments.

As stated above, however, the logic is clear: if service growth options cannot be wholly funded through new monies and revenue generation, and operational efficiency gains have been exhausted, then some services must be scaled back or stopped in order for additional growth items to be pursued. Proposed service reduction items are not necessarily 'bad' in their own right, and indeed may be producing some value. The point here though is that if a service reduction option is producing less value than a service growth option *at the margin*, resources should be shifted accordingly.

Supporting evidence and information

In order to support the PBMA process, information can be obtained from available sources including evidence from the literature such as outcomes studies, economic evaluations or health technology assessments, quality reports from the Internet, regional or government policies and guidelines, local utilization data, informal input from staff, clinicians and members of the public, and reports/guidelines from government health departments, to name just a few. In some cases, collection of primary evidence as part of the PBMA process may be warranted (Astley and Wake-Dyster 2001). If obtaining specific information from the public is of particular interest, eliciting such information through public consultation can also be carried out and included. Guidelines can be drawn up within the organization providing details on the various sources of information available, and how this information is best used. As a final check, as per table 5.2, the last stage of PBMA is to conduct a round of consultations with a wider group of relevant stakeholders, including clinicians or members of the public, in order to test the validity of the recommendations. At this point, any concerns can be taken back to the advisory panel and final decisions made.

Summary

No matter how much or how little actual evidence is available, in the end the members of the advisory panel are responsible for making recommendations as to whether resources should be shifted (Peacock 1998). Where evidence is lacking, group members can base recommendations on their own 'expert' opinion. Decisions in most health organizations are currently being made implicitly. The PBMA approach attempts to make the process transparent, enables explicit comparison of options based on set criteria, and provides a forum through which various pieces of information can be considered by the relevant decision-makers. One of the advantages of the approach is that it can be as sophisticated or as pragmatically oriented as is required, but is still based on the fundamental economic principles of opportunity cost and the margin. Despite the basis on principles, the above discussion has, hopefully, shown how such principles can be enacted in terms of a management process.

Researching the process

In recent years, much progress has been made, internationally, on developing economics-based frameworks in the ways described above (Scott *et al.* 1998; Mitton and Donaldson 2002; Mitton *et al.* 2002). The process has now been 'evaluated' in several contexts through open-ended interviews, conducted following PBMA exercises, with managers stating that such a process allows: all proposed service developments to be treated equally, according to pre-defined criteria; consideration of whether, once development monies are spent, the authority concerned would like to consider weighing up currently unfunded developments against potential areas for disinvestment.

Much of this progress is also due to economists adopting a different research paradigm; that of qualitative research. For example, it could be argued that one reason for a lack of uptake of economics frameworks is that academics have not spent enough time 'listening to the bureaucrats' (Mooney and Wiseman 1999). Instead, at least in health economics, there has been a focus on improving technical aspects of evaluatory tools such as CEA, rather than ensuring that what is technically sound is also practically applicable. As Jan (2000) suggests, consideration of the institutional context is a key factor in uptake and application of health economics in real-world settings.

Such qualitative research can be based on interview-type work of the sort described above or even more detailed participatory action research (PAR). For example, between late 2001 and mid 2002, a PAR project was conducted in a single, urban health region in Alberta, Canada (Mitton *et al.* 2003). The primary objective of the project was to develop and implement a macro-level approach to priority setting across major service areas within the Calgary Health Region (CHR) for the 2002/3 budget. The advantage of using a PAR approach in this context was that not only were the researchers in a position to influence priority setting processes in the CHR, but decision-makers also had ample opportunity to engage in the creation of the processes so that the resulting framework catered to the environment in which the priority setting activity was to be carried out.

The results of the Alberta-based PAR project are reported in detail else-where (Mitton and Donaldson 2003). In brief, a multi-disciplinary working group within the CHR proposed service growth (i.e. investment) options totalling approximately $20M (CAN), as well as operational efficiency gains in the order of $45M and genuine service reductions (i.e. disinvestments) of about $1M. The Board had initially earmarked $12M for new growth initiatives, leaving about $8M in unfunded options. With a $42M deficit, most of the internally released resources were taken up, but a remaining $4M was allocated for additional investment options. It was argued that such a large-scale reallocation process, across major service areas within a single health region, had not previously been conducted.

The major hindrance of PBMA at this level, i.e. releasing resources to reinvest elsewhere, was overcome in part due to the fiscal imperative, but was also fostered through a genuine desire of decision-makers to see the health of the population improve within available resources. In this respect, while some 'turf wars' persisted, due to the integrated nature of the Health Region, the CHR was able to shift resources across major service areas to improve benefit overall. Following this first application of macro-level PBMA in the CHR, during which the researchers had an active role in guiding the priority setting process, decision-makers then adopted and carried out the PBMA process without the assistance of researchers, for the 2003–4, 2004–5 and 2005–6 budget cycles. In each round, the process has been continually improved; an example of this being an attempt to refine the process of weighting criteria through the application of discrete choice experiments (Ryan 2004). To assess the ethics of the PBMA process, Accountability for Reasonableness (A4R) has been used to evaluate a PBMA exercise (Gibson et al. 2006). A future step may involve tying both ethics and economics together in managing scarcity.

Other public sector initiatives: 'Balanced Scorecard' and 'Best Value'

It is important at this stage to reflect on how priority setting and management of resources have developed slightly differently in health as compared with other sectors. To do this, we will review two important developments which have also been used to examine resource use and assess, in some sense, how performance matches expectations in the public sector: 'Balanced Scorecard' and 'Best Value'. Each has become more popular throughout the 1990s and 2000s in the public sector internationally. The former, in particular, has been adopted in some health care organizations whilst the latter has not really figured in health care. Indeed, it could be argued that 'Best Value' is a PBMA-type process that has been used in non-health areas of the public sector.

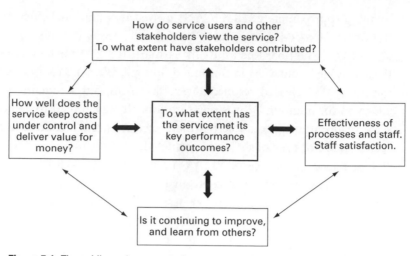

Figure 5.1 The public sector scorecard

Balanced Scorecard

As with many performance measures in the public sector, the Balanced Scorecard stemmed from work in the private sector which was based on concerns that financial measures alone were insufficient for managing a company. Developed by Kaplan and Norton (1992), from work conducted with several corporate entities, the Balanced Scorecard tries to develop a balanced and integrated set of performance measures to assess how to reach a common set of goals (Kaplan and Norton 1992; 1996; 2000).

The history of the Balanced Scorecard is well known, although there is little rigorous evidence as to its effectiveness (Neely *et al.* 2004). Despite this, it has been adopted on a relatively widespread basis in the public sector in the UK. An example, of a public sector scorecard, developed by Moulin (2004), is shown in figure 5.1. Such scorecards take many forms, but the basics are similar. Issues related to costs and value for money are addressed in the left-hand box, stakeholder views of the organization at the top, effectiveness of processes to the right and effectiveness as a learning organization at the bottom. Each of these would be reviewed in relation to how well they are helping the organization meet its strategic goals, found in the middle of figure 5.1.

The cause-and-effect relationship of each element of the scorecard is represented by the arrows in figure 5.1. However, the notion of scarcity is not mentioned in the presentations in the scorecard. Although it is useful to acknowledge the causal relationship of inputs with outputs, as might be the case with a Balanced Scorecard, we would argue that it is also important for a model to explicitly recognize the fact that choosing to put more of the organization's inputs into one action may mean that, at the margin, another activity has to be scaled back. This is particularly the case in the public sector, where most organizations are operating on a fixed budget which might vary only very slightly from year to year.

A less positive interpretation of the above might then be that schemes such as the Balanced Scorecard help management avoid the real issues; these being the challenges of making tough choices, and therefore, of priority setting. Another, more positive, view is simply that activities such as Balanced Scorecard and PBMA are complementary in the sense that it is important to identify weaknesses and strengths of an organization with respect to how it is meeting its goals, but that a choice to act on a particular aspect in an attempt to improve performance is likely to have resource consequences which should be considered within a framework which recognizes that such resources are scarce. At a minimum, the Balanced Scorecard can serve to highlight organizational objectives which may form the basis of a set of decision-making criteria upon which trade-offs are considered in a PBMA-like approach.

Best Value

Best Value was introduced into the public sector on a voluntary basis in the late 1990s and is now statutory within local government. In line with attempts to 'modernize' other areas of the public sector, Best Value seeks to ensure that management and business practices in local government deliver better and more responsive public services (Scottish Executive 2003). Laudable objectives are espoused in the name of Best Value, such as allowing local government to: balance quality service provision against costs; achieve sustainable development; be accountable and transparent by engaging with the local community; ensure equal opportunities; and continuously improve the outcomes of services provided.

At the same time, Best Value is both broader than PBMA but also, it could be argued, not as challenging in terms of the questions it poses about resource use. For example, in terms of breadth, Best Value might involve reviewing an authority with respect to the following factors which are described in more detail in table 5.3: commitment and leadership, responsiveness and consultation, sound governance at strategic, financial and operational levels, and effective performance management systems. A 'Best Value Authority' would also develop cultures which encourage equal opportunity, sustainable development and consideration of impacts of decisions on local business communities.

Table 5.3: Broad review criteria for Best Value

Criterion	Description
Commitment and leadership	Acceptance of the principles of Best Value and development of a vision of how Best Value will contribute to the corporate goals of the authority which informs the direction of services and is communicated effectively to staff
Responsiveness and consultation	In particular, responsiveness to the needs of, and communication with, communities, citizens, customers, employees and other stakeholders, such as public sector partners and the local business, voluntary and community sectors
Sound governance at strategic, financial and operational levels	Involving a framework for planning and budgeting that includes detailed and realistic plans linked to available resources, to achieve the authority's goals at service delivery level
Effective performance management systems	Including the use of external comparison, through which performance issues can be identified, monitored and addressed

The more specific part of Best Value relates to the economics of the process. It is important under Best Value to have sound management of resources, which involves making the best use of public resources and maintaining an appropriate balance between cost and quality. The process involves the use of options appraisal which can be used within any area of work to ensure competitiveness with regard to quality and potential for improvement. The process involved here is similar to PBMA, whereby a service area can be 'challenged' to provide evidence of Best Value. However, the process differs slightly from PBMA in that it tends to concentrate on a particular service area and examines issues such as quality obtained for the resources put in and, for example, whether the service could be provided more competitively (i.e. more cheaply). The focus here on achieving Best Value within one service area (referred to as technical efficiency) is narrower than that adopted in a PBMA. Little or no recognition is given to the possibility that trade-offs might have to be made between service areas in order to achieve a better outcome for the community overall. Therefore, in this sense PBMA may be viewed as a more comprehensive framework, but there may well be lessons to learn from the implementation of Best Value which, we think, is more widespread in local government than PBMA is in the NHS. For example, the Best Value methodology places a substantial emphasis on rigorous benchmarking of existing services and practices in order to identify options for service change within the organization undertaking the Best Value review.

Development of an empirical framework and future research programme

Based on the empirical evidence from the research on PBMA reported above, a model of the PBMA process has been depicted as per figure 5.2, which draws out some of the important organizational barriers and facilitators to the initial uptake of the framework and implementation of recommendations emanating from applying the framework (Mitton and Donaldson 2004). This model encompasses key issues highlighted by Peacock (1998) for the development and application of PBMA as a practical decision-making aid, and serves as a summary of important issues identified in this Alberta-based research project. The point to take from the model as outlined is that while a PBMA exercise can be conducted perfectly in a 'technical' sense, an understanding of the context in which the application of PBMA – or any explicit, evidence-based

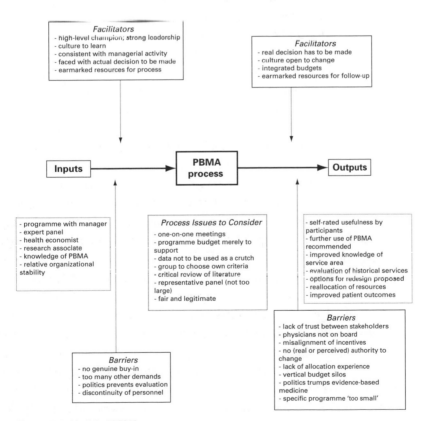

Figure 5.2 Model of PBMA process

decision-making framework – takes place is required in order for the exercise to have a chance at being successful, however 'success' is defined.

To date, the PBMA process has essentially been examined in the priority setting literature in isolation. That is, the focus has been on going through the seven stages outlined above. The hypothesis here is that one of the main reasons for the lack of even greater proliferation of PBMA in Western Europe and North America, to this point, has been due to the PBMA process being applied without an understanding of the decision-making context of health organizations. Similarly, Best Value has been criticized for providing structure, process and systems relating to performance review, but without an understanding of the cultures in which the framework is applied, and, perhaps, the need to change such cultures (Martin *et al.* 1999; Sanderson 2001). Figure 5.2 attempts to set the PBMA process within the context in which it is to be applied, to provide a more complete description of this type of priority setting activity. It was first published in Mitton and Donaldson (2001). The model is also put forth as an 'evaluation framework' for future PBMA studies, as well as those on Best Value, which will require prospective application and validation. Indeed, innovative designs, through which comparison to the depicted model can be made, should be pursued.

A description of the model is presented below. Following this we outline how it can be used to evaluate further priority setting exercises and present a summary of a review of the management and organizational behaviour literature to determine if the model is representative of other decision-making processes.

So, turning to figure 5.2 more explicitly, the empirical model was depicted to portray a number of 'inputs' which should be in place for the PBMA process to be conducted. These can be viewed as prerequisites to conducting a PBMA exercise; without any one of these, application of the framework may still proceed, but success is more likely if all are present for a given exercise. Highlighted under the 'PBMA process' box are a number of the key 'lessons learned' from previous applications to illustrate that sound methodology must be applied for the process to move forward. For example, one-on-one meetings are useful for generating ideas for scaling back services which people may be reluctant to bring forward initially in group situations. Issues about the programme budget and not using data as a crutch are to do with emphasizing that PBMA is as much a thought process as a technical exercise and, therefore, can still proceed without perfect information. From there, numerous 'outputs' can potentially result from any given PBMA process. These outputs include resource reallocation and improved patient outcomes, but are expanded to also include other items such as the evaluation of historical services and improved knowledge of a given service area. The outputs were generated from decision-makers who have used the PBMA approach, and helps to move the understanding of PBMA from a purely economic technique (concerned with measuring marginal costs and benefits) to a management process which contributes to strategic planning.

Barriers and facilitators to the PBMA process were also empirically observed from previous work and are included in the model. In some cases PBMA exercises will not even get off the ground, thus an accurate depiction of the process requires that barriers and facilitators be highlighted after the input box but before the process commences. Similarly, factors following the PBMA process may prevent recommendations from being reached or followed through to the point of being put into practice, and other factors may serve as facilitators. The depiction of barriers and facilitators in this manner actually has its roots in psychology, whereby Lewin (1951) examined factors influencing change in individuals, and coined the term 'force field analysis'.

Considering the literature reviewed, a number of key points can be taken away for future priority setting exercises, specifically with respect to the empirical model outlined in this chapter. First, an understanding of the 'antecedent conditions' which exist in a given health organization must be obtained and used to strategically plan whether the time and setting are most receptive to explicit priority setting activity. Second, there must be one person with overall 'change' responsibility, and there must be an environment where learning and innovation are key values. Third, identifying the organizational culture and determining processes to work through the challenges are clear prerequisites for any priority setting study. Finally, the reviewed literature emphasizes the importance of group training, which is particularly relevant for the PBMA process which is to be used by health region personnel, and the need to develop a unified vision for the expert panel at the outset of an exercise.

In summary, the broader literature has many references to decision-making processes, and barriers and facilitators to change (Daley and Kettner 1986; Mink et al. 1993; Shortell and Kaluzny 1994; Rogers 1995; Grol and Grimshaw 1999; Spasoff 1999) but explicitly setting the process within the context of the organization was not found elsewhere. Thus use of the empirical model as an evaluative framework for future priority setting exercises would represent a major contribution of this work.

The literature reviewed above brings us to two research questions: what conditions are required to be in place prior to the implementation of a framework such as PBMA; and can possible barriers be identified and overcome before embarking on the implementation process?

Coming back to the point on evaluation of the framework itself, the broader set of outputs can be taken as evaluative criteria on which PBMA exercises can be rated. Future case studies may use this list of criteria, first to test the validity of the model, particularly noting that it was created following the compilation of results from this research project (i.e. developed retrospectively), but further, with refinement, to use it in judging the success or failure of future PBMA studies. In this way, a standardized evaluation tool for PBMA studies – and perhaps other evidence-based decision-making processes – can emerge and be used in health regions internationally. Coupled with work comparing the use of PBMA to other alternative uses of managerial time, this can help to develop an understanding of both how best to use PBMA (i.e. is it doing what it should be doing?) and whether it is a worthwhile activity for managers.

Further, it would be important to build on the Alberta work discussed above in examining priority setting, through the use of a framework like PBMA, across major segments of an integrated health organization.

Conclusions

PBMA provides a frame to guide managers in having to make choices between competing claims on limited resources and in critiquing existing services vis-à-vis a new service alternative. Along with other innovations in the public sector, such as Best Value, it can be viewed as an improvement over historical and/or political allocation processes commonly used in health care and, relative to other frameworks used to manage scarcity in the public sector, it is the only one which builds its process on an explicit recognition of this reality. This, however, raises challenges for implementation of such processes. In particular, their use is not as widespread as it could be and they are not actively promoted by government as having a central role in the myriad of reforms which have beset the public sector in the past ten to fifteen years. Despite this, such frameworks offer great potential for reconciling central direction with local needs.

Culture change is the key and economists must learn the value of other research paradigms to our understanding – by both adopting these alternative methods and also working with others who specialize in such methods. If PBMA and Best Value are part of the solution for sustainable public services, then large investments are required in training programmes and action research that will allow researchers and managers to work together to ensure that such schemes are based in reality whilst still being based on rigorous principles. We hope that the model we have outlined here will provide a framework around which to build such research.

REFERENCES

Astley, J. and Wake-Dyster, W. (2001) Evidence-based priority setting. *Australian Health Review* **24**(2): 32–9.

Bate, A., Donaldson, C. and Hope, A. (2004) *Priority Setting and Health Care Commissioning: Is there a Case for a UK Network?* in Littlejohns, P. and Rawlins, M. (eds.) *Delivering Quality in the NHS*. London, Radcliffe Medical Press.

Blaug, M. (1998) Where are we now in British health economics? *Health Economics* **7**(Suppl. 1): S63–S78.

Cohen, D. (1994) Marginal analysis in practice: an alternative to needs assessment for contracting health care. *BMJ* **309**(6957): 781–4.

Crisp, N. (2004) *The NHS Improvement Plan: Putting People at the Heart of Public Services*. London. Department of Health (also available at www.dh.gov.uk/assetRoot/04/08/83/76/3).

Daley, J.M. and Kettner, P.M. (1986) The episode of purposive change. *Journal of the Community Development Society* **17**(2): 54–72.

Donaldson, C. and Farrar, S. (1993) Needs assessment: developing an economic approach. *Health Policy* **25**: 95–108.

Donaldson, C., Bate, A. and Bryan, S. (2005) Practice-based commissioning: a treatment without a diagnosis?. *Health Service Journal* **21** (April): 21.

Gibson, J.L., Mitton, C., Martin, D.K., Donaldson, C. and Singer, P.A. (2006) Ethics and economics: does program budgeting and marginal analysis contribute to fair priority setting? *Journal of Health Services Research and Policy* **11**(1): 32–7.

Grol, R. and Grimshaw, J. (1999) Evidence-based implementation of evidence-based medicine. *Journal on Quality Improvement* **25**(10): 503–13.

House of Commons (2002) *Second Report of Session 2001–02*, National Institute for Clinical Excellence. HC 515-1. London: House of Commons Health Committee.

Jan, S. (2000) Institutional considerations in priority setting: transactions cost perspective on PBMA. *Health Economics* **9**: 631–41.

Kaplan, R.S. and Norton, D.P. (1992) The Balanced Scorecard: measures that drive performance. *Harvard Business Review* **70**: 71–9.

(1996) *The Balanced Scorecard – Translating Strategy into Action*. Boston, MA: Harvard Business School Press.

(2000) *The Strategy-Focussed Organization – How Balanced Scorecard Companies Thrive in the New Business Environment*. Boston, MA: Harvard Business School Press.

Lewin, K. (1951) *Field Theory in Social Science: Selected Theoretical Papers*. New York: Harper.

Mabin. V., King, G., Menzies, M. and Joyce, K. (2001) Public sector priority setting using decision support tools. *Australian Journal of Public Administration* **60**(2): 44–59.

Martin, D. (2005) Half a billion and counting: the NHS's black hole revealed. *Health Service Journal* **6** (January): 12–15.

Martin, S., Davis, H., Bovaird, T. *et al.* (1999) *Improving Local Public Services: Interim Evaluation of the Best Value Pilot Programme*. London: Department of the Environment, Transport and the Regions.

Maynard, A., Bloor, K. and Freemantle, N. (2004) Challenges for NICE. *British Medical Journal* **329**: 227–9.

McDonald, R. (2002) *Using Health Economics in Health Services: Rationing Rationally?* Buckingham: Open University Press.

Miller, P. (1997) Managing informed purchasing: a survey of decision-makers. *Journal of Management in Medicine* 11(1): 35–42.

Mink, O. G., Esterhuysen, P. W., Mink, B. P. and Owen, K. Q. (1993) *Change at Work: A Comprehensive Management Process for Transforming Organizations.* San Francisco: Jossey-Bass Publishers.

Mitton, C. and Donaldson, C. (2001) Twenty-five years of programme budgeting and marginal analysis in the health sector, 1974–1999. *Journal of Health Services and Research Policy* 6(4): 239–48.

(2002) Setting priorities in Canadian regional health authorities: a survey of key decision makers. *Health Policy* 60(1): 39–58.

(2003) Setting priorities and allocating resources in health regions: lessons from a project evaluating program budgeting and marginal analysis (PBMA). *Health Policy* 64: 335–48.

(2004) *Priority Setting Toolkit: A Guide to the Use of Economics in Health Care Decision Making.* London: BMJ Books/Blackwells.

Mitton, C., Donaldson, C., Halma, L. and Gall, N. (2002) Setting priorities and allocating resources in regional health authorities: a report from two pilot exercises using program budgeting and marginal analysis. *Health Care Management FORUM* 15: 39–47.

Mitton, C., Peacock, S., Donaldson, C. and Bate, A. (2003) Using PBMA in health care priority setting: description, challenges and experience. *Applied Health Economics and Health Policy* 2(3): 121–34.

Mitton, C., Patten, S., Donaldson, C. and Waldner, H. (2005) Priority setting in regional health authorities: moving beyond the barriers. *Health Care Quarterly* 8: 47–53.

Mooney, G. and Wiseman, V. (1999) *Listening to the Bureaucrats to Establish Principles for Priority Setting.* Sydney: University of Sydney.

Moulin, M. (2004) Using the public sector scorecard in health and social care, in Neely, A., Kennerley, M. and Walters, A. (eds.) *Performance Measurement and Management: Public and Private. Papers from the Fourth International Conference of the Performance Measurement Association.* PMA, Centre for Business Performance, Cranfield School of Management.

Neely, A., Kennerley, M. and Martinet, V. (2004) Does the Balanced Scorecard work? An empirical investigation, in Neely, A., Kennerley, M. and Walters, A. (eds.) *Performance Measurement and Management: Public and Private. Papers from the Fourth International Conference of the Performance Measurement Association.* PMA, Centre for Business Performance, Cranfield School of Management.

Peacock, S. (1998) *An Evaluation of Program Budgeting and Marginal Analysis Applied in South Australian Hospitals.* Melbourne: Centre for Health Program Evaluation, Monash University.

Preskill, H. and Torres, R. T. (1999) The role of evaluatory enquiry in creating learning organizations, in Easterby-Smith, M., Burgoyne, J. and Aruajo, L. (eds.) *Organizational Learning and the Learning Organization: Developments in Theory and Practice.* London: Sage.

Rogers, E. M. (1995) *Diffusion of Innovations*, 4th edn. New York: The Free Press.

Ryan, M. (2004) Discrete choice experiments in health care. *British Medical Journal* 328: 60–1.

Sanderson, I. (2001) Performance management, evaluation and learning in 'modern' local government. *Public Administration* **79**: 297–313.

Scott, A., Currie, G. and Donaldson, C. (1998) Evaluating innovation in general practice: a pragmatic framework using programme budgeting and marginal analysis. *Family Practice* **15**: 216–22.

Scottish Executive (2003) *Local Government in Scotland Act*. Edinburgh: HMSO.

Spasoff, R. A. (1999) *Epidemiologic Methods for Health Policy*. New York: Oxford University Press.

Shortell, S. and Kaluzny, A. eds. (1994) *Health Care Management: Organization Design and Behaviour*. New York: Delmar Publishers Incorporation.

Wanless, D. (2002) *Securing Our Future Health – Taking a Long-Term View*. London: HM Treasury.

Part II

Performance metrics

6 Public service productivity: new approaches to performance measurement in health sectors

Mary O'Mahony, Philip Stevens and Lucy Stokes

Introduction

Measures of output and productivity in the total economy and broad sectors of this aggregate have been useful tools for policy analysis. These performance indicators form the background for evaluating both the extent to which providers of goods and services benefit consumers and the effectiveness of government policy. International comparisons of output and productivity performance are seen as particularly useful benchmarking exercises and are employed in a wide range of contexts in the private sector. For example, the analysis of the impact of information technology in driving growth in EU industries (O'Mahony and van Ark 2003) points to significant lags in achieving productivity benefits compared to those currently enjoyed in the US. Aggregate performance indicators are seen as an important test of an economy's performance; while changes occur at the level of the firm or provider, their importance needs to be evaluated in terms of their benefits to consumers. Such aggregate indicators are often the starting point by which commentators in academia and the media judge government policy. Hence it is important that reliable, well-measured indicators are constructed.

In the private sector nearly a century of research by academics and statisticians has produced aggregate indicators that are considered both reliable and internationally comparable, if by no means perfect. However, at the same time, little effort was devoted to methodology to measure the output of services provided by the public sector. While measurement is difficult, not least due to the lack of prices that can be employed to measure marginal benefits to consumers, the lack of progress is difficult to understand given the importance of public services in modern industrial societies. Thus the combined education, health and public administration sectors accounted for 19 per cent of gross domestic product in the EU-15 in 2005 and 21 per cent in the US.[1] Recently academics and national accounts statisticians have turned their attention to addressing this deficiency (e.g. The Atkinson Review 2005; Dawson *et al.* 2005; O'Mahony and Stevens 2006) and work is underway to develop and analyse these aggregate indicators so that they are both reliable and comparable.

Our purpose in this chapter is to consider the methods that might be employed to measure output and productivity performance in public services, using performance evaluation in the health sector as an example. The final output of the health sector – ensuring a healthy population – has a direct impact on consumers' well-being but also has an indirect impact on the productive capacity of the workforce in general. This chapter examines the economic, organizational and innovation characteristics of health sectors; critically reviews existing evidence on performance; and sets out a measurement strategy that might be employed in future work.

To place current trends in context, the next section begins with an account of how health care systems have developed over time, outlines the nature of the production process, the determinants of performance and the impact of technology. It presents a brief overview of the structure of the health care systems in the EU and US. Available evidence on performance of the health care sectors in an international context is then reviewed in the following section; this highlights the paucity of information at present. The subsequent section considers how one might measure performance in the health sector, drawing from theoretical developments in measuring productivity for private sectors. The chapter ends with a discussion of the use of numbers for performance management.

The characteristics of the health sector

The system of health provision: historical developments

The health care sector is subject to a high degree of government intervention, both directly, through provision and funding, and indirectly, through regulation. Governments have to balance the goals of equity and efficiency of health provision, and understanding the potential conflict between these two goals is fundamental to understanding both the development of systems

---

[1] Updates of data underlying O'Mahony and van Ark (2003) – downloadable from www.emblems.net.

of provision and attempts to reform these systems. In a recent overview of international trends in health care performance, Cutler (2002) argues that the origins of medical care systems in most countries were fundamentally driven by equity considerations, with little concern about efficiency, since medical care was relatively cheap. Guarantees of equal access to medical care for all citizens led to the development of universal insurance coverage. However, beginning with the development of antibiotics, the postwar period has been one of rapid change in treating illness and in understanding of the causes of illness. This rapid change brought rising costs, with new treatments and increasing demand, as citizens became more aware of the benefits of medical interventions. In turn these increases in costs and demand led to greater conflict between the two goals of equity and efficiency.

Cutler (2002) suggests that, since the 1960s, the rapid increase in medical care expenditure has led to severe financial constraints for governments and has made a commitment to complete equality unaffordable. Many countries' first response in the 1970s and 1980s was to put regulatory limits on costs, reducing provider fees and rationing access. While these policies had some success in cost containment, the controls led to increased waiting times. This led to a greater emphasis on efficiency, with many countries moving away from regulation towards more market-oriented solutions in the 1990s. As a result, some systems have become less equitable, although there is considerable variation across countries in the extent to which market-based reforms have been implemented.

The nature of the production process

In some ways, the health sector is just like any other service sector. Inputs such as capital, labour and materials are employed to produce health care outputs. However there are reasons why standard methods employed to measure productivity in private market services do not translate easily to measuring performance in the health sector. First, in terms of output measurement, public provision means that market prices for outputs are not readily available. Health care is a sector where information asymmetries abound, since service provision through public funding or insurance schemes creates a wedge between the final consumers and service providers. It is relatively easy to measure the activities of the sector, e.g. number of medical treatments, but the extent to which alternative treatments lead to improvements in the health of the consumer is more difficult to gauge. Compounding this is the fact that the output of medical care treatments is difficult to disentangle from other influences on health, such as lifestyle and diet. In the health care sector extraneous influences tend to be very large and often dominate changes in medical care provision. Finally, the nature of technological change also distinguishes the health care sector from other services – advances in knowledge have increased the capabilities of medical interventions, and so have led both to rapidly rising costs and increased demand.

Productivity is defined as the ratio of outputs to inputs. Measuring inputs also presents problems. The health care sector is regarded as being highly skill-intensive so measurement is complicated by the need to take account of the different types of workers distinguished by their skill levels. Drug use is an important intermediate input and rapid technological change in the pharmaceuticals sector will be an important contributory factor to performance. Similarly, the use of new treatments frequently requires new capital equipment. Hence, it is important to take account of both the quality of inputs used as well as their quantities in evaluating productivity performance across countries.

Structure of the health care system in the EU and US

The structure of the health care system is a key factor for its efficiency. Across the EU, and indeed internationally, a number of different approaches to providing health care are apparent. An overview of the EU and US systems, including the ways in which health care is both financed and delivered, is provided in table 6.1.

Ensuring that all residents have access to health services is an important goal in all EU countries, leading to almost universal coverage. This is in stark contrast to the US, where 16 per cent of the population aged under 65 years is uninsured. Most health care in the EU is publicly financed through taxation or social insurance schemes. Although one system will generally predominate, most countries use a combination of insurance and taxation to finance health care. In the US, most health care is funded by private insurance, although public sector funding, in particular for the elderly, is significant.

Individuals are increasingly required to pay part of the cost of medical care received. This cost-sharing may, for example, comprise co-payments (the payment of a fixed amount for a service) or co-insurance (where the individual takes on a proportion of the cost risk). Their use varies between countries, with countries such as the UK restricting cost-sharing to services such as pharmaceuticals, dental and optical care, while countries such as Finland also

Table 6.1: Health systems: the EU and the US

	Finance			Delivery		
	Social insurance	Private insurance	Tax	Public	Private	Out-of pocket ^{a} (%)
Belgium	✓			✓	✓	17.0
Denmark			✓	✓		15.3
Germany	✓			✓	✓	10.4
Greece	✓		✓	✓	✓	42.0
Spain			✓	✓		23.6
France	✓			✓	✓	9.8
Ireland			✓	✓		13.1
Italy	✓		✓	✓	✓	20.3
Luxembourg	✓			✓	✓	11.9
Netherlands	✓	✓			✓	10.1
Austria	✓			✓	✓	17.5
Portugal			✓	✓		44.6
Finland			✓	✓		20.0
Sweden			✓	✓		<1.0
UK			✓	✓		11.6*
Cyprus				✓	✓	†
Czech Rep.	✓			✓	✓	8.6
Estonia	✓			✓	✓	11.6
Hungary	✓			✓		21.3
Lithuania	✓		✓	✓		20.0
Latvia			✓	✓		21.1
Malta			✓	✓	✓	†
Poland	✓			✓	✓	27.0
Slovenia	✓			✓	✓	†
Slovakia	✓			✓	✓	7.9
US		✓	✓		✓	14.0

Source: European Observatory on Health Systems and Policies, 'HiT' country profiles and OECD Health Data 2004.

Note: ^{a} Out-of-pocket expenditure comprises cost-sharing, self-medication and other expenditure paid directly by private households, irrespective of whether the contact with the health care system was established on referral or on the patient's own initiative. † Not available. All figures for 2001 except * 2000.

extend it to ambulatory and inpatient care. Cost-sharing can help to reduce unnecessary demand for services by making consumers bear some of the expense of treatment. This may help to improve efficiency but it can have negative implications for equity.

Health care can be delivered by either the public or private sector, or a combination of both. Increasingly, contracts are used whereby purchasers contract with either public or private providers to deliver services. Some countries allow free choice of both doctor and hospital, which may serve to increase competition and is also partly aimed at increasing patient choice and satisfaction. Some allow direct access to all levels of health care, while others employ a gatekeeping system where a referral is necessary to obtain hospital care.

EU enlargement has introduced even greater diversity into the range of health care systems here. In general the new Member States have moved from highly centralized, planned systems to a much more decentralized approach with reforms ongoing. Although some provide universal coverage, others are yet to achieve this completely.

The payment system used for physicians is an additional important point of difference, and may affect productivity. Some doctors receive salaries, some are paid on a fee-for-service basis and some are paid on a capitation basis, which is payment of a fixed amount per patient. Fee-for-service systems tend to be more expensive as they can lead to over-supply of services. Salaries tend to be better at containing costs but may provide little incentive to increase output. In response to these problems, some countries have introduced payment systems that combine two or more of these methods.

EU countries have instigated many reforms to their health care systems – a comprehensive review is available in Docteur and Oxley, 2003. For example, many countries have implemented budget caps in an attempt to contain spending, with varying degrees of success. Others have attempted to overcome the lack of a functioning market by introducing wage or price controls or by creating some form of pseudo-markets. Decentralization, defined as the transfer of management and decision-making from the national level to organizations at the sub-national level, has also been tried in many countries. Decentralizing decision-making to a lower level is designed to ensure health care is more responsive to the needs of patients but this may be at the expense of economies of scale. Finally, many reforms have attempted to improve patient choice in order to increase quality and accountability of services, improve patient satisfaction and ultimately raise health outcomes.

While policy interventions continue apace, there is little evidence on the extent to which they are beneficial for both efficiency and equity. Policy evaluation requires assessment of performance of health care systems across a range of settings and/or before and after reform and this means comparing performance across countries and time. The next section considers the existing evidence on performance across EU countries and the US and whether any differences can be linked to systems of provision.

Existing performance measures applied to the health sector

This section presents a brief overview of the performance measures readily available as comparators of health sectors across countries. It begins with broad 'macro' measures and then considers some recent research at the 'micro' level, in this instance, related to individual diseases. The first group of measures concentrates on total expenditures on health, aggregate mortality rates and survival from major diseases. For example total health spending per capita at purchasing power parity (PPP) exchange rates,[2] shown in figure 6.1 for EU

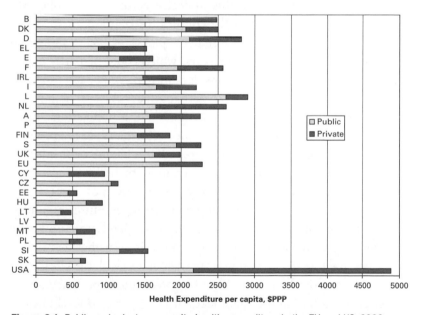

Figure 6.1 Public and private per-capita health expenditure in the EU and US, 2000
Source: WHO European Health for All Database, 2004 and OECD Health Data 2003, 2nd edition.
Note: EU refers to EU-15; B = Belgium; DK = Denmark; D = Germany; EL = Greece; E = Spain; F = France; IRL = Ireland; I = Italy; L = Luxembourg; NL = Netherlands; A = Austria; P = Portugal; FIN = Finland; S = Sweden; UK = United Kingdom; CY = Cyprus; CZ = Czech Republic; EE = Estonia; HU = Hungary; LT = Lithuania; LV = Latvia; MT = Malta; PL = Poland; SI = Slovenia; SK = Slovak Republic.

---

[2] PPP exchange rates convert values in national currencies to a common metric (usually US$) using estimates of relative prices of the goods and services being compared. The market exchange rate is generally considered inappropriate for such adjustments given its sensitivity to short-term capital movements.

countries and the US, illustrates both the considerable variation across countries and the unique position of the US. This chart also presents the division into public and private sector provision; showing that although public expenditure in the US accounts for a considerably smaller proportion of total health expenditure than in EU countries, US public health expenditure per head is higher than for all EU countries except for Luxembourg.

The reasons for the variations in health expenditure are unclear. Expenditure may be greater because the output of its health sector is higher, but also because it does not operate efficiently or its population are generally more prone to illness. Both output and efficiency may be a function of the type of system in place.

The second most common macro indicator employed in international comparisons is life expectancy, an outcome measure, shown in table 6.2. There is little variation in this indicator across EU Member States but the US is at the bottom end of the country distribution, in stark contrast to its position in terms of expenditure per capita. The US fares more favourably in terms of life expectancy at 65 years, which could be partly explained by the observation that the US has considerably higher neonatal mortality rates than the EU (Baily and Garber 1997), perhaps due to the lack of universal insurance coverage amongst the poorer sections of the population and immigrants. Clearly, if the sole interest were in the performance of the providers of health care then the US position is not too bad. But if equity considerations are also given a weight in performance measures, then the relevant outcome (life expectancy) shows the US in a very poor relative position.

Figure 6.2 plots the relationship between expenditure and life expectancy at age 65. The data suggest that countries that spend more on health per capita record higher life expectancy. However, it is clear that there are two distinct groups, the EU-15 and the new Member States, with the US an outlier. For the EU-25, the correlation coefficient between life expectancy and expenditure per capita is 0.75 and is significant at the 5 per cent level but for the EU-15 alone there is no evidence of such a relationship. Given that many other factors contribute to life expectancy beyond the health care system, it is difficult to determine whether there is a significant relationship just by plotting life expectancy against health expenditure measures.

An alternative to crude life expectancy is to consider evidence on the relationship between spending and age-standardized death rates (SDR) for major diseases such as ischaemic heart disease, cerebrovascular disease and malignant neoplasms, as shown in figure 6.3. Within the new Member States, there appears to be a weak negative relationship between health expenditure

Table 6.2: Life expectancy in the EU and US

	Male life expectancy at birth, years		Female life expectancy at birth, years		Life expectancy at 65 years, male and female	
	1990	2000	1990	2000	1990	2000
Belgium	72.8	74.2[a]	79.6	80.8[a]	16.9	17.6[a]
Denmark	72.3	74.1[b]	78.0	78.9[b]	16.2	16.8[b]
Germany	72.1	75.2	78.6	81.3	16.4	18.1
Greece	74.8	75.8[b]	79.6	81.0[b]	17.1	18.0[b]
Spain	73.4	76.0	80.6	83.0	17.5	19.0
France	73.4	75.2[b]	81.8	82.8[b]	18.7	19.2[b]
Ireland	72.1	74.0	77.7	79.3	15.2	16.5
Italy	73.8	76.8	80.5	83.0	17.3	19.0
Luxembourg	72.2	75.0	78.7	81.9	16.5	18.5
Netherlands	73.9	75.7	80.4	80.8	17.1	17.6
Austria	72.5	75.6	79.1	81.5	16.8	18.4
Portugal	70.5	72.6	77.5	79.7	15.7	16.7
Finland	71.0	74.3	79.1	81.3	16.2	17.9
Sweden	74.9	77.5	80.7	82.3	17.5	18.7
United Kingdom	73.1	75.7	78.7	80.5	16.4	17.7
EU-15	73.1	75.6	79.8	81.7	17.1	18.4
USA	71.8	74.1	78.8	79.5	17.2	18.0
Cyprus	n.a.	75.6	n.a.	80.2	n.a.	17.3
Czech Republic	67.6	71.8	75.5	78.6	13.8	15.8
Estonia	64.7	65.4	75.0	76.3	14.5	15.3
Hungary	65.2	67.6	73.9	76.3	14.0	15.2
Lithuania	66.5	66.8	76.4	77.6	15.7	16.3
Latvia	64.2	64.9	74.6	76.1	14.5	15.3
Malta	73.8	76.0	78.4	80.3	15.7	17.0
Poland	66.6	69.8	75.6	78.1	14.6	15.9
Slovenia	70.0	72.3	78.0	80.1	15.8	17.0
Slovak Republic	66.8	69.3	75.8	77.6	14.4	15.2

Source: OECD 2003b; WHO 2004; National Center for Health Statistics 2003.
Note:
[a] indicates 1997 data,
[b] indicates 1999 data.
n.a. means not available.

per capita and SDRs for ischaemic heart disease and cerebrovascular disease but this relationship is much weaker within the EU-15. There is no evidence of a relationship between expenditure and the SDRs from malignant neoplasms at any level. However, in the case of SDRs, expenditure on health care is

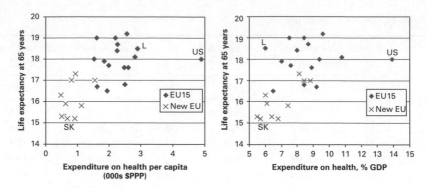

Figure 6.2 Life expectancy at 65 years and expenditure on health, in $PPP per capita and as a percentage of GDP

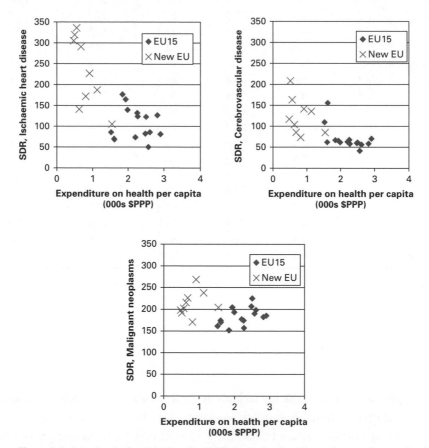

Figure 6.3 Age-standardized death rates (SDR) for major illnesses and expenditure on health

frequently palliative, relieving symptoms rather than life-enhancing, so outcomes should also take account of quality of life.[3]

The health of a country's population is both an input to and output of the health sector. This is because the health status of a population reflects not only the quality of health care in the country, but also its dietary and other socio-economic factors. Countries with higher consumption of alcohol and tobacco, for example, are likely to place a heavier burden on their health sectors than others. Some have argued that differences in health are mostly due to differences in socioeconomic and demographic factors rather than medical interventions (Navarro 2000). Given this, the aggregate indicators based on mortality discussed above are unlikely to be useful in measuring output and productivity that can be attributed to health care providers.

One attempt to build an overall performance measure that would account for the many – often conflicting – goals of health systems was made by the World Health Organization (WHO) in the *World Health Report 2000*. The WHO considered overall attainment in terms of three goals – not only better health, but also the fairness of financial contribution and the responsiveness of the health system in terms of respecting an individual's dignity, autonomy and confidentiality. These indicators were then weighted and added to create a single index of 'attainment'. The data suggest that, as with the individual outcome indicators, the main difference is between the EU-15 and new Member States. In particular, there is little to separate many of the original EU-15 countries, since the differences that are recorded fall within the data's uncertainty intervals.

The *World Health Report 2000* also considered the efficiency of health provision – an indication of a country's performance in relation to its expenditure. Two measures are shown in table 6.3 – the first panel is based on the overall attainment referred to above and, in the second panel, performance is measured by level of health using disability-adjusted life expectancy (DALE), defined as 'expectation of life lived in equivalent full health'.[4] The countries are ranked according to the resulting performance indicator.

On both measures some countries show better than average performance (France, Italy) and others score less well (Denmark, Finland). Nevertheless, as

---

[3] Note that the US tends to perform relatively better on these major disease measures than on crude life expectancy without adjustments for age.

[4] The *World Health Report 2000* was the first concerted attempt to provide a comprehensive comparative analysis of health systems. However, it has been criticized at many levels in many respects (e.g. Mulligan *et al.* 2000; Navarro 2000; Williams 2000).

Table 6.3: Ratio of WHO attainment and health levels to health expenditure

	Performance	Health level
France	0.994	0.974
Italy	0.991	0.976
Malta	0.978	0.989
Spain	0.972	0.968
Austria	0.959	0.914
Portugal	0.945	0.929
Greece	0.933	0.936
Luxembourg	0.928	0.864
Netherlands	0.928	0.893
UK	0.925	0.883
Ireland	0.924	0.859
Belgium	0.915	0.878
Sweden	0.908	0.89
Cyprus	0.906	0.885
Germany	0.902	0.836
Finland	0.881	0.829
Denmark	0.862	0.785
Slovenia	0.838	0.797
USA	0.838	0.774
Czech Republic	0.805	0.765
Poland	0.793	0.742
Slovakia	0.754	0.742
Hungary	0.743	0.698
Lithuania	0.722	0.724
Estonia	0.714	0.677
Latvia	0.63	0.655

Source: WHO 2000.

with the overall WHO attainment index, the main difference is between the EU-15 and the new Member States.

The difficulties in tying macroeconomic indicators to resource use, as outlined above, and a desire to understand the process of technology diffusion and links with supply-side constraints has in recent years led to a focus on disease-specific microeconomic studies. These studies concentrate on persons diagnosed with specific diseases, and frequently also particular population cohorts, thus controlling to some extent for extraneous influences. The analysis is generally based on micro data from administrative records, individual data and surveys.

The McKinsey Global Institute published one of the first international comparative studies in 1996 (McKinsey 1996, summarized in Baily and

Garber 1997). This study aimed to assess differences in relative productivity at the disease level, comparing the US, the UK and Germany in the 1980s. In this study, productivity is defined as the physical inputs used to achieve a given level of health outcomes. Outcome measures were derived by comparing the expected health outcomes with treatment in each country to the outcomes without treatment. The project focused on four specific common diseases – diabetes, gallstones, breast cancer and lung cancer. The report showed that for diabetes, productivity was higher in the UK than the US, but for the remaining three diseases the US was the most productive country. In explaining the differences across countries, the McKinsey report emphasizes differences in regulation and competition. It suggests that the per-diem payment system in Germany gave greater incentives to extend hospital stays than the generally fee-for-service payment system in the US. In addition, McKinsey points to the separate control and regulation of primary and hospital care in Germany which hampers substitution of outpatient for inpatient treatments. It also emphasizes the lower diffusion of technological changes in Britain and links this again to provider payment systems and lack of competition. Note the McKinsey finding of higher productivity in the US relative to other countries seems to contradict the impression using macroeconomic indicators. Explanations include higher costs of inputs in the US, in particular payments to physicians and drugs.

Grieve *et al.* (2001) in a study of stroke units found, on the basis of detailed patient data from European hospitals, a very wide variation in costs and outcomes and in the amount of staff time allocated. The evidence suggests some positive relationship between resource use and outcomes. The authors conclude that the way resources are organized, in addition to the level of resources used, may be important in explaining variations in outcomes.

Perhaps one of the most systematic and detailed international comparative studies of the performance of health sectors was the OECD age-related disease (ARD) project (OECD 2003a). This focused on a particular age cohort, the elderly, and three diseases, ischaemic heart disease (IHD), breast cancer and stroke. For IHD, the ARD project showed that while there was little cross-country correlation between intensity of use and outcomes, the US showed lower fatality rates than other countries (Moise 2003). Results for stroke (Moon 2003) suggested a positive relationship between the use of resources and health outcomes, with the important exception of the UK where high fatality rates went hand-in-hand with high resource use. Confirming the findings of Grieve *et al.* (2001) the ARD project suggests that it is not just how much money is spent but how it is spent that is important. In the case of breast cancer the results suggest that there is no clear association between technological inputs and survival rates, and that state-of-the-art machinery alone is not sufficient to achieve high performance rates; better performance arises from well-organized screening programmes and following the latest clinical guidelines.

In summary, the microeconomic studies highlight the difficulties in matching resource use and technological diffusion to outcomes. This in turn could explain why so little hard evidence can be gleaned using macroeconomic indicators, leading many to suggest that much of the observed improvements in health outcomes are likely to fall outside the influence of health care systems. Results from micro studies are in the future likely to yield interesting results regarding the relationship between outcomes and resources but it is difficult to see how these can be aggregated to give a picture of the whole sector.[5]

Lessons from the theory of productivity measurement

The previous section highlighted the difficulty of measuring performance relative to resources, due both to the difficulty of controlling for extraneous influences and to the fact that the aggregate indicators used relate only to a small sub-section of the health sectors' services. Most treatments affect quality of life rather than having a significant impact on longevity, for example data for the UK National Health Service (NHS) for 2003 show nearly 70 per cent of expenditure is on activities where mortality following treatment is a rare event.

However the problem with existing performance measures is more than just the lack of readily available data; there is also no consistent theoretical framework in which to evaluate performance measures. In fact to a large extent quantitative assessment of public sector performance, both in aggregate and across producing units, tends to rely on composite indicators that combine data from a range of sources, frequently with arbitrary weighting schemes (Jacobs *et al.* 2003). The WHO measures outlined above are examples of composite indicators. This lack of theoretical rigour is surprising given the vast economics literature on measuring productivity, developed since the 1950s and still being refined today. Although this literature tends to link to a private sector model of production, it is worth examining if the theoretical

---

[5] Micro disease studies that involve international collaboration are becoming increasingly the norm e.g. the TECH Global Research Network 2003 study of heart disease (McClellan and Kessler 2003).

framework and analysis are also applicable to the provision of public services that are not sold in private markets.

This section asks whether there are lessons that can be drawn from theoretical research on measuring productivity, in the past mostly concerned with provision of goods and services in the private sector, that can aid in devising robust measures of performance. The discussion draws on AIM-funded research on how approaches designed for national accounts purposes be employed to measure output of publicly provided services (summarized in O'Mahony and Stevens 2006), and work by the authors on measuring NHS productivity, jointly conducted with the Centre for Health Economics, University of York, available in Dawson *et al.* (2005).

To begin it is helpful to distinguish between *activities* (operations, GP consultations), *outputs* (courses of treatment which may require a bundle of activities) and *outcomes* (the characteristics of output which affect utility). In the measurement of private sector productivity growth the focus is on outputs rather than the characteristics they produce, because of the assumption that the market price of the output measures the consumer's marginal valuation of the bundle of characteristics from consuming the output. In the NHS there are no final markets where patients buy outputs from producers. Since there are no prices to reveal patients' marginal valuations of NHS outputs, we have to find other means of estimating their value. Measurement of health output requires quantification of the attributes of output valued by individuals. Research drawing lessons from productivity measurement in private market services argues that information on outcomes can be employed as an alternative to prices to measure these attributes.

The UK Department of Health has traditionally measured output change by an index that weights activities by average unit cost, the cost-weighted output index (CWOI). This implies that costs reflect the value that society places on these activities at the margin, i.e. that resources are optimally allocated across procedures. This strong assumption is unlikely to hold in the NHS but nevertheless the cost-weighted index is a useful starting point. The analysis in Dawson *et al.* (2005) suggests combining the data in the CWOI with information on outcomes. Health gain is the most obvious outcome from NHS activity and so an ideal output measure would incorporate estimates of the change in health state following an NHS intervention relative to what it would have been without the intervention. In practice we can only observe changes in health before and after treatment, using the concept of quality-adjusted life years (QALYs) which takes account of both morbidity and mortality (see chapter 5 by Donaldson *et al.*, this volume).

There are a number of challenges to measuring health gain in practice, not least of which is the lack of data on gains before and after treatment, collected on a routine basis. Nevertheless, the research shows how such information could be incorporated in an output index. In addition there is the issue of how to attribute changes in health status to NHS activity. Dawson *et al.* (2005) present calculations combining the CWOI with a readily available health gain measure, short-term mortality. It suggests that the latter cannot be seen in isolation but rather needs to be evaluated relative to patient health outcome if treatment had been foregone. The impact was to raise the annual average growth rate of output over the period 1998/9–2003/4 from 2.8 per cent to between 3.3 and 3.7 per cent, depending on the assumptions employed. This is a significant upward adjustment.

Health gain is only one attribute valued by consumers. Dawson *et al.* (2005) also consider how changes in waiting times for treatment might be incorporated by modelling waiting times as a delay in receiving health gain on which interest is charged. This approach however yields very little by way of quality adjustments when applied to the actual CWOI. Partly this reflects the fact that waiting times (cost weighted) did not change very much in the period under consideration and the small size of the delay in days relative to the length of time patients enjoy health gain after intervention.

An alternative approach discussed in Dawson *et al.* (2005) was to estimate the volume of different outcomes generated by the outputs and to value the outcomes. The authors identify five key outcomes of NHS output which it may be possible to measure: health outcomes; waiting times; choice and certainty of date of treatment; patient satisfaction and environment. Information from a number of sources was employed to attempt to take account of these attributes but none other than health gain were found to have a large impact on NHS output growth. The valuations put on attributes such as waiting times and cleanliness tend to be small relative to the values placed on health gains. The research highlights the need for additional information, in particular data on health gains, for the majority of procedures that affect quality of life rather than life expectancy. In addition the report emphasizes the need for estimates of the value of attributes, in particular the valuation of QALYs; the subject of chapter 8 by Baker *et al.*

Accurate measures of changes in the volume and quality of inputs are required to estimate productivity growth. These can be combined with quality-adjusted output growth using the growth accounting method which weights diverse inputs by their shares in the value of output (see e.g. Jorgenson *et al.* 1987). In the NHS study, Dawson *et al.* (2005) advocate a method that involves a decomposition of inputs into changes in volumes (e.g. number of NHS employees) and the quality of inputs (e.g. greater use of highly skilled nurses). This report highlights the importance also of correctly measuring input growth.

Conclusions

What are the implications of the method outlined in the previous section for measuring performance in public services in general? The most important message is that measurement methods need to be embedded in a theoretical framework which has benefits to consumers at its core. This is the framework underlying measurement for private services and at its root is the notion that goods and services which have little value (command a low price) should not be given an overly large weight in performance evaluation. In practical terms the method suggests that research should begin with data on quantity indicators and unit costs of providing services. Information on outcomes can be employed to achieve quality-adjusted output indexes using weights that arise from the theoretical framework. To date much of the aggregate performance measurement literature is based on direct outcome measures with consequent attribution problems or on combining readily available indicators using arbitrary weights.

It is important to acknowledge that the information requirements to undertake such an exercise, especially in international comparisons, are daunting. And many of the complexities of measurement remain to be addressed, e.g. defining attributes valued by consumers in areas such as criminal justice. However similar issues have also affected measurement in the private sector and many problems remain unresolved. In the private sector research, data deficiencies were addressed once research pointed to the importance of knowledge in a range of areas. Tracing changes in services outputs to inputs and underlying productivity growth would then give a broad-brush picture of performance variations across countries, which could then be compared to differences in structure and changes due to reforms. Many countries are reforming systems of provision of public services without any hard evidence on the impacts of these changes in raising the welfare of citizens. It may be possible to point to improvements in specific areas of concern but only comprehensive measures that calculate benefits against costs are capable of determining whether policy is moving in the right direction.

The primary concern of this chapter has been measures of performance at the sector level but the arguments have as much force when performance indicators are employed to make relative judgements across producing units. Management by numbers, whereby providers are judged according to some quantitative index of performance, is frequently seen as a recent British disease, although it has been used both in the past and in many areas of public provision world wide (Hood, 2006). Composite performance indicators are now commonly used both as a management tool and for resource allocation. Examples include the star ratings in the health sector and the Research Assessment Exercise for universities but there are few areas of public sector provision in England that are not subject in some way to this form of management. The consequences for providers such as NHS Trusts or local authorities of receiving a low rating are serious. Yet the methods underlying such measures are suspect, lacking theoretical rigour, and often use inappropriate data and methods (Stevens *et al.* 2006). Quantitative data can contain information useful for managing public services but if used inappropriately may hinder rather than aid performance improvement.

REFERENCES

Atkinson, T. (2005) *Atkinson Review: Final Report. Measurement of Government Output and Productivity for the National Accounts.* Basingstoke: Palgrave Macmillan.

Baily, M. and Garber, A. (1997) Health care productivity. *Brookings Papers on Economic Activity: Microeconomics* 1997: 143–202.

Cutler, D. (2002) Equality, efficiency and market fundamentals: the dynamics of international medical care reform. *Journal of Economic Literature* **40**: 881–906.

Dawson, D., Gravelle, H., O'Mahony, M. *et al.* (2005) Developing new approaches to measuring NHS outputs and productivity. Final Report. *NIESR Discussion Paper* 264 and *CHE Research Paper* 6.

Docteur, E. and Oxley, H. (2003) Health-care systems: Lessons from the reform experience. *OECD Economics Department Working Papers* 374. Paris: OECD.

Grieve, R., Hutton, J., Bhalla, A., *et al.*, (2001) on behalf of the Biomed II European Study of Stroke Care (2001) A comparison of the costs and survival of hospital-admitted stroke patients across Europe. *Stroke* **32**: 1684–91.

Jacobs, R., Smith, P. C. and Goddard, M. (2003) *Measuring Performance: An Examination of Composite Performance Indicators, A Report for the Department of Health.* York: Centre for Health Economics, University of York, December.

Jorgenson, D. W., Gollop, F. M. and Fraumeni, B. (1987) *Productivity and US Economic Growth.* Cambridge, MA: Harvard University Press.

McClellan, M. B. and Kessler, D. P. (eds.) (2003) *Technological Change in Health Care. A Global Analysis of Heart Attack.* Ann Arbor: University of Michigan Press.

McKinsey Global Institute and the McKinsey Health Care Practice (1996) *Health Care Productivity.* Los Angeles: McKinsey and Co. Inc.

Moise, P. (2003) The heart of the health care system: summary of the ischaemic heart disease part of the OECD ageing-related diseases study. in OECD 2003a, pp. 27–52.

Moon, L. (2003) Stroke treatment and care: a comparison of approaches in OECD countries, in OECD 2003a, pp. 53–76.

Mulligan, J., Appleby, J. and Harrison, A. (2000) Measuring the performance of health systems. *British Medical Journal* **321**: 191–2.

National Center for Health Statistics (2003) *Health, United States, 2003*. Hyattsville, MA, Department of Health and Human Services, Center for Disease Control and Prevention.

Navarro, V. (2000) Assessment of the World Health Report 2000. *The Lancet* **356**: 1598–1601.

OECD (2003a) *A Disease-based Comparison of Health Systems. What is Best and at what Cost?* Paris: OECD.

(2003b) *OECD Health Data 2003*. Paris: OECD.

(2004) *OECD Health Data 2004*. Paris: OECD.

O'Mahony, M. and van Ark, B. (2003) *EU Productivity and Competitiveness: An Industry Perspective. Can Europe Resume the Catching-up Process?* Luxembourg: Office for Official Publications of the European Communities.

O'Mahony, M. and Stevens, P. (2006) International comparisons of output and productivity in public services provision: a review in Boyne, G. A., O'Toole, L. J. Jr., Meier, K. J. and Walker, R. M. (eds.) *Public Service Performance: Perspectives on Management and Measurement*. Cambridge: Cambridge University Press, pp. 233–53.

Stevens, P., Stokes, L. and O'Mahony, M. (2006), Metrics, targets and performance. *National Institute Economic Review*, July.

Williams, A. (2000) Science or marketing at WHO? A commentary on 'World Health 2000. *Health Economics* **10**(2): 93–100.

World Health Organization (2000) The World Health Report 2000. *Health Systems: Improving Performance*. Geneva: World Health Organization.

(2004) *European Health for All Database*. Copenhagen: WHO Regional Office for Europe.

7 Performance measurement systems and the criminal justice system: rationales and rationalities

Barbara Townley

This chapter examines the role and function of performance measures within the Scottish criminal justice system (CJS), and more specifically considers the responses to a political initiative that there should be overarching measures for the CJS as a whole. But its lessons are broader than this. The underlying curiosity driving the research stems from the observation that although performance measurement systems have been part of the political agenda since their adoption in the post-war period (National Audit Office 2001), they have failed to live up to their initial promise. Studies document the disappointments: the routinization of measures with little impact on policy; distortion of operational goals and programmes; the creative reporting of results; the encouragement of a 'measurement mentality' with the collection of information rather than knowledge; and irrational expectations of what targets may achieve (Carter *et al.* 1992; Smith 1993; Meyer 2002; Paton 2003; Townley 2005). The House of Commons Public Administration Select Committee commented of the target setting regime 'it does not appear to be particularly effective at motivating people. Few of our witnesses claimed that in themselves, targets were inspirational and . . . some saw them as obstacles to professional satisfaction and improved performance' (2003: 32). The report concluded, however, 'the measurement culture cannot and should not be abolished'. How may one explain the continuing disappointments that result and the eternal optimism of their continued recommendation? And, crucially, why is it important to ask this question?

Performance measures: their rationale

The aims of performance measurement systems are deceptively simple. They are introduced to achieve a number of objectives: to provide a 'clear public statement of what the Government is trying to achieve'; to provide a 'clear sense of direction'; 'used wisely', to provide a focus for delivering improved services; to provide a basis for monitoring what is and what isn't working; to spread and reward good practices; and to allow poor performance to be addressed. Reporting progress against targets also provides public accountability (Treasury 2004).

Performance measurement systems are thus recommended as a rational management tool, part of the rational panoply of effective management and organizational functioning (Townley 2002b). A curious aspect of the above claims, however, is that there is no statement as to how these aims are to be achieved. Their purpose is clear; the means whereby this is achieved are not. Their recommendation lies in their rationality. No rational individual could deny that the objectives are desirable and rational. Ergo performance measures are rational. And therein lies the difficulty. Rationality does not inhere in an action, recommendation, tool or policy. It is ascribed (Weber 1978). Rationality is ascribed by those who encounter a recommendation, tool, action, request, etc. on the grounds that it meets the requisite conditions of warranty for the context of its operation (Toulmin 1958). In other words, something is rational, reasonable or meaningful 'in context', and warrants recognition or response as such. This is the basis of a continuing presumption of rationality that informs social coordination. The work in making or rendering something rational, however, involves choosing the form of rationality from a range of repertoires (for rationality, being ascribed in context, is not a singular quality), applying and measuring against the appropriate warrants, and forming a conclusion as to whether something is or is not 'rational'.

This chapter recounts the rationalities that are brought into play in the attempt to make performance measures 'rational'. An analysis of performance measures in terms of multiple and often conflicting rationalities is favoured for several reasons (Townley 2002a). Conventional explanations for problems with performance measures point to operational difficulties of the lack of time, understanding and commitment given to their introduction; political issues surrounding conflicting objectives of stakeholders; the problems of devising technically robust measures that capture the complexity of practice; and tensions between the institutional and operational demands of measures, their political or managerial purpose. Without doubt these all play their part, but these explanations remain unsatisfactory. First, they are partial. They take as their starting point the presumption of performance measures as a rational, neutral technology. Second, they involve an asymmetry in explaining failure. Success reflects performance measures as a good thing; failure is the result of circumstances (Bloor 1991). Third, they fail to progress debate. Those who fail to appreciate their functioning are misguided. Recourse is to the eternal optimism of 'next time'. Fourth, and most important, they fail to address the reported frustrations of those who are obliged to work with them and cope with the dysfunctions their operation entails. Empirical material, and the voices of those who work within the CJS, are drawn from over eighty interviews conducted with those involved with the criminal justice system: members of the judiciary, prosecution service, police, barristers, solicitors, legal aid, court service, prison service, social work, charities associated with the criminal justice system, civil servants and political representatives. The exceptions, it must be noted, were any interviews with victims of crime or convicted criminals.

Crime and the criminal justice system

Crime has risen dramatically on the political agenda of all the main political parties and with this has come an increased spotlight on the criminal justice system. Scotland has its own legal system, separate and distinct from that of England and Wales (Young 1997). Under the Scottish system, crime is investigated under the direction of the Procurator Fiscal's (PF) office (the equivalent of the English Crown Prosecution Service, the CPS). The PF determines what the subsequent process will be: no proceedings (where there is insufficient evidence); a warning; a fine; to prosecute before a Sheriff or the High Court, depending on the seriousness of the crime. Unlike the CPS, the PF is obliged to prosecute cases if it is in the public interest even if success is unlikely, or where a complaint is not pursued, for example, in race crimes. Cases (criminal and civil) are allocated court time by the court service, cognizant of the legal requirements that criminal cases are to be heard within certain stipulated times; if not they must, by law, be dismissed. Sheriffs and judges hear cases and are responsible for sentencing within general guidelines, although they are obliged to have social work reports before sentence is passed. Sentences can range from drug treatment orders heard before a special court, or community service orders, to imprisonment.

Principal agency relationships organize much of the CJS structure, governing the relationship between the executive and agencies such as the prison and court services, and local authorities and voluntary agencies. Targets are ubiquitous. All organizations have their own performance measures, whether these are part of a formal principal agency contract or not, with audits monitoring agency or service performance. The objectives of the Justice ministry are to make Scotland a place where people are safer and feel safer (measured by the reduction of serious violent crime, increased drug seizures, and reduced fear of crime); to create a fair and more efficient justice system that commands confidence of customers and public (court case completion and access to legal aid); and to achieve a reduction in offending and the provision of more effective non-custodial penalties (prisoner places, rehabilitation programmes and community disposals) (Scottish Executive 2002).

A number of different agencies are involved in the CJS: the police, the prosecution service, the courts, solicitors and barristers, the judiciary, prisons, criminal justice, social work and voluntary agencies. This highlights some of the problems encountered in 'joined up' government, ensuring that agencies deliver that for which they are responsible, but also delivering 'collective' services (Perri 6 *et al.* 2002, Sullivan and Skelcher 2002). Operationally there have been problems with the coordination and effective joint working in the delivery of what has been termed 'end-to-end' justice, i.e., from the point of detection of an offence to case disposal, including: the uncertainty of trial sittings and delays in cases coming to trial; the non-attendance of the accused and witnesses; late pleas, adjournments and delays in court proceedings, thus impacting on witnesses, victims and jurors. Reviews of CJS agencies have identified problems with a lack of inter-agency communication; a failure of 'organizational empathy' (asking: 'what does this mean for our partners?'); the lack of knowledge of each other's work; and insufficient direct contact between staff. Similar problems have been identified in England and Wales (National Audit Office 1999; Auld 2001), leading to overall targets for the CJS as a whole, while Northern Ireland has seen a major revision of its criminal justice process.

Given the complexity of the CJS, there have been a number of reviews of legal practice and court procedures with the aim of improving cross-system liaison (Bonomy 2002; MacLean 2002; Price-Dyer 2002; McInnes 2004).[1] In the management of court cases, however, it must be recognized that unpredictability is built into the process:

Basically there are always more trials than courts can deal with. It works on the assumption that a number of cases will settle at the last minute. There is a rough idea on trials. This comes with paying attention to cases that are brought in and judgement and experience. A lot of times this comes off, but sometimes it doesn't happen. There are always going to be cases adjourned, whether this suits the accused or not. There are always going to be witnesses not turning up, on holiday, ill and so on. (Court Service)

---

[1] For ease, reports are cited by reference to the principal author.

As McInnes (2004: 192) notes, 'it is impossible to predict which cases will not go ahead on the day of the trial in advance of the day of the trial and not easy to calculate how long the trial is likely to take.'

It was against this background of operational difficulties and problems with the administration of the system; the political objectives of a newly devolved Scottish Executive and Parliament; developments in England and Wales and Northern Ireland and the institutional pressures for similar initiatives that this prompted, that a review was established for the design of overarching objectives and targets for the criminal justice system, hereafter the Normand report, after its chair (2003). Its remit was:

Having appropriate regard to the interests of justice, to make proposals for the integration of the aims, objectives and targets of the principal agencies which make up the criminal justice system in Scotland, in order to ensure the more efficient, effective and joined-up operation of the system and to secure delivery of the criminal justice priorities of the Scottish Executive. (Normand 2003: 1)

As part of its work, Normand held a number of focus groups with staff from the various CJS agencies who identified a number of serious concerns including: low staffing levels, inexperienced staff and a lack of resources; the feeling of working within an 'initiative' work organization; increased workloads, scrutiny and a blame culture; lack of understanding of operational concerns by senior management; tension in bilateral relationships and failures of inter-agency communication. Generally, frustration with the CJS as whole.

The Normand report recommendations were for the establishment of a National Criminal Justice Board to oversee the operation and performance of the CJS against overarching aims, objectives and targets and to ensure coordination and consistent planning across the system. Local Criminal Justice Boards were also recommended for coordination and liaison at a local level. Suggested objectives for the system as a whole were: to reduce the level of crime, disorder and offending; to improve people's feeling of safety and the confidence of the whole community in the CJS; to improve the treatment of victims and witnesses; to protect the rights of the accused and to improve efficiency and deal with cases at appropriate speed. Suggested targets were crime reduction, and reducing persistent offending; increased public confidence; the number and percentage of crimes committed, action taken and the number of no proceedings; waiting times; monitoring the European Convention on Human Rights devolution; and time target for cases i.e. length of time to disposal, rates of adjournment, timing of guilty pleas.

Curiously, there is a failure to define precisely what 'the problem' is, to which performance measures are a response. As in most debates on the Criminal

Justice System its use is as a short-hand phrase to encompass several different referents that coalesce around the concept of crime: the institutions and agencies involved; statistics about; experiences of; political bravura surrounding; the construction of a system; those who commit a crime; those who have a crime committed against them; a social problem; a social problem affecting certain socioeconomic classes and circumstances (Hacking 2001). There are thus a range of issues to which performance measures are presented, even within the terms of the Normand remit, as an aid, if not as a solution. It is garbage-can decision-making: solutions in search of a problem (Cohen *et al.* 1972). Normand's conclusion: 'an overarching set of aims and objectives [with appropriate measures] should help encourage a greater sense of common purpose and to secure more efficient and effective performance of the system as a whole' (2003: 45), assumes that a performance measurement framework can and will act as a steering or a coordinating mechanism for a network or a system.

A measured response

The National Board was established in 2003, with two pilot local boards established later the next year. In quite stark contrast to the route chosen in England and Wales where Local Criminal Justice Boards were presented with elaborate measurement systems and specified targets on confidence and satisfaction figures, an approach based on the establishment of objectives, measures and targets was deliberately eschewed:

There is an interest in overarching aims and objectives. But the Board is opposed to targets. We don't want to be target driven. There is an interest in practicalities. The intention is to remove where the system rubs. If you do this then the system can become a system. But it is easy to put measures into place … measures on an overarching system but this leads to blaming agencies. We have managed to avoid this. This is not why we're doing this. (Criminal Justice Board)

The reasons for this response are explored below.

Rationalized myths: measurement matters

Within institutional environments, politics, the law, the arts, the economy, etc. 'rationalized myths' or an institutional rationality informs what is appropriate or 'rational' in a particular sphere, legitimating actions and behaviour (Meyer and Rowan 1978). A number of rationalized myths inform the rationale for performance measures in government. First is the importance of government being able to 'deliver' outcomes. Second is the role of performance measures as an indicator of responsible and accountable government. Third is the capacity of performance measures to improve outcomes. All generate expectations and political pressure for demonstrated change and results. Finally, as crime has ridden higher in the political agenda, the 'management' of crime and allaying 'fears of crime' have become a more urgent political priority. The media in particular is a powerful force in stimulating concerns demanding 'that something be done'. These pressures were perceived by respondents as generating the need for 'good measures' and 'good news' stories, and fostering a tendency to 'initiatives':

Government wants to meet targets because it wants to demonstrate that things have changed. The reason why it [a target] is in there is because it is a good political headline. It's a soundbite. It looks good for politicians. There are so many initiatives around. (Policy)

'Political' responses were seen as placing more demands on the CJS already perceived as having heavy demands made of it, while raising the problematic issue of 'long-term' versus 'short-term' time frames for effective interventions.

The political warranty of performance measures is the obligation to be legitimate and publicly accountable:

It is very easy to abuse simplistic measures and because of this it is easy to justify not having measures. But if you have no measures, you don't know what you are doing with the resources that you have got. What the outcome is for the resources that have been put in. But what is society getting for spending this money on prosecuting this type of cases? A lawyer may answer that 'this is not my concern'. But they are getting a lot of resources that they need to justify. How effective is this if you don't know how much things are costing and the resources that are consumed in dealing with aspects of work? (Sheriff)

Measures (re)present the public face of an accountable, functioning organization. A large element of public services, however, rely on ambiguous technologies and produce outputs that are difficult to appraise – the CJS is a prime example. Where there is ambiguity and a lack of tangible outcomes, organizations rely on what Meyer and Rowan (1978) refer to as a logic of confidence and good faith. Professionalization is taken as the guarantee of organizational competence and functioning. However, when faced with a loss of faith in the institutionalized support for the professions, there is a crisis of legitimacy. The current political context, to which performance measures are both a response and a contributing cause, reflects this crisis of legitimacy. There is a move from the logic of appropriateness, based on professionals' understandings of the situation and their own professional identity, to the logic of consequentiality, a demand for 'evidence', objective outcomes and means–end causality. Demands for legitimacy are now posed in epistemological terms: 'how does one know?'

You have standards, but does this improve quality? How do you ensure quality? How do you make an argument to Treasury for more money for salaries, more money for buildings if you can't show evidence? What have we learnt? There have been huge increases in funding, but how do we know that this makes a difference? (Politician)

Acceptable responses must now rely on the quasi-scientific recourse to performance measures. Rationality is ensured through a rational account of how resources are used, activities controlled, and purposes achieved. Public services are no longer a store of collectively accumulated knowledge of structures, rules, procedures, technologies and methods of interaction that are taken for granted; but a *tabula rasa* on which inputs, throughputs, outputs and outcomes, means–end relationships around purposes must be mapped.

The obligation to be legitimate and publicly accountable, however, is in danger of shading into the need to *appear* legitimate and accountable. It is politically important and therefore rational for every organization to present itself in the best light. It makes those managing organizations very aware of the political significance of measures, with the institutional concerns of senior managers coming into conflict with the operational concerns of frontline staff, often exacerbating existing communication difficulties. There is the danger that management becomes defined as the ability to manipulate administrative systems rather than deal with the substantive issues of organizations (Power 1997): 'Targets are taking the force away from the primary focus of our organization . . . we are here to provide a police service not to meet targets.' (Police). This 'political rationality' sometimes outweighs the technical rationality of measures being reported or recorded accurately, with the attendant difficulties this introduces: 'if you're fiddling figures, how can you say to a police constable, "you're crossing the line"' (Police)?

These are the recognized tensions between institutional and managerial demands that performance measures raise. There is, however, another dimension of the 'political' functioning of measures. Objectives and measures by their very nature make the ambiguous tangible (Townley 1995; 2002b). This requires a basic statement as to what is to be measured and what appropriate definitions are. Categories and definitions 'write the world into being', prescribing and proscribing identities and the possibilities of action. They are not neutral technologies but inherently political: the operation of power through knowledge (Townley *et al.* 2003). This is perhaps nowhere more apparent than in the term CJS itself.

A rose by any other name?

Criminal justice has traditionally referred to the stages through which criminal behaviour is dealt with through the state agencies: charge, prosecution, trial, sentence, appeal, punishment. The processes and agencies responsible for these are referred to collectively as the CJS. What is encompassed by the criminal justice system and the extent of its jurisdiction, however, influences debates as to its performance, its problems, its needs for reform, etc. It also influences perceptions of the degree of control over factors measuring its 'success'. Although intuitively understood by those who practise in it, ask for definitions or precise boundaries and the CJS becomes more nebulous. Lord Justice Auld (2001) considers the term CJS misleading, but identifies three understandings of its boundaries: the principal agencies of the police, prosecution and the courts; the wider CJS which includes voluntary bodies and legal practitioners; and the system 'as a whole' that includes government departments. He also identifies a possible fourth, 'the context of CJS' which includes the community as a whole.

The CJS depends for its effectiveness on the coordination of the respective agencies:

A happy police officer is when they are arresting people. An unhappy police officer is when they are writing warrants and police reports. The police have a clear up rate target. The quality of the evidence gathered and how they present the information then gets overlooked, naturally so. The indicator is 'crimes cleared up' against a benchmark. But then low quality, iffy reports are sent to the PF. The number of 'no proceedings' goes up and the police get annoyed. This is an example of the two targets fighting each other. That tension runs through the entire system. What is really called for is system definition and understanding. You can't be blind. Your actions impact on other agencies. (PF)

The work of one agency impacting on another is taken to imply a 'system'. 'System' however, may be understood in a number of different ways: as an input/throughput/output mechanism; a series of linked, but loosely coupled, chains; a series of objects that circulate (case files, suspects/offenders); or as a consistency of practice. Each has implications for how the CJS should be managed, may be measured, and the nature of interventions that can be made.

In using the term 'system' it is all too easy to construct the metaphor as a technical or mechanical artefact, an extant empirical or tangible scientific entity that may be managed like a tightly coupled cybernetic system. The CJS, however, refers to an institution, or a series of institutions, which reflect a number of different tensions: criminogenic or welfare orientations; private, local authority or central government sources of funding; and managerial versus practitioner emphasis within the same agencies. The different CJS agencies interact in a very complex manner, often neither understood nor appreciated by those working within it, even those at a high level with a lot of experience. Given this complexity, small changes have serious 'knock on' effects elsewhere in the system. For example, changes in legal aid procedure resulted in legal firms hiring fewer trainees with a subsequent impact several years later on the number of criminal lawyers available to work on an increasing criminal case load; privatization of prisoner transport from jail to courts, introduced to relieve police workload, resulted in limiting access to court records for criminal justice social workers thus delaying the number of sentencing reports for judges, causing further delays in the disposition of cases. Interventions based on a stimulus–response model can thus result in unforeseen and sometimes deleterious consequences for the 'system' as a whole.

Given its complexity, the CJS is sustained by, and some would argue, functions through a contextual rationality, the beliefs and actions sustained by a community of professions and occupations and the context that legitimizes them. Strong organizational, agency and professional identities among the police, prosecution, lawyers, judges, etc., inform views of their purpose and role within the CJS. Challenges to these identities come from calls that emphasize the need to 'manage' the system. For some, one of the aims of the National Criminal Justice Board with its objectives and performance measures, is an attempt to change this 'culture', and to introduce thinking that sees beyond the confines of the immediate role. For others, there are concerns as to whether overarching measures are the attempt to introduce a new fledgling institution, 'the CJS', as something distinct from the operation of its constituent, independent agencies and bodies. The ambiguity of the term 'system', and the ascription to all those working within it of having the same overarching purpose, is never clarified. Normand, for example, refers to the CJS as 'a collective entity serving a common purpose, whose many elements should work together' (2003: 7). In an abstract sense, the CJS works for the acquittal of the innocent and the speedy conviction of the guilty, but to imply a common purpose in more concrete terms is a characterization resisted by many practising within it for compromising statutory responsibilities: 'I'm not sure what an integrated system would be. Police and prosecution are on one side of the fence. Then there is the accused and the accused's representatives. There are standards for agencies, the crown office, the prosecution system and social workers' (Advocate).

The system exists in common parlance: 'There is a CJS. You turn up at High Court and there it is.' To the extent that a system exists, it exists through the circulation of documentation that ensures that the processes of charge, prosecution, trial, sentence, appeal, and punishment may be secured. Through having objectives and targets ascribed to it that encompass crime levels and reoffending rates, its traditional boundaries are extended to Auld's fourth sense of the term. The 'system' is an artefact, brought into being through the objectives and measures ascribed to it. It must then be made to function as such.

Technical matters: identifying targets

One of the rationales for a performance measurement system is the attempt to remove 'politics' by introducing robust measures that give an indication of progress and do not mislead. It is to substitute a technical rationality for a political rationality (Oakeshott 1991). Measures are also important because they support an 'evidence-based' approach to policy and focus on outcomes (Smith *et al.* 2000). Devising the 'right' measures, however, confronts the vexed question of how events, activities, practices taking place over space and time may be represented in a manner that can be taken to be an accurate account.

The attempt to introduce a quasi-scientific approach to performance measures is undermined by arbitrary measures that reflect the easy to measure; give simplistic views of what goes on; ignore the nature and realities of work; and fail to address quality and process issues – criticisms levelled at performance measures within the CJS, especially those perceived as being outwith the direct control of agencies, i.e. to reduce the level of crime, disorder and offending, and to improve people's feeling of safety and the confidence of the community in the CJS. Even basic measures, for example crime levels, are problematic (Coleman and Moynihan 2003). Links between the operation of the CJS and crime levels are very loosely coupled. Fear of crime (taken to be an indicator of safety) is affected by a range of experiences unrelated to recorded crime levels (Reiner 2002). 'Satisfaction' and 'confidence', perceived to have an impact on fear of crime, the willingness to report crime, provide local intelligence to the police, and willingness to act as witnesses, can be problematic: 'if the CJS treats the individual badly [in the sentence passed on the accused], then it doesn't matter how helpful or how good we were. It's as though we hadn't bothered' (Voluntary agency)

Reoffending (reconviction) measures, and their interpretation, are particularly contentious:

> How do you measure the effectiveness of community service orders (CSOs)? Is effectiveness going through the order? If someone is reconvicted but for a lesser offence, this could still count as successful. It has taken years for people to get to the stage where they offend. There are so many expectations of quick returns. (Voluntary agency)

The attempt to develop robust measures often foundered on the ease with which data could be collected or the extent to which the measures would be understood by a general public for whom they were in the large part designed.

> Some of the targets looked at were opaque, as for example, the monitoring of racist incidents. This came out as a figure with a decimal place per 1,000 of the population. To make sense of this figure you would have to be familiar with the density of the population, the total population and then multiply ... On racist incidents, you obviously want to encourage the reporting of this. Although after a while you obviously want this to go down. How long is a while? (Policy)

The measure lying wholly or largely within the CJS is that of improving efficiency and dealing with cases at appropriate speed. This can be addressed by the police, prosecution, court service and legal aid. However, independent professionals, solicitors, advocates, the sheriffs and judges who also impact on the progress of cases lie outside the purview of a performance target system. The measures with the most significance and meaning for those working within the CJS were statutory time limits, dating back to the seventeenth century and unique to Scottish law, where cases must be heard within prescribed legal time limits or be dropped. Resistance to other measures was prompted by their failure to concur with the situated rationality of operational experience.

A situated rationality

A situated rationality is a located, interactional rationality that sustains a sense of organizational rationality. It addresses the 'what nextness' of work (Boden 1994), focusing on making activities within an organization work (Suchman 1987). Knowing the nature of work organization and work flows within the CJS is essential to any understanding of the process. This is not easy, as short-hand terms, for example the 'filing of police reports' or the 'use of postal citations', hide complex work operations and much tacit knowledge:

[on postal citations to appear in court] the legislation says you have to use recorded delivery. If you use recorded delivery you try and get it delivered on Saturday. Otherwise the postie goes, and if they're out, then leaves a note. But most people know that recorded delivery is something they don't want to know. The letter delivery officer (LDO), ex police officers, know the areas. They may know the people. If you want [court attendance] figures to be higher, then you might have to do them all through the LDO. The police don't want that impact on their budget. (Police)

For operational staff the most useful exercise was a process known as 'mapping the system', introduced in response to an information technology problem. It involved tracking the progress of the 'paper trail' through the various agencies in the CJS to get full knowledge of how the 'system' operates and identify blockages. The 'trail' of paper is the only thing that truly circulates within the CJS, and it is this that constitutes it as a system. Its tracking or mapping is complex:

70% of the cases reported by the police come in clusters or groups. A shop lifter usually has drugs and will be a case of breach of the peace. Police will caution and charge. But the PF will roll up charges or will add others, or decide some are 'no pros' because there is not enough evidence. So you are progressing different types of report from the original charge. (Policy)

The complexity of the processes involved highlights the importance of local knowledge and experienced support staff who are relied on to 'keep the system going'. A situated rationality indicates the importance of informal, day-to-day interactions. 'When we used to be in the same building, at tea break, the PF would come down to the [court] clerks. This is when you chewed the fat and issues were resolved. You didn't call it a management meeting then, but this is what it was' (Court Service). Within this context, change, for example favouring technological solutions over personnel, was seen by those on the ground as a false economy, leading to a loss of knowledge or 'common sense', and the need for the continual retraining of temporary staff. In some organizations there was a real perception of management not knowing the details of work organization, not seeing it as their role to need this information, and therefore not understanding the impact of measures and their concrete effects, further exacerbating internal divisions between frontline and more senior staff.

If you do not have an in-depth knowledge of how it all works, then you shouldn't touch it. Once you know how the system works in detail, you know the work organization, then you can make changes. And to make changes without this information is immoral. You can't impose targets unless you know how the system works. (Anonymous)

It is a position reinforced by McInnes (2004: 254): 'setting targets is pointless unless the right management information is available'. For the system 'as a whole', this information is lacking. It remains widely dispersed in people's heads.

Within the situated rationality of the immediate work context, performance measures can be seen as an irrelevance, a hindrance, or detrimental to 'getting the job done': 'The main issue is the daily issue of will there be enough clerks? Is somebody going to phone in sick? Are there going to be enough Sheriffs? . . . That's not to say you don't feel good when you reach a target but that you are too caught up managing meteorites that crash through the ceiling' (Court Service). Certainly there is an opportunity cost to collecting and recording measures dictated by the finite resource of time. There is resistance when measures conflict with understandings of what the job entails. Voluntary organizations, increasingly relied upon to deliver CJS objectives, for example satisfaction measures, reported:

We have difficulties getting hold of ethnic monitoring data [on those affected by crime]. People hate asking this and hate being asked. They also have to ask how many people in the household. This gets information on how many people were affected by the offence. But there are very few circumstances where this information would be naturally recorded or asked. It is a political measure. You can see why it's important from a political point of view. But it impacts the engagement with clients. (Voluntary agency)

But what happens when the 'reforming ought' confronts the 'recalcitrant is' (Bloor 1991)? Reporting on focus group responses to overarching aims, objectives and measures, Normand reported scepticism. Optimism, however, prevails: 'an important part of the process will be to ensure that there is appropriate consultation and that organizational communication and training are effective in explaining the relevance and value of this approach' (2003: 7). Exhortation or pleas for ownership, however, must confront the ultimate test of relevance that comes from the 'reality' of the context. Performance measures are not seen as core if they cannot speak to the immediate context of 'keeping the show on the road'. Co-location of personnel from different agencies (e.g. police and PF, PF and court); regular meetings; task-based problem-solving; training beyond the immediate prerequisites of the job; and the ability to maintain support staff who have a lot of local knowledge were viewed as much more valuable than meeting targets and performance measures.

Communicative rationality

There is a strong belief that performance measures will act as a stimulant to a communicative rationality, an enhanced communication between agencies leading to more effective work organization: 'Basically targets are a means to enforce cooperation between the agencies on ensuring targets. It gets partners around a table. It gets data out on the table, and it's a forum for asking questions, and it's a basis, an opportunity for gaining commitment' (Policy). Measures may indeed serve this function, the irony of an enforced coopera- tion notwithstanding, enhancing communication intra-organizationally; inter-organizationally for cross-agency collaboration; or as a broader demo- cratic engagement, whereby civil society is engaged in some discussion of the concept of public interest.

Measures, however, do not axiomatically operate in this manner. Where there is already a lack of intra-organizational communication between oper- ating levels and more senior managerial levels, they may exacerbate this, impacting on inter-agency cooperation: 'It's management's job to fix the targets; it's yours to meet them. You find a way to fix it, even though it may cause problems for others down the line' (Anonymous). Nor do measures axiomatically provide a common vocabulary for debate:

Earlier debates, for example, with the Trots, was valuable because it was couched in terms of 'this is what we want from the police and this is what you should do'. Now it's in terms of numbers and targets. From debates about gender, domestic violence, racial attacks, demands for safer communities, politicization 'this is what the police should be doing and how they should be doing it', is now politicization based on performance measures. 'Have your PIs gone up or down?' The political is not about values. The political is devalued. There is a narrowing. (Policy)

The effective and efficient functioning of public service organizations is not only a political but also a moral obligation. A failure to secure its effective functioning impacts on those who encounter the service, employees and ultimately the polis itself. This was the deeply felt sentiment expressed by those working within the CJS. Lessening emotional distress; helping the vulnerable; giving protection from fear; helping people who are caught up by crime; a moral commitment to the CJS as a public good; what it is to live in a 'just' society; maintaining the ethos of CJS; protecting the accused; and preserving the integrity of CJS institutions, were all factors that ensured that the 'system' functioned and that extra effort was forthcoming when things had to be made to work. These values do not hide complacency but are the foundation of appeals for change within the CJS so that it may achieve these ends. To be critical of the means chosen to secure a more effective functioning of CJS – overarching objectives and measures – is not to imply criticism of the ends.

Conclusions

In the introduction I argued that an analysis of some of the difficulties encountered with performance measurement systems has to go beyond explanations of the 'usual suspects': conflicting stakeholders, institutional versus managerial objectives, measurement versus learning. Instead, I have offered an analysis of conflicting rationalities that are brought into play in the attempt to flesh out what is involved in a rational technology. My argument is a simple one. Performance measures do not work. They are made to work (Townley 2004; Townley and Doyle 2006). A performance measurement system is a theoretical construct. It operationalizes in a set of concrete practices. It has to be socially accomplished. To become an acceptable and accepted technology, performance measures must be able to address *reasons* for their introduction. They are introduced to focus on 'what's the goal, purpose, objective of what we do?' But performance measures simultaneously prompt questions of 'what to measure?' (a bureaucratic rationality); 'how to measure accurately?' (technocratic); 'how do these help me understand what my job is and know what to do?' (institutional and contextual rationalities); 'how does this help me now?' (a situated rationality); 'how do we all under-stand what it is we're doing?' (a communicative rationality); and 'how do we make wise decisions?' (practical reason) (Townley 2008). Exhortations that to be successful a performance measurement system should distinguish between measures and targets (confused here by all respondents); that performance measures must be 'owned' by the organization; must be credible; resist manipulation; lie within the control of the organization, etc., that often accompanies their introduction, fail to capture the significance of their social accomplishment and in doing so easily become understood as being a tech-nical exercise.

It is interesting to note that improvements in the CJS came in response to the Bonomy recommendations on High Court legal practice and procedure, changes that are also percolating to Sheriff Courts, thus addressing institu-tional, contextual, and practical reasons for change. Changes were also brought about through the findings of the mapping exercise, addressing a situated and practical reason. Wisdom in these circumstances would indicate that measures should act as indicators of a 'direction of travel', rather than as a tightly connected cascade of targets and measures. It is however unfortunate that the Scottish Executive has moved away from a 'direction of travel'. The institutional rationalities that pervade politics, as it is currently understood, emphasize targets instead.

So what are managers to do? The answer to this question is equally simple: manage. That is, they need to ensure that the work for which they are responsible is conducted in an efficient and effective manner and that it secures the broader objectives of the organization. A range of operational information will be necessary to ensure that this is being carried out, of which measures will be one. Measures which support this are part of the normal management information of 'getting the job done', and as such rarely register as a discrete entity of 'performance measures'. They are incorporated into the ongoing narrative through which managers reflect on and reaffirm work. Measures which intrude on this, or distort this, should be jettisoned. Where political reasons make this inoperable, it should be made clear that this is the reason for their continued existence, with those sanctioning their adoption accepting responsibility for this. Such suggestions, of course, stress the importance of people having an adequate knowledge and understanding of job functions and their overall integration into an organization; the importance of, and support for, voice and the ability to speak out within organizations at all levels; managerial integrity in response to demands placed on the managerial role; and political integrity in relation to managerial or operational demands. Such issues are rarely addressed in relation to performance measures. But measures are no substitute for their operation and rarely, if at all, a catalyst to secure them.

REFERENCES

Auld, R. (2001) *Review of the Criminal Courts of England and Wales*. Report by the Right Honourable Lord Justice Auld. London: Stationery Office.

Bloor, D. (1991) *Knowledge and Social Imagery*. Chicago: Chicago University Press.

Boden, D. (1994) *The Business of Talk*. Cambridge: Polity Press.

Bonomy Report (2002) *Review of the High Court*. Report by the Honourable Lord Bonomy. Edinburgh: Scottish Executive.

Carter, N., Klein, R. and Day, P. (1992) *How Organizations Measure Success*. London: Routledge.

Cohen, M. D., March, J. G. and Olsen, J. P. (1972) A garbage can model of organizational choice. *Administrative Science Quarterly* 17: 1–25.

Coleman, C. and Moynihan, J. (2003) *Understanding Crime Data*. Maidenhead: Open University Press.

Hacking, I. (2001) *The Social Construction of What?* Cambridge, MA: Harvard University Press.

House of Commons Public Administration Select Committee (2003) *On Target? Government By Measurement*. London: Stationery Office.

MacClean Report (2000) *Quality and practice review unit review of the Crown Office and Procurator Fiscal Service Systems for the processing, preparation and prosecution of High Court cases*. Edinburgh: Scottish Executive.

McInnes Report (2004) *Summary Justice Review Committee, Report to Ministers*. Sheriff Principal McInnes. Edinburgh: Scottish Executive.

Meyer, M. (2002) *Rethinking Performance Measurement*. Cambridge: Cambridge University Press.

Meyer, J. and Rowan, B. (1978) Institutionalized organizations: formal structure as myth and ceremony. *American Journal of Sociology* **83** (1): 340–63.

National Audit Office (1999) *Criminal Justice; Working Together*. London: Stationery Office.
    (2001) *Measuring the Performance of Government Departments*. London: Stationery Office.

Normand Report (2003) *Proposals for the Integration of Aims, Objectives and Targets in the Scottish Criminal Justice System*. Report by Crown Agent Andrew Normand. Edinburgh: Stationery Office.

Oakeshott, M. (1991) Rationalism in politics, in Oakeshott, M. (ed.) *Rationalism in Politics and Other Essays*. Indianapolis; Liberty Fund, pp. 5–42.

Paton, R. (2003) *Managing and Measuring Social Enterprises*. London: Sage.

Perri 6, Leat, D., Seltzer, K. and Stoker, G. (2002) *Towards Holistic Governance*. London: Palgrave.

Power, M. (1997) *The Audit Society*. Oxford: Oxford University Press.

Price-Dyer Report (2002) *Review of the Planning, Allocation and Management of Resources in the Crown Office and Procurator Fiscal Service*. Edinburgh: Scottish Executive.

Reiner, R. (2002) Media made criminality; the representation of crime in the mass media, in Maguire, M., Morgan, R. and Reiner, R. (eds.) *The Oxford Handbook of Criminology*. Oxford: Oxford University Press, pp. 376–416.

Scottish Executive (2002) *Building a Better Scotland*. Edinburgh: Stationery Office.

Smith, P.C. (1993) Outcome-related performance indicators and organizational control. *British Journal of Management* **4**: 135–51.

Smith, H.T.O., Nutley, S. and Smith, P.C. (2000) *What Works?* Bristol: Policy Press.

Suchman, L. (1987) *Plans and Situated Actions*. Cambridge: Cambridge University Press.

Sullivan, H. and Skelcher, C. (2002) *Working Across Boundaries*. London: Palgrave.

Toulmin, S.E. (1958) *The Uses of Argument*. Cambridge: Cambridge University Press.

Townley, B. (1995) Managing by numbers: accounting, personnel management and the creation of a mathesis. *Critical Perspectives on Accounting* **6**(6): 555–75.
    (2002a) The role of competing rationalities in institutional change. *Academy of Management Journal* **45**(1): 163–79.
    (2002b) Managing with modernity. *Organization* **9**(4): 549–73.
    (2004) Managerial technologies, ethics and management. *Journal of Management Studies* **41** (3): 425–45.

(2005) Critical views of performance measurement, in *The Encyclopaedia of Social Measurement* Vol. I. Amsterdam: Elsevier, pp. 565–71.

(2008) *Reason's Neglect: Rationality and Organizing*. Oxford: Oxford University Press (forthcoming).

Townley, B., Cooper, D. J. and Oakes, L. (2003) Performance measurement and the rationalization of organizations. *Organization Studies* **24**(7): 1045–71.

Townley, B. and Doyle, R. (2006) Performance measures, in Ritzer, G. (ed.) *The Blackwell Encyclopaedia of Sociology*. Oxford: Blackwell, pp. 3396–9.

Treasury (2004) *The UK Government's Public Service Agreement Framework*. London: Stationery Office.

Young, P. (1997) *Crime and Criminal Justice in Scotland*. Edinburgh: Stationery Office.

Weber, M. (1978) *Economy and Society*. Berkeley, CA: University of California Press.

8 Valuing public sector outputs

Rachel Baker, Helen Mason, Cam Donaldson
and Michael Jones-Lee

Introduction

Recent government policy and pronouncements show that the drive to improve performance and achieve value for money in our public services goes on. Value for money cannot be measured – and therefore improved – without a clear agreement on how this should be done. This is the overarching theme of this chapter.

Despite the common perception that economic metrics of value are well established, it is in fact not so clear cut. Significant methodological challenges remain, plus the area is seen by some as ethically controversial. Nevertheless, if the challenges implicit in the measurement of productivity in the public sector were to be resolved (see chapter 6 by O'Mahony *et al.* in this volume), it could be possible to provide a valid measure of the value of any demonstrated gains in productivity in monetary terms. This measure of value could be used at the national level, for example in project appraisal, in choosing between a new road safety improvement scheme that saves lives or a new health care treatment which might prolong survival or enhance quality of life. Although the focus here is on such national-level decision-making, there are other levels of decision-making, such as patients choosing between different treatment options and health authorities deciding how to allocate their limited resources across different patient groups, to which such valuation methods might be applied (Olsen and Donaldson 1998; Donaldson 2001; Donaldson *et al.* 2006).

Two of the areas of the public sector which have made significant progress in such valuation are safety, especially transport safety, and health. The area of environmental economics is also at the forefront of development and application of such valuation methods. However, the strong links between health and safety with respect to their impacts on life-saving and quality-of-life improvements make it useful to focus this chapter on these areas, although developments in the environmental area, where pertinent, will also be referred to.

The aims of the chapter, therefore, are to describe the current 'state of the art' in estimating monetary values for health and safety and to suggest important next steps for research in these fields. This is done by reviewing previous theoretical and empirical work in the health field before moving on to do the same for research on valuation of safety policies. As priority setting in the health care arena was the focus of the AIM Fellowship held by one of the authors (CD) during 2003–4, the review focuses on health first, and indeed it is in this area that much recent debate has occurred about the need for monetary valuation. Having raised issues in the health area, it seems natural to then discuss how some of these have been addressed in an area in which monetary valuation seems to be more accepted (though it is still controversial); that of safety. An important aspect of the AIM Fellowship in this context was to review the literatures concerned, a review which forms the bulk of this chapter, but then to take the lessons learned from these fields into a discussion of the extent to which methods and results in one area can be brought together with those from the other and, indeed, more broadly across the public sector, so setting a research agenda as to how this might be achieved. This latter objective is briefly touched upon towards the end of the chapter.

Valuing health

'QALYs' and 'willingness to pay'

The issue of valuing health in monetary terms has recently come to the fore in UK health policy as a result of the creation of the National Institute for Health and Clinical Excellence (NICE) (Devlin and Parkin 2004; Loomes 2002). In offering guidance to the National Health Service (NHS) about the uptake or maintenance of an intervention, NICE has to weigh up the costs and benefits involved. If it is thought necessary to have these costs and benefits expressed in a common metric, usually money, the question is raised as to what value to place on improvements in length and quality of life. This is similar to the need of the Department for Transport to place a value on human life saved and non-fatal injuries avoided by reductions in risk arising from road safety improvements.

When NICE was first conceived, amongst its stated aims was, 'to produce a common currency of effectiveness for the NHS' (House of Commons Health Committee 2002). The 'quality-adjusted life year' (QALY) is currently the preferred outcome measure (of effectiveness) used by NICE (National

Coordinating Centre for Research Methodology 2003). QALYs are a generic metric which combine measures of quality of life and length of life. If quality of life can be valued on a 0–1 scale (where 0 = death and 1 = full health) then existing and additional life years can be adjusted for their quality, reflecting levels of impairment in which such years are spent. In the UK, there is a national 'tariff' for making such adjustments based on a five-dimensional health state classification system known as the EQ-5D (Dolan *et al.* 1995). The aim of developing the QALY was to have a more complete measure of health gain than one based on survival alone (Williams 1985). To make a recommendation as to the implementation of an intervention, competing interventions can be compared on the basis of their cost per QALY gained. In most cases, the intervention with the lowest cost per QALY gained would be implemented. This would reflect the dominant evaluation paradigm in health economics to date, whereby cost–utility analyses, using the QALY as a measure of benefit, are conducted.

However, returning to NICE, many of their recommendations involve considerations of the costs and benefits of single interventions, where there is no comparison between alternatives. In such cases the decisions about which intervention to provide are not obvious and the question of what value to place on QALY gains is raised. This question is complicated by the challenge of considering aspects beyond the health effects captured by QALYs and how benefits produced by health care can be compared with those arising from investments in other areas of the public sector which are not (and often cannot be) valued in terms of QALYs. Hence the need for a monetary measure to reflect the value of a QALY.

The monetary measure which forms the basis of the review in this chapter is 'willingness to pay'[1] (WTP). In standard welfare economics, maximum WTP represents the theoretically correct measure of 'strength of preference' for, or value of, a commodity (Mishan 1971; Pauly 1995). In areas of public sector activity, such as health care, in which conventional markets do not exist, decisions still have to be made about how best to use limited resources. This requires valuation of both resource costs of interventions and their benefits (the benefits being health gain and other sources of well-being), elicited in surveys by the use of hypothetical WTP questions (essentially the contingent valuation approach in which respondents state values for the good in question rather than reveal them as a result of real market-based choices). WTP focuses on the valuation of benefits, whereby a health care option is described to a

---

[1] Or willingness to accept compensation.

respondent and the person is asked what is his/her maximum WTP for it. In principle, with this type of information, the combination of NHS interventions could be chosen which maximizes the value of benefits (possibly distributionally weighted) to the community.

It is important to distinguish WTP, as a measure of benefit, from the cost of a good. Many people would be willing to pay more than the market-clearing price of a good. For any individual, the difference between benefit, as represented by his/her maximum WTP for the good, and the price paid by him/her for the good represents a gain in well-being from having the good provided.

WTP for a QALY: the health economics literature

The WTP method was first applied in the health area in the famous study of WTP to avoid heart attacks (Acton 1973). Subsequent to that, there were relatively few studies in the area of health (Diener *et al.* 1998), probably as a result of the QALY being perceived as a more acceptable measure of benefit than one which valued life in monetary terms.[2] Although QALYs may appear to have been introduced to health economic evaluation after Acton's initial WTP study (Torrance 1986; Williams 1985), they have emerged as the dominant valuation paradigm in this field. It was not until the publication of two empirical papers in the *Journal of Health Economics* in the early 1990s (Donaldson 1990; Johannesson *et al.* 1991) and the conceptual paper by Gafni (1991) that the feasibility of using the WTP approach in health economics was once again recognized and more studies began to be undertaken (Diener *et al.* 1998; Klose 1999; Olsen and Smith 2001). In fact, Gafni was one of the few people to undertake empirical work in the health field during the 1980s, with his small study of the WTP of women on a kibbutz for contraception services (Gafni and Feder 1987). More recently, two strands of literature have emerged on WTP for a QALY, one theoretical and one empirical. These are summarized in the following sections. However, as will be seen, the empirical literature is not strong or large, thus reinforcing the case for further research in this area.

---

[2] On the face of it, it would seem that it is problematic to use WTP measures to inform decisions about the allocation of resources for commodities, such as health care, for which such allocation is supposed to be on the basis of (some notion of) need. This is because WTP is obviously associated with ability to pay. However, it has been shown that this need not impede the use of WTP in health care economic evaluations (Donaldson 1999) and also that whatever method is use to value benefits, including QALYs, it will suffer from the same distributional concerns (Donaldson *et al.* 2002).

Theoretical perspectives on WTP for a QALY

Alongside the need within policy-making for a WTP-based value of a QALY, a theoretical debate has arisen as to why we need a monetary value of a QALY and what conditions are needed for this to occur. Within the theoretical literature the need for a WTP based value of a QALY is driven by an interest in the link between cost–utility analysis[3] and cost–benefit analysis and whether this link can provide a basis for cost–utility analysis within welfare economics.

Within the literature this link is referred to as the equivalence (or non-equivalence) of cost–benefit analysis (CBA) and cost-effectiveness analysis (CEA):

> Cost-effectiveness analysis should then be interpreted as an estimation of the cost function to produce health effects . . . In order to decide whether a treatment is cost-effective or not the estimation of the cost function has to be supplemented with information about the willingness to pay per unit of health effects to decide whether benefits exceed costs or not. (Johannesson 1995: 489)

In simple terms, from the above quote, CEA might be interpreted as estimating cost per QALY, whilst CBA might be interpreted as putting a monetary valuation on the QALY so as to indicate in one unit of account (money) whether benefits outweigh costs. In health care, the CBA–CEA equivalence debate has been developing since the original discussion of the issue by Phelps and Mushlin (1991). A major part of the debate has been about the conditions under which CBA and CEA are equivalent.[4] The basic argument presented by Phelps and Mushlin (1991) is that CBA typically determines in advance the marginal value of a QALY and uses this to calculate net benefit, whereas CEA calculates the 'price' (or 'cost') of obtaining a QALY but leaves unstated the crucial issue of whether benefits are greater than costs. The question of whether cost is greater or less than the marginal value of a QALY in a CEA (essentially rendering CBA equivalent to CEA) generates the requirement for a societal valuation of (WTP for) a QALY.

This then spawned a technical literature examining the conditions under which CBA is equivalent to CEA. Johannesson (1995) suggests that such conditions are where the WTP per unit of effectiveness is constant and the same for all individuals. If this assumption is relaxed (e.g. when WTP per unit of effectiveness is allowed to vary with the size of the health effects) the equivalence

---

[3] The term cost–utility analysis (CUA) is used to refer to the type of economic evaluation which has QALYs as its outcome measure. However, this is often replaced by the term cost-effectiveness analysis within this literature.

[4] Another line of debate addresses the issue from the point of view of defining economic evaluation types according to the original efficiency question to be addressed, whether one of technical or allocative efficiency (Donaldson 1998). This is less relevant in the context of the research being considered here.

will no longer hold. Thus, as highlighted in the above quote, WTP per QALY data may still be required, but it may also have to be more context-specific.

Garber and Phelps (1997), in discussing the welfare economic foundations of CEA, again show that CEA is equivalent to CBA under certain conditions, a crucial factor being the degree to which QALYs represent individuals' preferences. Bleichrodt and Quiggin (1999) and Dolan and Edlin (2001) extend the argument further, their principal aim appearing to be to examine the conditions under which the CBA of proposed health care expenditure decisions (based on WTP) and CEA (based on QALYs) would produce consistent conclusions.

While Bleichrodt and Quiggin allow the possibility that WTP per QALY gained may increase with income or wealth and derive conditions under which CEA (based on constrained QALY maximization) would be consistent with CBA, Dolan and Edlin argue that these conditions are excessively restrictive and unrealistic and instead examine the possibility of producing a WTP per QALY gained that is constant and, in particular, independent of income/wealth. Dolan and Edlin then proceed to demonstrate the impossibility of the latter under circumstances in which the marginal utility of consumption is taken to be an increasing function of health status – a result which is, on reflection, hardly surprising.

Despite the debate highlighted above, this does not render the quest for a single, defensible, WTP-based monetary value of a QALY doomed to failure. In particular, seeking an individual WTP-based monetary value of a QALY that is independent of income or wealth is about on a par with the aspiration that individual WTP for a reduction in the risk of premature death would be independent of income or wealth when both theory and empirical evidence point strongly in the direction of the conclusion that safety is a *strictly normal* good. But this does not prevent the UK Department for Transport, as well as other government departments in this country and abroad, from employing WTP-based values for the prevention of a statistically premature fatality (VPF) that are based on central tendency measures (typically arithmetic means) of the population distribution of individual WTP for risk reduction. The fact that these VPFs are then applied *uniformly* to all groups in society *whatever the income levels of members of the group* clearly implies the use of inverse-income distributional weights. Furthermore, it should not be forgotten that it has been shown recently, at least theoretically, that QALYs also 'suffer' from not being independent of income/wealth (Donaldson *et al.* 2002 – also, see footnote 2). Similar arguments apply to the relationship between WTP-based values of a QALY and age.

It would therefore appear that not only are all economics-based valuation methods subject to the 'distributional problem' but also that there is already a precedent in UK public sector decision-making for applying distributional weights to individual WTP for reductions in risks to life in order to arrive at an overall value in the form of a population mean (or possibly median) of individual values. This represents the state of the art of dealing with any such biases.

WTP for a QALY: statements and estimates

Several studies report monetary values and QALYs, but none of these has directly estimated a value of a QALY (Thompson 1986; Barrett *et al.* 1994; O'Brien and Viramontes 1994; Coley *et al.* 1996; Kobelt 1997; Krabbe *et al.* 1997; Swan *et al.* 1997; Zethraeus *et al.* 1997; Bala *et al.* 1998; Blumenschein and Johannesson 1998; Olsen and Donaldson 1998; Zethraeus 1998; Lundberg *et al.* 1999; Sorum 1999; Cunningham and Hunt 2000; Kupperman *et al.* 2000; Voruganti *et al.* 2000; Smith 2001). Although a WTP per QALY value can, in principle, be calculated from such studies there are several problems with such estimates. The range of health care contexts and valuation techniques used vary; some studies elicit values from patients and others from the general public and none of these studies were designed for this purpose. Furthermore (and perhaps as a result of some of these issues), the values which are indirectly obtained from these studies turn out to be wide ranging and in some cases implausible (Baker *et al.* 2003). Indirect estimates from existing studies should, therefore, be interpreted with caution.

Other tentative attempts at placing a value on a QALY have been made recently by Rawlins and Culyer (2004) and Willams (2004). Based on their experience and observations of the NICE process, Rawlins and Culyer state that values of over £25,000–£35,000 would need special reasons to be accepted, which could be interpreted as the revealed preference of NICE. Williams proposes a much lower figure of £18,000 based on the premise that in the UK this is the amount that we have in real resources to provide all the needs of the average citizen. He implies that, with this amount available to spend on meeting all needs, it is excessive to spend almost twice that (assuming a £30,000 benchmark) on health care alone and reinforces this by stating that a £30,000 benchmark represents more than twenty times the UK average health care expenditure per person per annum. However, given that payments to health care are based on many contributing so that few can benefit and that relatively few people use the NHS (at least as an inpatient and, thus, for more serious conditions) each year, such a benchmark of £30,000 (or one based on the more scientific approaches proposed later in this chapter) might be defensible.

In summary it is quite clear that the bases of these two sets of estimates could be stronger. In the short term one way of estimating a value of a QALY might be to take established values of life from the safety literature and attempt to 'model' an estimate from these values. This has actually been done in the US context by Hirth *et al.* (2000); an example of a UK-based calculation is shown in the fourth section of this chapter. Another approach is to conduct survey research to directly estimate a value of a QALY, using methods which are again similar to those used previously in the safety literature. A Danish study, by Gyrd-Hansen (2003), has been conducted along such lines.

Learning from safety

It has been argued, in the preceding sections and sub-sections of this chapter, that in order for policy-makers such as NICE to make decisions about resource allocation in the health sector, there needs to be a societal valuation of the benefits yielded by health care. In a review of the theoretical and empirical health economics literature, attention has been drawn to the gaps and weakness with respect to estimates of a societal value of health benefit.

There are obvious parallels between the need, in the health sector, for a value of a QALY and the work that has been done in the area of safety (in particular transport safety) on the value of a statistical life. Overall, it seems that there is great potential for the transfer of methods and results from the valuation-of-safety field to address issues in health. Amongst other issues, this potential relates to whether the value of a prevented statistical fatality (VPF) used in safety can be used as the basis of the value of a QALY, whether the methods used to estimate the VPF can be transferred over to the health care context and how distribution and altruism are dealt with when eliciting and using values for safety expressed by the public.

Valuing Safety

The first empirical application of WTP, published in a journal, was in the area of environmental policy evaluation (Davis 1963). During the 1970s, the method was further developed in studies of the valuation of human life, as applied to safety and transport policies (Jones-Lee 1974; 1976; Mooney 1977). Of great relevance to the issues faced currently in health has been the valuation work in the context of safety policies. This work has involved the development of methods to elicit a 'value of statistical life' and, thus, is more closely related to the challenge of valuing a QALY (or 'healthy year').

Until the 1980s most countries that explicitly addressed the public sector safety-valuation issue tended to use some variant of the so-called 'gross output' or 'human capital' approach. Under this approach the primary component of the 'cost' of the premature death of an individual is treated as the discounted present value of that individual's future output extinguished as a result of his or her premature demise. In some countries (including the UK) a further more-or-less arbitrary allowance was then added to the gross output figure to reflect the 'pain, grief and suffering' of the victim and/or his/her surviving dependents and relatives. Values for the prevention of premature death are then defined in terms of the costs avoided.

To give an example of the costs and values that emerge under the gross output approach, the UK Department for Transport's most recent gross output-based value for the prevention of a road fatality was £180,330 in 1985 prices, of which about 28 per cent was an allowance for pain, grief and suffering. Updated for inflation and growth of real output per capita this figure would stand at some £500,000 in 2004 prices.

Not surprisingly, many economists have objected to the gross output approach on the grounds that most people almost certainly value safety largely because of their aversion to the prospect of their own and others' death and injury as such, rather than because of a concern to preserve current and future levels of output and income (Schelling 1968; Mishan, 1971; Jones-Lee 1989). Given this, it has been argued that values of safety ought ideally to be defined so as to reflect people's 'pure' preferences for safety, *per se*, rather than in terms of effects on output and income, as in the gross output approach. However, in order to define and estimate values of safety in this way we clearly require some means of measuring people's preferences for safety and, more particularly, their *strength* of preference. How can one do this? Arguably, the most natural measure of the extent of a person's strength of preference for anything is the maximum amount that he or she would be willing to pay for it. This amount reflects not only the person's valuation of the desired good or service relative to other potential objects of expenditure, but also the individual's *ability* to pay – which is itself a manifestation of society's overall resource constraint.

So, under what has naturally come to be known as the 'willingness-to-pay' (WTP) approach to the valuation of safety, one first seeks to establish the maximum amounts that those affected would individually be willing to pay for (typically small) improvements in their own and others' safety. These amounts are then simply aggregated across all individuals to arrive at an overall value for the safety improvement concerned. The resultant figure is a clear reflection of what the safety improvement is 'worth' to the affected group, relative to the alternative ways in which each individual might have spent his or her limited income. Furthermore, defining values of safety in this way effectively 'mimics' the operation of market forces – in circumstances in which markets typically do not exist – insofar as such forces can be seen as vehicles for allowing individual preferences to interact with relative scarcities and production possibilities to determine the allocation of a society's scarce resources.

In order to standardize values of safety that are derived from the WTP approach and render them comparable with values obtained under other approaches (such as gross output), the concept of the prevention of a 'statistical' fatality or injury is applied. To illustrate this concept, suppose that a group of 100,000 people enjoy a safety improvement that reduces the probability of premature death during a forthcoming period by, on average, 1 in 100,000 for each and every member of the group. The expected number of fatalities within the group during the forthcoming period will thus be reduced by precisely one and the safety improvement is therefore described as involving the prevention of one 'statistical' fatality. Now suppose that individuals within this group are, on average, each willing to pay £w for the 1 in 100,000 reduction in the probability of death afforded by the safety improvement. Aggregate WTP will then be given by £$w \times 100,000$. This figure is naturally referred to as the WTP-based *value of preventing one statistical fatality* (VPF) or alternatively as the *value of statistical life* (VOSL).

Clearly, in the above example, average individual WTP, £w, for the average individual risk reduction of 1 in 100,000 is a reflection of the rate at which people in the group are willing to trade off wealth against risk 'at the margin', in the sense that the trade-offs typically involve small variations in wealth and small variations in risk. Empirical work on the valuation of safety thus tends to focus upon these individual marginal wealth/risk trade-off rates.

On a somewhat more cautionary note, it is extremely important to appreciate that, defined in this way, the VPF is not a 'value (or price) of life' in the sense of a sum that any given individual would accept in compensation for the certainty of his or her own death – for most of us, no finite sum would suffice for this purpose, so that in this sense life is literally priceless. Rather, the VPF is aggregate WTP for typically very small reductions in individual risk of death (which, realistically, is what most safety improvements really offer at the individual level). Importantly, as argued below, this is probably also most appropriately viewed as a group-aggregate willingness to pay for *marginal* gains in quality of life or life expectancy given that, at least in the case of a randomly selected sample of the public, such gains *will* typically be marginal, though of course the same cannot necessarily be said for those already suffering from health impairments.

Before outlining the various ways in which researchers have sought to obtain empirical estimates of values of safety using the WTP approach, two further points should be noted. First, so far only passing reference has been made to people's concern – and hence WTP – for others, as well as their own safety. Insofar as people do display such 'altruistic' concern then one would naturally expect that it would be appropriate to augment the WTP-based VPF to reflect the amounts that people would be willing to pay for an improvement in others' safety. However, it turns out that under plausible assumptions about the nature of people's altruistic concern for others' safety on the one hand and their material well-being on the other (the latter being reflected by their wealth or consumption), augmenting the VPF to reflect WTP for others' safety would involve a form of double-counting and would therefore ultimately be unjustified. For example, suppose that individual A is concerned not only about individual B's safety, but also about the latter's wealth or consumption. Furthermore, suppose that individual A's altruistic concern for B is 'pure', in the sense that it respects B's preferences. While A will then regard a reduction in B's risk of premature death as a 'good thing', he or she will also regard the increase in B's taxation (or other expenditure) required to finance the risk reduction as an *exactly offsetting* 'bad thing'. Taking account only of A's WTP for B's safety improvement would therefore quite literally involve double-counting. Thus, the issue of whether and how people's concern for others' safety ought to be taken into account under the WTP approach hinges on the essentially empirical question of the relationship between such concern and concern for others' wealth or consumption. For a more detailed discussion of the issue of altruism and safety, see Jones-Lee (1992). Given all of this, it would seem that similar arguments apply to the WTP-based monetary value of a QALY.

A further important aspect of the WTP approach involves recognition of the fact that safety improvements also have 'direct' economic effects, such as avoidance of net output losses (i.e. losses of the excess of an accident victim's future output over and above his/her future consumption), material damage, medical and police costs and so on. To the extent that people appear in the main not to take account of such factors in assessing their WTP for improved safety (and there is some evidence that they tend not to – see Jones-Lee *et al.* (1985)), then an allowance for these factors should clearly be added to WTP-based values of safety. However, such additions tend to be relatively modest in relation to the typical magnitude of aggregate WTP for safety *per se*, at least in the case of risks of premature death.

But how, in fact, are WTP values of safety estimated in practice? Broadly speaking, three variants of empirical estimation procedure have been employed to derive WTP-based values of safety. These are known respectively as the 'revealed preference' (or 'implied value'), the 'contingent valuation' (or 'expressed value') and 'relative valuation' approaches.

In essence, the revealed preference approach involves the identification of situations in which people actually do trade off income or wealth against physical risk – for example, in labour markets where riskier jobs can be expected to command clearly identifiable wage *premia* (Smith 1983; Viscusi and Moore 1989). By contrast, the contingent valuation approach involves asking a representative sample of people more or less directly about their individual WTP for improved safety (or, sometimes, their willingness to accept compensation for increased risk).

The difficulty with the revealed preference approach when applied to labour market data is that it depends on being able to disentangle risk-related wage differentials from the many other factors that enter into the determination of wage rates. The approach also presupposes that workers are well informed about the risks that they actually face in the workplace. In addition, those whose jobs do carry clearly identifiable wage *premia* for risk may not be representative of the work force as a whole, in that such people almost certainly have a below-average degree of risk-aversion (Gegax *et al.* 1991).

The great advantage of the contingent valuation approach is that it allows the researcher to go directly and unambiguously to the relevant wealth/risk trade-off – at least, in principle. On the other hand, the contingent valuation approach has the disadvantage of relying upon the assumption that people are able to give considered, accurate and unbiased answers to hypothetical questions about typically small changes in already very small risks.[5]

By contrast, unlike the revealed preference and contingent valuation approaches, the relative valuation approach does *not* involve an attempt to

---

[5] Equally contentious to placing monetary values on safety and health policies has been that area of environmental economics research involving assessment of so-called 'non-use' and 'existence' values. It is in this area that most work has been conducted on the extent to which values derived in such contingent-valuation surveys reflect 'real-world' behaviour. In the early 1990s, the literature on this issue was split, with five studies showing WTP values elicited from surveys to be greater than those from real behaviour whilst five studies gave consistent results (Hanemann 1993). Since then, Carson *et al.* (1996) have shown in a systematic review of the literature that, compared with revealed preference methods, contingent valuation WTP estimates tend to be lower (on average 0.89 of revealed preference estimates), which is the opposite of what many people might expect. One study in the health economics literature has shown that a revealed preference and contingent valuation method arrive at similar valuations (Kennedy 2002), whilst others have shown the opposite to the Carson *et al.* review (Clarke 1997), with one also making the claim that it may still be possible to correct for any overestimation (Blumenschein *et al.* 2001).

estimate wealth/risk trade-off rates directly, but rather seeks to determine the value of preventing one kind of physical harm *relative to* another. Thus, for example, the UK Department for Transport's current monetary values for the prevention of non-fatal road injuries of various levels of severity were obtained by applying estimates of such relative valuations to an absolute monetary 'peg' in the form of the Department's existing WTP-based roads VPF.

Turning to the question of the figures that are actually applied in practice, WTP-based values of safety are currently used in road project appraisal in the UK, USA, Canada, Sweden and New Zealand, with several other countries employing values that have been substantially influenced by the results of WTP studies. More specifically, in the UK the Department for Transport (DfT) employed a figure of £1.31 million in June 2003 prices for the prevention of a statistical fatality in its roads project appraisal. This figure was based on the findings of a study which obtained estimates of the roads VPF using a variant of the contingent valuation approach – see Carthy *et al.* (1999). In turn, the Department's values for the prevention of serious and slight non-fatal injuries are £147,460 and £11,370 respectively, again in 2003 prices, these figures having been obtained using the relative valuation approach to estimate non-fatal/fatal valuation relativities – see Jones-Lee *et al.* (1995), and Department for Transport (2002).

In the USA, the US Department of Transportation currently values the prevention of a statistical road fatality at US$ 3 million (though it will increase to $5m this year), this being an update of a figure originally recommended in 1991 following a survey of the then-existing literature on empirical estimation of WTP-based values of safety – see The Urban Institute (1991).

In turn, Transport Canada applies a WTP-based value for the prevention of a statistical fatality of CAN$ 1.5 million in 1991 prices based on a survey of the literature. Updated for inflation and growth this would be very close to the current DfT UK value.

Finally, the WTP values used in Sweden and New Zealand were derived under the contingent valuation approach and in 1999 prices are SEK 14.30 million (roughly £1.07 million) and NZ$ 2.5 million (roughly £820,000), though in the latter case it should be noted that the New Zealand Land Transport Safety Authority is considering increasing the figure to NZ$ 4 million (roughly £1.32 million) on the basis of recommendations following an extensive contingent valuation study carried out in New Zealand in 1997–8 – see Guria *et al.* (1999).

Recently, both quantitative and qualitative research have cast doubt on the reliability and validity of WTP values for safety derived through the above direct contingent valuation method. As well as sequencing and framing effects, a prominent issue has been the lack of ability of the method to account for embedding and scope. That is, respondents tend to view safety improvements as a 'good thing' and, therefore, will often state much the same WTP for different sizes of risk reduction, whether for fatal or non-fatal injuries (Jones-Lee *et al.* 1995; Dubourg *et al.* 1997; Beattie *et al.* 1998). It may be unreasonable to expect respondents to give accurate answers to hypothetical questions which involve direct trade-offs between wealth and small reductions in risk. Therefore, Carthy *et al.* (1999) have suggested a less direct contingent valuation (CV)/standard gamble (SG) 'chained' approach which breaks down the valuation process into a series of more manageable steps which involve chaining together responses to WTP and SG questions.

First, respondents are presented with a question asking them about their WTP for the certainty of a complete cure for a given non-fatal road injury and their willingness to accept compensation for the certainty of remaining in the impaired health state (the combination of which, based on some reasonable assumptions about underlying preferences obeying minimal conditions of consistency and regularity, it is argued, gives a reasonable estimate of the marginal rate of substitution of wealth for the risk of the non-fatal injury). Second, respondents are presented with an SG question aimed at determining the ratio of the health state value for death to that for the non-fatal injury. The monetary value from the first stage can then be combined with the ratio from the second stage to obtain a WTP for reduced risk of death.

The approach is, perhaps, more realistic in that most people can relate to giving a monetary value for avoiding a non-fatal injury of the sort they are likely to have experienced, and people are not asked directly to place a monetary value on a small risk reduction. The method has shown promise in terms of being subject to less marked embedding effects and other biases than earlier approaches (Beattie *et al.* 1998). It should also be noted here, however, that another major focus in the environmental literature with respect to validity has been on scope effects: especially whether split samples of respondents are willing to pay more for greater amounts of the good being valued, as one would expect. Carson (1997) shows that most studies (31 of 35 reviewed) reveal sensitivity to scope. It has also been argued that discrete choice experiments (DCEs) can overcome the scope problem as they force respondents to think more about the individual attributes of the commodity being valued (Hanley *et al.* 2002). Despite such positive results, doubts still remain about WTP values elicited through hypothetical surveys, and scope tests have taken on the status of being the 'acid test' for any particular study.

Also, this has led to more qualitative methods being used to examine the thought processes underlying respondents' stated values (Schkade and Payne 1994; Chilton and Hutchison 1999), a trend which is likely (and justifiably) to continue. Comparisons of all such approaches in the health arena would seem to be important, therefore.

Bringing safety and health together: the future research agenda

From life to quality-adjusted life years: modelling the value of a QALY

A straightforward way to combine work in health and safety valuation areas is to take the well-established roads VPF for the UK and, from it, attempt to model the value of a QALY. For example, based on similar approaches used elsewhere (Hirth et al. 2000), if we take a representative death avoided as being that of a person aged 35, assume that the VPF is £1.31M and that the person concerned would have lived for another 40 years, a rough calculation of the value of a life year gained by that person would be as follows:

$$(1) \quad V = \frac{£1.31 \times 10^6}{40}$$
$$(2) \quad = £32,750$$

Conveniently, V is close to the value of a QALY espoused by Rawlins and Culyer (2004). However, if one were to assume that not all of the 40 years gained would be spent in full health (especially later years) and a discount rate, the denominator in (1) would fall, thus raising the value of a QALY above £32,750. For example, if the discount rate was taken to be 5% then the annualized sum that would have a discounted present value of £1.31 million over 40 years would be £76,700.[6]

A further crude assumption of the approach outlined above is that of linear proportionality between an individual's WTP and future remaining life years. More specifically, it would appear that those who have advocated this approach have thought of the VPF upon which the approach is based as a value of (on average) 40 years of life expectancy and then have simply divided this figure by 40 (with appropriate discount factors and quality of life adjustments) to obtain the value of a life year. To the naïve or casual reader this

---

[6] In this estimate, life years are not discounted.

would then be naturally interpreted as the average sum that an individual could be expected to be willing to pay for a one-year gain in life expectancy. On careful reflection, however, this is plainly not the case and if the resultant sum is to be given any sort of credible justification it really has to be thought of as the kind of *group aggregate* WTP for a risk reduction that, taken across a large group of people, entails an expected gain of one year in life years lived.

Furthermore, the approach outlined also relies upon the rather doubtful assumption that WTP for a reduction in the risk of immediate premature death is no more and no less than WTP for the preservation of a given number of equally valued future life years (e.g. for our 35 year old, 40 more years). However, it would not be surprising if many people's WTP to reduce mortality risks depends on a *great deal more* than future lifespan and could, for example, be substantially influenced by considerations such as the emotional costs of premature death to those who would be bereaved; the will to live and a concern about failing to achieve specific lifetime aspirations, such as desire to see one's children and grandchildren grow up. In view of this, Loomes (2002) suggests that, at least beyond middle age, the VPF may be better viewed as comprising the sum of a constant component that is independent of age and reflects the pure value of living *per se* and a component that declined as the remaining life expectancy falls. This would imply estimation of the parameters of such a function using existing empirical estimates of WTP for safety by age which tends to take an inverted-U life cycle form, peaking in middle age and declining thereafter. Intuitively, such a method would pull the value of a QALY back down from that which would arise after discounting and quality adjusting the value expressed at (2), as the value of life would now be based on a fixed element as well as future QALYs gained.

Taking all of the above into account, and adding in a more accurate estimate of survival than that used in the simple calculation at (1), it can be seen that it might be possible to improve on current methods published in the literature and also compute a value (or set of values) for use in UK-based policy-making.

Survey research on the value of a QALY

In the medium term it might be more prudent to move to an estimate of the value of a QALY based on actual survey research, in the same way that the VPF used in the safety field was derived. All of the above points to the need for such research to take place. Although such an estimate has been derived by Gyrd-Hansen (2003), it is limited to the extent that it examines values of gains in quality of life only and does not account for uncertainty. Also, the quality-of-life values used in the study were those from a pre-existing tariff and not those of the respondents surveyed.

The method we would propose should use up-to-date techniques aimed at overcoming some of the cognitive problems associated with deriving estimates of WTP. In view of the promise shown by the CV/SG chained approach, it would seem to be a natural candidate for estimating a WTP-based monetary value of a QALY. This method appears to have the potential to overcome some important problems: first, it breaks down the valuation process into a series of (hopefully) more manageable tasks; second, despite commencing with questions asking respondents to value certain gains in quality of life, the last stage of the chaining approach ensures that links to uncertainty and life years are incorporated.

However, we are conscious that there are also a number of other possible approaches to deriving a WTP-based value of a QALY based on the contingent valuation method. It might be that a more direct contingent valuation method would suffice, although it remains contentious in both environmental and health research as to whether lack of sensitivity to scope is an issue (Olsen *et al.* 2004). The case for a DCE-based approach to the valuation of a QALY has also been made. Given the uncertainty as to which method would prove the more valid, and the challenges in demonstrating this quantitatively, it is important to address aspects of the validity of the approaches by the use of carefully constructed qualitative studies prior to, and alongside, surveys and to assess plausibility by comparing results obtained with those derived through the use of similar methods in non-health fields, especially (in the case of the methods proposed here) valuations of life derived from studies of safety improvements.

It is also important to account for theoretically relevant informational and societal aspects which have been shown in health and other applied literatures either to have an impact on values or, as in the case of scope effects/embedding, to be both controversial and important to test for. In addition to scope tests, these aspects include the information presented to respondents, age, health status, accounting for both quantity as well as quality of life, and adjusting values for broader societal factors such as age, initial health state (or severity) and culpability.

On the latter issue, it would seem that it may be necessary to have different values of a QALY for different sets of circumstances. Indeed, in the case of safety it has long been supposed that factors such as voluntariness, control, responsibility, catastrophe potential and so on – or to use a catch-all term, 'dread' – may well lead to substantially different VPFs in different contexts – see, for example, Mendeloff and Kaplan (1990), McDaniels, Kamlet and Fischer (1992), Savage (1993) or Sunstein (1997). However, recent work by a team including one of the authors of this chapter (Chilton *et al.* 2004) found that for a range of hazards involving risks of immediate death – such as road or rail accidents, fires in public places or drowning – where there are significant differences in the degree of dread associated with such hazards by members of the public, these effects are largely offset by the fact that high dread hazards typically have lower levels of baseline risks, thus resulting in preference-based VPFs that do not differ greatly across the hazards concerned.

Conclusions

Despite appearances to the contrary, there is still much work to be done in developing economics-based methods for valuing outputs of the public sector. The challenges outlined in this chapter are immense, but so too has been the progress which we have also described. In the context of safety, the values that exist are now routinely used in policy-making in the UK, Canada, New Zealand, Sweden and the US. This research work, essentially addressing the fundamental issue of the 'value of life', has the rare distinction in social and management research of being both path-breaking and having fed directly into policy.

Extension and replication of the work in the health field has the potential to be equally profound in terms of scientific quality and use in policy. The policy applications can be not only within organizations such as NICE but also in terms of valuing NHS productivity. Attempts are currently underway to measure such productivity in terms of the health gains produced by the NHS (see O'Mahony *et al.*, chapter 6 in this volume). If successful, and the research on valuing a QALY is equally so, it will be possible to value such gains in monetary terms. This will raise questions about to the possibility of further endeavours across the public sector. If the notion of 'joined-up government' is to have any meaning in measurement terms, one avenue might be to attempt to use such money metrics to aid resource allocations across the public sector as well as within its component parts. More realistically, if more accurate estimates of the value of life and health can be obtained, then resource allocation decisions which follow from their application will also be more efficient, leading to better health and more lives saved from our public sector resources. What can be more important than that!

REFERENCES

Acton, J. P. (1973) *Evaluating Public Programs to Save Lives: The Case of Heart Attacks.* Santa Monica: RAND Corporation, Report No R950RC.

Baker, R., Chilton, S., Donaldson, C. *et al.* (2003) *Determining the Societal Value of a QALY by Surveying the Public in England and Wales: A Research Protocol.* Birmingham: NCCRM Publications.

Bala M. V., Wood, L. L., Zarkin, G. A., Norton, E. C., Gafni, A. and O'Brien, B. (1998) Valuing outcomes in health care: a comparison of willingness to pay and quality adjusted life years. *Journal of Clinical Epidemiology* **51**(8): 667–76.

Barrett, B. J., Parfrey, P. S., Foley, R. N. and Detsky, A. S. (1994) An economic analysis of strategies for the use of contrast media for diagnostic cardiac catheterization. *Medical Decision-Making* **14**: 325–35.

Beattie, J., Covey, J., Dolan, P. *et al.* (1998) On the contingent valuation of safety and the safety of contingent valuation: part 1 – caveat investigator. *Journal of Risk and Uncertainty* **17**: 5–25.

Bleichrodt, H. and Quiggin, J. (1999) Life cycle preferences over consumption and health: when is cost-effectiveness analysis equivalent to cost-benefit analysis? *Journal of Health Economics* **18**: 681–708.

Blumenschein, K. and Johannesson, M. (1998) The relationship between quality of life instruments, health state utilities and willingness to pay in patients with asthma. *Annals of Allergy, Asthma and Immunology* **80**(2): 189–94.

Blumenschein, K., Johannesson, M., Yokoyama, K. K. and Freeman, P. R. (2001) Hypothetical versus real willingness to pay in the health sector: results from a field experiment. *Journal of Health Economics* **20**: 441–57.

Carson, R. T. (1997) Contingent valuation surveys and tests of insensitivity to scope, in Kopp, R. J., Pemmerhene, W. and Schwartz, N. (eds.) *Determining the Value of Non-Marketed Goods: Economic, Psychological and Policy Relevant Aspects of Contingent Valuation Methods.* Boston: Kluwer.

Carson, R. T., Flores, N. E., Martin, K. M. and Wright, J. L. (1996) Contingent valuation and revealed preference methodologies: comparing the estimates for quasi-public goods. *Land Economics* **72**: 80–99.

Carthy, T., Chilton, S. M., Covey, J. *et al.* (1999) On the contingent valuation of safety and the safety of contingent valuation: part 2 – the CV/SG 'chained' approach. *Journal of Risk and Uncertainty* **17**: 187–213.

Chilton, S. M. and Hutchison, W. G. (1999) Do focus groups contribute anything to the contingent valuation process? *Journal of Economic Psychology* **20**: 465–83.

Chilton, S. M., Jones-Lee, M. and Metcalf, H. (2004) *Valuation of Health and Safety Benefits: Dread Risks.* Final report on the Newcastle study. Report to the Health and Safety Executive.

Clarke, P. M. (1997) Valuing the benefits of health care in monetrary terms with particular reference to mammographic screening. PhD Thesis, Canberra: Australian National University.

Coley, C. M., Li, Y. H. Medsger, A. R. *et al.* (1996) Preferences for home versus hospital care among low-risk patients with community-acquired pneumonia. *Archives of Internal Medicine,* **156**: 1565–71.

Cunningham, S. J. and Hunt, N. P. (2000) Relationship between utility values and willingness to pay in patients undergoing orthognathic treatment. *Community Dental Health* **17**: 92–6.

Davis, R. K. (1963) Recreation planning as an economic problem. *Natural Resources Journal* **3**: 239–49.

Department for Transport (2002) *Highway Economics Note*, No.1. London: Department for Transport.

Devlin, N. and Parkin, D. (2004) Does NICE have a cost-effectiveness threshold and what other factors influence their decisions? A binary choice analysis. *Health Economics* **13**(5): 437–52.

Diener, A., O'Brien, B. and Gafni, A. (1998) Health care contingent valuation studies: a review and classification of the literature. *Health Economics* **7**: 313–26.

Dolan, P. and Edlin, R. (2001) Is it really possible to build a bridge between cost-benefit analysis and cost-effectiveness analysis? *Journal of Health Economics* **21**: 827–43.

Dolan, P., Gudex, C., Kind, P. and Williams, A. (1995) *A Social Tariff for the EuroQol: Results from a UK General Population Survey*. Centre for Health Economics, Discussion Paper 138. York: Centre for Health Economics, University of York.

Donaldson, C. (1990) Willingness to pay for publicly-provided goods: a possible measure of benefit? *Journal of Health Economics* **9**: 103–18.

(1998) The (near) equivalence of cost-effectiveness and cost-benefit analysis: fact or fallacy. *Pharmaco-Economics* **13**: 389–96.

(1999) Valuing the benefits of publicly-provided health care: does 'ability to pay' preclude the use of 'willingness to pay'? *Social Science and Medicine* **49**: 551–63.

(2001) Eliciting patients' values by use of 'willingness to pay': letting the theory drive the method. *Health Expectations* **4**: 180–8.

Donaldson, C., Birch, S. and Gafni, A. (2002) The pervasiveness of the 'distribution problem' in economic evaluation in health care. *Health Economics* **11**: 55–70.

Donaldson, C., Shackley, P. and Mason, H. (2006) Contingent valuation in health care, in Jones, A. M. (ed.) *Elgar Companion to Health Economics*. Cheltenham: Edward Elgar.

Dubourg, W. R., Jones-Lee, M. and Loomes, G. (1997) Imprecise preferences and survey design in contingent valuation. *Economica* **64**: 681–702.

Gafni, A. (1991) Willingness to pay as a measure of benefits: relevant questions in the context of public decision-making about health care programmes. *Medical Care*, **29**: 1246–52.

Gafni, A. and Feder, A. (1987) Willingness to pay in an equitable society: the case of the Kibbutz. *International Journal of Social Economics* **14**: 16–21.

Garber, A. M. and Phelps, C. E. (1997) Economic foundations of cost-effectiveness analysis. *Journal of Health Economics* **16**: 1–31.

Gegax, D., Gerking, S. and Schulze, W. (1991) Perceived risk and the marginal valuation of safety. *Review of Economics and Statistics* **73**: 589–96.

Guria, J., Jones, W., Jones-Lee, M. *et al.* (1999) The values of statistical life and prevention of injuries in New Zealand. Draft report to the New Zealand Land Transport Safety Authority.

Gyrd-Hansen, D. (2003) Willingness to pay for a QALY. *Health Economics* **12**: 1049–60.

Hanemann, W. M. (1993) Valuing the environment through contingent valuation. *Journal of Economic Perspectives* **8**: 19–43.

Hanley, N., Adamowicz, V. and Wright, R. (2002) Do choice experiments pass the scope test? A test of scope in a choice experiment examining the benefits of water quality improvements. Paper presented at EAERE/AERE World Congress, Monterey, 2002.

Hirth, R. A., Cherner, M. E., Miller, E., Fendrick, M. F. and Weissert, W. G. (2000) Willingness to pay for a quality-adjusted life year: in search of a Standard. *Medical Decision Making* **20**: 332–4.

House of Commons Health Committee (2002) *National Institute for Clinical Excellence. Second Report of Session 2001–2002 Volume I: Report and Proceedings of the Committee.* London: Stationery Office.

Johannesson, M. (1995) The relationship between cost effectiveness analysis and cost benefit analysis. *Social Science and Medicine* **41**: 483–9.

Johannesson, M., Jonsson, B. and Borgquist, L. (1991) Willingness to pay for anti-hypertensive therapy – results of a Swedish pilot study. *Journal of Health Economics* **10**: 461–74.

Jones-Lee, M. W. (1974) The value of changes in the probability of death or injury. *Journal of Political Economy* **82**: 835–49.

(1976) *The Value of Life: an Economic Analysis.* London: Martin Robertson and Chicago: University of Chicago Press.

(1989) *The Value of Safety and Physical Risk.* Oxford, Blackwell.

(1992) Paternalistic altruism and the value of statistical life. *Economic Journal* **102**: 80–90.

Jones-Lee, M. W., Hammerton, M. and Philips, P. R. (1985) The value of safety: Results of a national sample survey. *Economic Journal* **95**: 49–72.

Jones-Lee, M. W., Loomes, G. and Philips, P. R. (1995) Valuing the prevention of non-fatal road injuries: contingent valuation vs standard gambles. *Oxford Economic Papers* **47**: 676–95.

Kennedy, C. (2002) Revealed preference compared to contingent valuation: radon-induced lung cancer prevention. *Health Economics.*

Klose, T. (1999) The contingent valuation method in health care. *Health Policy* **47**: 97–123.

Kobelt, G. (1997) Economic considerations and outcome measurement in urge incontinence. *Urology,* **50**(6A): 100–7.

Krabbe, P. F. M., Essink-Bot, M.-L. and Bonsel, G. J. (1997) The comparability and reliability of five health-state valuation methods. *Social Science and Medicine* **45**: 1641–52.

Kupperman, M., Nease, R. F., Ackerson, L. M. *et al.* (2000) Parents' preferences for outcomes associated with childhood vaccinations. *Paediatric Infectious Disorders Journal* **19**: 129–33.

Loomes, G. (2002) Valuing life years and QALYs: transferability and convertibility of values across the UK public sector in Towse, A., Pritchard, C. and Devlin, N. (eds.) *Cost Effectiveness Thresholds: Economic and Ethical Issues.* London: King's Fund and Office of Health Economics.

Lundberg, L., Johannesson, M., Silverdahl, M., Hermansson, C. and Lindberg, M. (1999) Quality of life, health state utilities and willlingness to pay in patients with psoriasis and atopic eczema. *British Journal of Dermatology,* **141**: 1067–75.

McDaniels, T. L., Kamlet, M. S. and Fischer, G. W. (1992) Risk perception and the value of safety. *Risk Analysis* **12**: 495–503.

Mendeloff, J. and Kaplan, R. M. (1990) Are twenty-fold differences in 'lifesaving' costs justi-fied?: a psychometric study of the relative value placed on preventing deaths from programs addressing different hazards, in Cox, L. A. Jr. and Ricci, D. F. (eds.) *New Risks*. New York: Plenum Press.

Mishan, E. J. (1971) Evaluation of life and limb: a theoretical approach. *Journal of Political Economy* **79**: 687–705.

Mooney, G. (1977) *The Valuation of Human Life*. London: Macmillan.

National Coordinating Centre for Research Methodology (2003) Commissioning Brief RM03/JH12: The Societal Value of Health Gains http://pcpoh.bham.ac.uk/publichealth/nccrm/PDFs%20and%20documents/Ongoing/RM03JH12CD_QALY_CB.pdf.

O'Brien, B. and Viramontes, J. (1994) Willingness to pay: a valid and reliable measure of health state preference? *Medical Decision Making* **14**: 289–97.

Olsen, J. A. and Donaldson, C. (1998) Helicopters, hearts and hips: using willingness to pay to set priorities for public sector health care programmes. *Social Science and Medicine* **46**: 1–12.

Olsen, J. A. and Smith, R. D. (2001) Theory versus practice: a review of 'willingness-to-pay' in health and health care. *Health Economics* **10**: 39–52.

Olsen, J. A., Donaldson, C. and Periera, J. (2004) The insensitivity of 'willingness to pay' to the size of the good: new evidence for health care. *Journal of Economic Psychology* **25**: 445–60.

Pauly, M. (1995) Valuing health care benefits in money terms. In Sloan, F. (ed.) *Valuing Health Care: Costs, Benefits and Effectiveness of Pharmaceuticals and Other Medical Technologies*. Cambridge: Cambridge University Press.

Phelps, C. and Mushlin, A. (1991) The (near) equivalence of cost effectiveness and cost benefit analysis. *International Journal of Technology Assessment in Health Care* **7**: 12–21.

Rawlins, M. D. and Culyer, A. J. (2004) National Institute for Clinical Excellence and its value judgement. *BMJ* **329**: 224–7.

Savage, I. (1993) An empirical investigation into the effect of psychological perceptions on the willingness-to-pay to reduce risk. *Journal of Risk and Uncertainty* **6**: 75–90.

Schelling T. (1968) The life you save may be your own, in Chase, S. B. Jr (ed.) *Problems in Public Expenditure Analysis*. Washington, DC: Brookings Institution.

Schkade, D. A. and Payne, J. W. (1994) How people respond to contingent valuation questions: a verbal protocol of willingness to pay for environmental protection. *Journal of Environmental Economics and Management* **26**: 88–109.

Smith, R. (2001) The relative sensitivity of willingness to pay and time trade off to changes in health status: an empirical investigation. *Health Economics* **10**: 487–97.

Smith, V. K. (1983) The role of site and job characteristics in hedonic wage models. *Journal of Urban Economics* **13**: 296–321.

Sorum, P. C. (1999) Measuring patient preferences by willingness to pay to avoid: the case of acute otitis media. *Medical Decision-Making* **19**: 27–37.

Sunstein, C. R. (1997) Bad deaths. *Journal of Risk and Uncertainty* **14**(3): 259–82.

Swan, J. S., Fryback, D. G., Lawrence, W. F. *et al.* (1997) MR and conventional angiography: work in progress towards assessing utility in radiology. *Academic Radiology* **4**: 475–82.

The Urban Institute (1991) *The Costs of Highway Crashes*. Report number FHWA-RD-91–055, Final Report. Washington, DC: The Urban Institute.

Thompson, M. (1986) Willingness to pay and accept to cure chronic disease. *American Journal of Public Health* **76**: 392–6.

Torrance, G. W. (1986) Measurement of health state utilities for economic appraisal. *Journal of Health Economics* **5**: 1–30.

Viscusi, W. K. and Moore, M. J. (1989) Rates of time preference and valuation of the duration of life. *Journal of Public Economics* **38**: 297–317.

Voruganti, L. N. P., Awad, A. G., Oyewumi, L. K. *et al.* (2000) 'Assessing health utilities in schizophrenia': a feasibility study. *Pharmacoeconomics* **17**: 273–86.

Williams, A. (1985) Economics of coronary artery bypass grafting. *British Medical Journal* **291**: 326–9.

Williams, A. (2004) What could be nicer than NICE? The Office of Health Economics Annual Lecture 2004.

Zethraeus, N. (1998) Willingness to pay for hormone replacement therapy. *Health Economics* **7**: 31–8.

Zethraeus, N., Johannesson, M., Henriksson, P. and Strand, R. T. (1997) The impact of hormone replacement therapy on quality of life and willingness to pay. *British Journal of Obstetrics and Gynaecology* **104**: 1191–5.

9 The use of geodemographics to improve public service delivery

Paul A. Longley and Michael F. Goodchild

Introduction

This chapter provides an overview of the construction and use of small-area geodemographic indicators, with an emphasis upon applications in the USA and UK. A number of fundamental issues arising out of the construction of these 'metrics' are discussed. We then describe the potential applications of geodemographics in public service delivery settings and review a range of impediments to their use in practice. Our conclusions address the potential contribution of the approach to management reform and improvements in service delivery to citizens.

The big picture of public policy today is dominated by issues of national and international migration, of demographic change, and of economic development and technological change. Yet each of these dynamics remains grounded in processes of socio-spatial differentiation at local (e.g. intra-urban) scales, and the development of appropriate metrics for measuring performance at such scales is core to management reform and improvements in service delivery to citizens. While the apparent consensus is that 'urban' lifestyles are becoming increasingly heterogeneous across a range of geographic scales, systematic and generalized assessment of lifestyle characteristics provides a daunting challenge to researchers and policy analysts. In this context, this chapter considers the demands that different groups place upon cities through collective consumption of public services at the local scale. The consumption of policing, education and health services in particular entails disbursement of large budgets at the local level, and we consider how geographic information systems (GIS) may be used to represent and manage relevant information pertaining to supply, demand and context, in the interests of efficient and effective delivery of public services.

For present purposes, GIS may be thought of as software tools that make it possible to reveal forms and processes that are otherwise invisible in geographic information: Longley *et al.* (2005: 16–17) provide extended definitions and a classification of the groups that find them useful. GIS is already widely used in local government: 70–80 per cent of local government work involves GIS in some way, and inventory applications are legion. In general terms, GIS make it possible to devise practical, rational measures of the demand for local services, as well as facilitating transparent assessment of current performance levels relative to locationally sensitive measures of need. In relation to specific urban services, GIS can be used to anticipate and accommodate the priorities and preferences of local communities in terms of how services are delivered, or to create the opportunity to achieve savings by targeting communication programmes to populations for whom their messages are most appropriate (as, for example, with neighbourhood watch schemes in policing, or primary health care interventions).

This chapter considers how the use of *geodemographics* in GIS may be used in quantitative analysis of the geography of public finance, and is set to fulfil a central role in understanding and hence managing geographies of public service consumption. We draw on international (particularly Anglo-American) experience to illustrate how a new generation of geodemographic indicators might be used to represent intra-urban geographies, in ways that are robust, defensible and generalized. However, there are important impediments to such adoption, centred upon issues of design, data and accountability. These are discussed, and recommendations made as to how wider dissemination geodemographics and GIS might be achieved through research-led applications.

Background and definitions

Geodemographic indicators are small-area measures of social, economic and demographic conditions. They have an established academic pedigree, although most of the important developments in the last thirty years have been made in the private sector. Commercial systems in the UK include Mosaic (Experian, Nottingham), ACORN (A Classification of Residential Neighbourhoods: CACI, London) and Cameo (EuroDirect, Leeds), and have been provided for census output areas (approximately 100 households) and for unit postcodes (a postcode covers approximately 15 households). US indicators are provided for block groups (approximately 100 households) and for ZIP+4 areas (approximately 15 households): there are counterparts to the Mosaic and ACORN systems, as well as others such as Tapestry (ESRI, Redlands, CA).

Historically, geodemographic indicators have been derived from census data, which are only disseminated in aggregate form for reasons of confidentiality. Different neighbourhoods are characterized by different densities of households, and so the extent of neighbourhood units is variable (suburban and rural areas have lower household densities and hence larger reporting zones). Different neighbourhoods may also be more or less heterogeneous in geodemographic conditions: it is important to be aware that any or all of the characteristics of a given household are unlikely to be identical to the neighbourhood average, and that a neighbourhood profile may not provide guidance as to the specific characteristics of individual households.

The Booth studies of the intra-urban geography of poverty in Victorian London are considered to be the earliest systematic measurements of population characteristics. The *conceptual* roots to geodemography are conventionally traced to the work of Park, Burgess, and the other 'Chicago ecologists' from 1916 onwards (Batey and Brown 1995). There is a rich academic literature on residential patterning, including *social area analysis* in the 1950s and 1960s, and *factor analysis* in the 1970s. What was essentially an inductive, data-led approach to urban geography became unfashionable from the late 1970s, largely because of the lack of theoretical grounding for the work and problems of data sourcing, management and display. However, as we discuss below, there are reasons to suggest that the trend may be reversing, leading to renewed interest in a data-led, quantitative and geographically detailed research tradition.

The first UK national classifications were developed by Richard Webber from the 1971 Census of Population, at four scales ranging from the enumeration district (census block) to the parliamentary (electoral) constituency. The classifications were initially intended to guide local government in neighbourhood policy implementation but the basic approach was subsequently successfully developed into commercial applications through proprietary systems such as Mosaic and ACORN (see above). Recently the circle has closed as interest has regenerated in public sector applications.

In the US, geodemographics has been popularized by a series of books by pioneer Michael Weiss (2000). Weiss makes the point that human geography is essentially *repetitive*, especially from a social and economic perspective. Residents of Bloomfield Hills, Michigan, for example, live in neighbourhoods of similar social structure and status to residents of Scottsdale, Arizona, or parts of Atlanta.

Historically, two methods have been used with similar objectives of simplifying the complex patterning of the human landscape. The *factorial ecology* of the 1960s attempted to discover the basic underlying dimensions of variability through the analysis of masses of census data. Just as factorial methods had originally been developed by psychologists in the 1930s to search for underlying dimensions of personality and behaviour, so the same methods

E29 City Adventurers (1.27%HH)   28 29 30 31 32 33 34

A 1-7
B 8-14
C 15-20
D 21-27
E 28-34
F 35-40
G 41-43
H 44-47
I 48-50
J 51-56
K 57-61

Weiss 1998 *The Clustering of America.*

Figure 9.1 Visual labelling of the 'City Adventurers' type of the 2001 Mosaic UK classification (© Experian Ltd)

could be used to reveal underlying dimensions of society – the basic dimension of wealth, for example, would be reflected in many census indicators, including house value, number of bedrooms, and occupation.

Cluster analysis searches not for basic underlying dimensions but for disjoint classes, arguing that because human geography is repetitive, neighbourhoods can be assigned to a manageably small number of groups. Like factorial ecology, it applies standard analytic methods to the massive tables provided by the census (both methods require intensive computation). But it is conceptually simpler than the factorial approach, which probably accounts for its much greater popularity and resilience. On the other hand it probably also accounts for a lack of uptake by the academic research and public policy communities, as we discuss below.

Both factorial and cluster methods extract composite indicators (dimensions and classes respectively). In both cases an important stage in analysis consists of *labelling*, through the attachment of simplistic but lucid descriptions that have popular appeal. This has developed into a fine art, and descriptions are often supplemented by simple graphic icons. Figure 9.1 shows the composite image used to characterize Type E29, City Adventurers, in the 2001 Mosaic clustering marketed in the UK. In effect, the detailed description of statistical distributions of individual characteristics is replaced in the user's mind with whatever associations are suggested by the images. Even text descriptions can have similar effect, such as this summary of the characteristics of Tapestry's (US) Urban Chic cluster: 'The Urban Chic are professional couples with an urbane, exclusive lifestyle. They are home owners, but city dwellers with a preference for expensive homes in high-rise buildings or townhomes (median value over $472,000). Median age is 41 years.' This description need not fit *any* household in any of the zones allocated to this cluster – instead, it describes only the national average of the characteristics of zones allocated to this cluster. Moreover, it is important to realize that areas are assigned to this class *because it is the most similar of the available options*, and that within each class there is substantial variation around any mean or median value.

Applications

Geodemographics has now been used for over three decades to inform and devise effective communications strategies in the private sector. The methods are used in operational, tactical and strategic decision-making by almost all customer-facing organizations. Numerous different systems exist for general and niche markets in North America and Europe, and systems are under development in much of Latin America, China, Europe and Japan.

The primary use of these products is in characterizing neighbourhoods. For example, a developer considering acquisition of a property for construction of a retail store will request a summary of the socioeconomic characteristics of the area surrounding the site, possibly in concentric rings. A geodemographic report will summarize the numbers of households in each cluster, in each area of interest. As well as zones made up of concentric rings, reports can also be generated by areas defined by the user, such as school districts or trade areas. With modern GIS capabilities it is possible for users to request raw census data for the same areas, or indeed to create their own bespoke geodemographic classifications using census and ancillary sources, although it is the simplicity of geodemographic products and the simple labels attached to them that often make them more attractive than counts or bespoke classifications.

More advanced applications use the same clustering to impute socioeconomic characteristics to customer lists. A customer living in a given ZIP+ 4 area can be inferred to have the characteristics of the population of the area, if one is willing to assume that all households in the area have characteristics identical to those of the cluster.

Rudimentary approaches to multivariate socioeconomic classification remain an important area of activity in the public sector, as in the calculation of standardized composite indices of levels of hardship and deprivation. The more elaborate approaches pioneered in the private sector are now under development in the public sector, in order to promote community engagement and to improve public service outreach. Geodemographic analysis can be used as an intelligence product for resource allocation/determination at the neighbourhood level. A very good example in this context is the UK Output Area Classification (OAC), which is a free geodemographic system of the UK that has the status of a national statistic (ONS 2006; Vickers and Rees 2007). It is interesting that, in promoting this national classification, the UK Office for National Statistics has avoided use of 'pen portraits' such as that shown in figure 9.1. This is indicative of a sensitivity in moving from private to public sector applications: graphic icons are important in selling commercial systems to the private sector, but might be considered pejorative or offensive in the public sector.

In summary, there are perhaps four distinct markets for geodemographics in the private sector:

- Purchasers of shrink-wrapped data and software packages – novice users with limited needs in the main
- Organizations with in-house geodemographics capability – and which perhaps use census-based geodemographics data along with their own lifestyles (customer data and other marketing and social survey data) sources
- Organizations that develop consultancy arrangements with outside firms, such as those between GMAP (Leeds) and Ford/Toyota in Europe
- To this one might add the market of organizations like Sears in the US that employ GIS software house ESRI to host and update their own data at remote sites. Logically the next step is for the likes of ESRI to supply a fuller range first of data and then of consultancy services, assuming of course that generic models can be adapted to work across industry sectors.

Fundamental issues in the creation of geodemographic indicators

Many private sector users of geodemographic systems are essentially consumers of 'black box' technology, and this is generally deemed appropriate by the sector so long as the classification is considered to be improving operational and tactical decision-making. However, prior to considering the impediments that are specific to adoption in public service applications, it is important to be aware of some of the generic limitations of the classification technology.

Within-cluster variability

In essence, clustering begins with data on the socioeconomic characteristics of aggregate reporting zones. Each zone is characterized by measures on a number of dimensions, and the *socioeconomic space* defined by these dimensions can be visualized as occupied by thousands of points, each representing the aggregate characteristics of a zone. Variation among individual households in each zone is ignored.

The clustering task consists of partitioning the space so that each point is assigned to one of a number of clusters. Ideally, the points assigned to a cluster will form a tight cloud of minimal variability, but in practice the density of points within the socioeconomic space varies continuously. The number of such clouds is subjectively determined by the analyst, on the basis of past experience, diagnostic statistics, and the intended end use of the classification. Each cluster is then described, either by describing the characteristics of a central point in the cluster (perhaps the centroid), or by describing the limits of the section of space occupied by the cluster. The exact choice of options depends on which of several clustering methods are being used. In summary, when an area's households are described as belonging to a specific cluster the following stages of information loss have occurred:

1. Variation within reporting zones, when aggregate characteristics were used to develop clusters
2. Variation assigned to one or another category, in the interests of devising a parsimonious classification that can be understood by users
3. Variation within clusters, when the specific characteristics of the zones assigned to each cluster were replaced by summary characteristics of the cluster
4. Information contained in the detailed characteristics of each cluster, when these were summarized by text, icons, or images

Nevertheless it is entirely feasible for much of this information to be retained, and made available to users. In the case of (3), summary statistics regarding within-cluster variation could be generated and made available. In the case of (4), users could be encouraged to use explicit information on cluster characteristics, rather than simplistic summary properties.

The zones used to develop clusters are typically the smallest zones for which detailed summary data are provided by the census. When clusters are reported for smaller zones (for example, for ZIP+ 4 zones in the US, where the larger block group is the smallest unit for detailed census summary data), it is done by a process of imputation which introduces further uncertainty.

Spatial heterogeneity

Cluster products have typically been developed and marketed by country, implying some degree of homogeneity in socioeconomic characteristics at the national level. There has also been some success at developing pan-European datasets. In the other direction, it seems reasonable to examine whether the makeup of clusters varies nationally, and whether better characterization can be obtained by separate cluster analyses of major regions – for example, the constituent states of the USA, or major conurbations and world cities such as London. Undoubtedly this would lead to a more refined product, though at the cost of greater complexity in analysis, application and user interpretation.

Choice of defining variables

Data availability and measurement issues have driven the development of geodemographics, and there has been an element of choice in the variables selected in rival systems. This is to some extent driven by the social constructs that they are deemed to represent and the end uses to which they are to be applied. But census-based systems are broadly similar to one another, and recent developments in data supply and access (notably the development of portals in the public sector: e.g. www.statistics.gov.uk/) make them a routine data product.

Other data sources

In recent years, census data have been increasingly supplemented with *lifestyles* data, which can be defined as quantitative measures of the varied consumption choices, shopping habits and practices of identifiable individuals (these characteristics are typically not collected by the decennial census). They are usually assembled by data-warehousing organizations. Some vendors have also included explicitly geographic measures of location in their classifications (e.g. accessibility to shopping centres or coastal resorts). Because these alternative sources often provide data at the level of the individual, they can be used to improve the accuracy with which very small areas are characterized. In the US, for example, they can improve the characterization of ZIP+ 4 areas, which are smaller than the block groups used to define the input data for traditional clusters. Alternative sources can also be used to cover constructs that are poorly represented in the census, such as affluence and rurality, and to provide frequent updates, ideally on annual rather than decennial cycles

Lifestyles datasets are now routinely used in commerce, and many enumerate salient characteristics of tens of millions of individuals. Although they are rarely collected to the same exacting standards as conventional public sector datasets, they are updated continuously and provide very detailed snapshots of the diverse lifestyles that are often to be found in quite small urban areas.

Lifestyles datasets vastly enrich the potential content of social classifications, yet their use raises a number of possibly frustrating issues of coverage and representation, not least because commercial organizations are unlikely to be motivated towards assembling detailed data inventories on the 'have nots' of society. This may frustrate the application of lifestyles data to some public service applications, although some datasets (such as court judgment and credit records) can be used to tackle this issue. There is a clear need to cross-validate small-area lifestyle measures with respect to external data sources, and this remains an important area for research.

Many retail organizations have developed in-house geodemographics teams. These same organizations often have customer loyalty programmes, the data from which are a very valuable input to market analysis. Thus UK retail corporation Marks and Spencer uses its own store card data alongside the PSYCLE geodemographic product, and the UK grocery retailer Tesco classifies customers into groups on the basis of purchasing behaviour. There remains a core need for geodemographic systems in order to supplement 'what is?' analysis of existing customer characteristics with 'what if?' understanding of new and existing markets.

Public sector research applications to date

In what follows we distinguish between different types of applications that can be characterized as public policy-oriented research. We use the following headings:

- Applications that go beyond the traditional ones outlined above, in the solution of well-defined problems

- Use of clusters as the basis for panel selection, stratified sampling, and other efforts to select or characterize populations
- Research on clustering and geodemographics, aimed at devising new and more useful products.

New applications

A recent development is the emergence of public sector applications – aided in the UK by a more enlightened approach to extracting value from government data sources. In the UK these include

- Policing: the National Reassurance Policing Programme, Young Offenders and operational analysis in a number of police forces
- Education: schools reorganization and widening participation initiatives in university admissions
- Inland Revenue: profiling of users of Inland Revenue Enquiry Centres
- Legal: analysis of magistrates' court fines, targeting of licence-fee evaders
- Regional government and development agencies: adoption of IT and other characteristics desired by inward investors

In each of these cases, clusters provide a convenient way of segmenting the population into approximately homogeneous groups, so that estimates can be made of various types of behaviour by group. Segmentation thus allows a more detailed and insightful analysis than would otherwise be possible. In the education area, for example, university application and acceptance rates are being tabulated and monitored by cluster, with clear implications for future university recruitment strategies. In essence, these applications mirror those pioneered decades previously in the private sector.

These public sector applications achieve several overlapping objectives:

- Leveraging research value of operational datasets
- Identifying which interventions might be used at different spatial scales
- Saving money by targeting interventions that operate at the fine levels of granularity, rather than 'blunderbuss' approaches
- Saving resources on local surveys
- Making evidence-based policy more sensitive to context

Table 9.1 shows how UK 2001 Mosaic Groups are used to classify neighbourhood crime profiles and levels of neighbourhood social capital, and thus inform policing strategies. There are several examples in the GIS literature of academic applications of similar techniques. A group from Ohio State University (OSU) led by Duane Marble reported at the 1997 ESRI User

Table 9.1: Results of geodemographic profiling local policing strategies, using the Mosaic (© Experian Ltd) geodemographic classification

Mosaic UK group	Crime profile		Level of fear	Social capital			Summary	Appropriate 'neighbourhood policing' strategies
	Common types of crime and disorder	Level of crime and disorder		Level of trust	Informal contacts	Formal association		
A Symbols of success	Fraud, traffic offences	Low	Low	Fairly high (excluding 'Global Connections')	Low	High	Networks are often instrumental and not locally based	Engage with local representatives. Leaflet drops to communicate information and promote campaigns.
B Happy families	Fraud, some marital violence	Moderate	Low	Fairly high	Moderate	Moderate	New communities tend to have shallow networks	Child safety orientation. School-based programmes.
C Suburban comfort	Traffic offences	Low	Low	High	Quite high	High	Well-established networks	Engage with local representatives. Establish 'Neighbourhood Watch' schemes. Leaflet drops to communicate information and promote campaigns.
D Ties of community	Alcohol related; domestic violence	Average	Moderate – low	High among local residents: apprehensive of outsiders	Quite high	Quite high	Tends towards 'self policing'.	Identify representatives and attempt to recognize parallel communities. Police Community Support Officers. Rapid response to environmental disorders such as abandoned cars
E Urban intelligence	Snatching; mugging; credit card theft	High	Considered fact of life	Low	Informal contacts are not local	Patchy : high for those who are not transient	Networks are often not local. Local networks are often transient and one dimensional	Reliance on communications programmes; target hardening; intelligence-led policing. Police Community

		Crime profile							Policing strategy
F	Welfare borderline	Drug dealing; child abuse; car crime	Very high	High	Low	Low	Very low	Low levels of social cohesion	Partnership work with housing department and social services; Community Support Officers.
G	Municipal dependency	Drug usage; marital disputes; vandalism; graffiti; petty theft	Very high	High	Low	Low	Low	People may know each other but not trust each other	Liaison with schools and social services. Increased surveillance. Target hardening. Rapid response to criminal damage and signal disorders
H	Blue collar enterprise	Alcohol-related offences; serious traffic offences	Moderately high	Above average	Moderate	Moderate	Below average	Not ideologically communitarian but are responsible on specifics	Default strategy
I	Twilight subsistence	None	Moderate	Quite high	Moderate	Moderate	Below average	Low level of mobility impairs social integration	Reassurance; high visibility policing, CCTV. Anti-fraud campaigns.
J	Grey perspectives	Few	Low	Underlying but unfocused need for reassurance	High among known people / low among outsiders	High	Above average	Highly responsible for local conditions. Are at home much of the day. Natural 'wardens'	Reassurance; high visibility policing; anti-fraud campaigns; neighbourhood watch.
K	Rural isolation	Theft of equipment; planned, high-value burglaries	Low	Anxiety about quality of police response	High among known people	High	High	High levels of responsibility to other community members	Reassurance on response times. More intensive communications with community leaders

Rows indicate the crime profile, levels of social capital and policing strategies appropriate to different Mosaic Groups.
(Source: Ashby 2005)

Conference on the use of PRIZM clusters in an analysis of admissions to OSU. Grant Thrall's review of Tapestry at www.geospatial-online.com dated 3/1/04 describes a suite of applications, many of which have academic relevance. In general, one would expect academic researchers to make routine use of geodemographic products as a source of simple baseline data on neighbour-hood characteristics, subject to the concerns expressed in the last section of this report.

Stratified sampling

Recently interest has developed in the use of clusters to support stratified sampling. For example, in testing a particular drug, it is likely that some social groups will be of more interest than others, because they have higher prob-ability of being customers for the drug, or because they are more likely to have the conditions the drug is designed to treat, or both. Clusters provide a ready basis for identifying areas and groups to sample, since they act as a substitute for individual-level data on social characteristics. They also act as a useful frame for analysing disease rates and the impacts of public health activities. In this spirit the US Center for Disease Control (CDC) has negotiated access by its researchers to PRIZM, which has 'proven useful in disease prevention and health promotion activities.' However, in some applications it will be of utmost importance to understand how the relevant geodemographic classifi-cation was devised, in order to understand its impacts upon the outcome of sampling.

Research on clustering

There will always be a need for improved methods of clustering, and improved products. The academic community has placed greater emphasis on factorial methods, since they are not as subject to the information-loss problems identified earlier. Much of the early research on clustering was conducted by academics, though the private sector has operationalized that research and added substantial practical improvements. Stan Openshaw conducted a public-domain clustering of the UK in the early 1990s, based on the 1991 census, and the results are freely available. They have also been linked to the Sample of Anonymized Records, a sample of individual census records, in an effort to refine the clusters. This work was in the same spirit as the Output Area Classification of Vickers and Rees (2007), described above.

Various efforts have been made to extend geodemographics to daytime distributions – the daytime geography of the workplace – to get away from excessive focus on night-time distributions, since place of work is obviously important in many purchasing decisions. Workplace PRIZM was developed by convolving night-time clusters with commuting data from the census, and data classifying workplaces by Standard Industrial Classification codes have been used to meet similar needs.

Why is geodemographics not yet pivotal to public service delivery?

The arguments presented above suggest that clusters can have major appeal to researchers in the social and health sciences, so it is reasonable to ask why there has not been more take-up of these methods in the academic and public policy sectors. In this section we present some possible explanations, and some recommendations to increase use. The first set of arguments is concerned with standards that are widely prevalent in all scientific communities.

When an activity is described as 'scientific', a number of tests are implied. First, the activity must be *replicable*, in the sense that a different researcher conducting the same activity would arrive at the same result. Second, the activity must be reported to *scientific standards of reporting*. These include the principle that sufficient detail must be provided about the activity to allow someone else to replicate it. Third, there must be concern for *accuracy*. Results must not be reported to levels of precision that are unjustified by the accuracy of measurements and calculations, and efforts must be made to determine and minimize any uncertainties associated with the results.

Unfortunately, traditional geodemographics fails several of these tests. The methods used to extract clusters are often proprietary, making it impossible to replicate them. Moreover, no information is provided on within-cluster variation, so it is impossible for the researcher to determine the amount of information lost through the use of clusters. These problems are compounded when lifestyles data are intrinsic to the classification process, because they are not collected to scientific standards.

This immediately suggests four strategies for increasing research applications of geodemographics:

1. *Publish details of the method used to define clusters, to meet the scientific standard of replicability.*

This might at first sight suggest that the cluster product would lose value, since it would be possible in principle for anyone else to create an identical product. But there are strong arguments against this notion. A competitor would incur substantial cost in doing so, equal to the cost of developing a different, and in the eyes of the competitor, superior product. Why would a competitor want to duplicate rather than improve? If the classification is based upon lifestyles data that are not in the public domain, access to these components of the classification might be restricted through licensing and data pricing agreements. If access were restricted to only the most recent updates of lifestyles data, such a strategy might encourage research and interest, whilst maintaining a competitive edge for the product with the most recent lifestyles updates. Related to this, it is important that lifestyles metadata are published, ideally to standards that are recognized industry-wide.

2. *Publish statistics on within-cluster variation, and on detailed characteristics of clusters.*

Several statistics would be very useful to researchers wishing to use cluster products in scientific research. First, statistics could be provided on the distribution characteristics of each cluster: means and standard deviations of zone measures on each of the defining dimensions; boundaries of each cluster in socioeconomic space; and differences for each zone between zone measure and cluster mean, on each defining dimension. These might be summarized into standard graphical indicators that could be appended to cluster pen-portraits as a numeric supplement to the existing text and graphics.

Hitherto the overwhelming number of geodemographic applications has concerned tactical and strategic decision-making in private sector applications (specifically retailing), and it is probably true to say that the clearest indicator of 'success' is the way in which improvements in targeting of goods and service offerings improve measured profitability. Geodemographics are fundamentally blunt-edged discriminators in terms of marketing activity – a 'successful' mailshot may achieve a 4% response rate as opposed to the 2% response of a non-targeted campaign. This may double the effectiveness of the marketing budget, but still represents a 'failure' rate of 96%. On the other hand such measures are irrelevant to the academic sector, which measures progress in terms of conceptual integrity, goodness of fit, and accuracy. One of the interesting challenges of the coming years will entail use of these techniques in public service applications, given the pressures to demonstrate value for money in targeting public funds according to local needs. This will require research into the content and coverage of the data sources that are used to create and update geodemographic profiles.

The fundamental issues facing the geodemographics industry resonate with broader secular changes in social survey research, data analysis, and GIS. First, digital data capture is now routine, but more and more of this capture occurs in the private sector, and without being subject to the rigorous standards normally required in the scientific and public policy communities. Second, the scale and pace of change to urban systems now makes the decennial snapshots of censuses increasingly irrelevant to policy needs. Instead, the focus is increasingly on monitoring change, and on collecting data not on the relatively static characteristics of residential neighbourhoods, but on the dynamic behaviours exhibited by individuals and households. Third, the fission of lifestyles amongst urban populations means that many urban geographies are increasingly heterogeneous at fine scales of granularity. This makes the limited content (attribute base) of censuses increasingly problematic in the analysis of urban systems.

On the positive side, there is currently a resurgence of interest in geodemographic systems, which is allied to the following developments:

1. Increased interest in the measurement and analysis of local or regional 'place' effects
2. Increased interest in making use of the vast volumes of data that are produced through routine interactions between humans and machines
3. Enlightened approaches to public data access (especially through on-line portals) making widespread dissemination of socioeconomic data a reality, and the creation of general-purpose and bespoke data systems straightforward
4. The greater ease with which geodemographic systems based on framework socioeconomic data can be successfully 'fused' to census sources to provide richer depictions of lifestyles
5. The improved abilities of GIS to match diverse data sources and accommodate the uncertainties created by scale and aggregation effects
6. Recognition that academics and policy-makers must not simply become passive consumers of increasingly sophisticated geodemographic systems
7. An increasing policy focus upon the neighbourhood and on adopting approaches that are place-sensitive

Just as government and the private sector have different traditions, so also does the academic sector. Academics are used to working with a limited range of rather boring (but free and uncontentious) public sector datasets like the census. This is no longer good enough in today's information-rich world, but it will take some time for change to permeate the academic community. At this time it is difficult to discern the leaders who will drive change. There are few if any textbooks, and little in the way of confidence-building and well-documented applications. Instead, academic promoters of geodemographics are often marginalized, and instead academics have tended to limit themselves to critique, typified by several chapters of John Pickles's collection *Ground Truth* (1995).

3. *Develop and publish examples of best research practice, showing how geodemographics can be used in support of scientific research.*

Academics in geography (and to a lesser extent in marketing) have been reluctant to include geodemographics in the curriculum. Little literature emerges from the private sector, for obvious reasons. Geodemographics is still seen as a 'black box' technology, for reasons outlined earlier. The situation is changing as data supply and access are improving, but progress is slow. There is a need for greater transparency, better metadata, and education about the provenance of geodemographic indicators.

The public sector itself has an important role to play in this. Many of the most important data sources that might be used to improve geodemographic classification are themselves collected by locally delivered public services. There is some irony that the most widely available classification systems use private sector lifestyles data for refresh and update, when these contain indicators that are often only of passing relevance to the consumption of public services.

4. *Develop instructional materials that can be incorporated into academic curricula, covering the theory and applications of geodemographics.*

Researchers considering using geodemographics must address a fundamental point about scale. Social scientists are concerned with robustness, and tend to use comparatively large areas to ensure sufficient numbers and sufficiently reliable statistics. Geodemographic indicators on the other hand are typically provided for very small areas, for which many measures of interest to social scientists would be considered hopelessly unreliable. There needs to be a middle ground, on topics such as the reliability of appending geodemographic codes to the individual records of national/state surveys in order to produce estimates at local scales.

Academics used to free data from census sources clearly face obstacles in acquiring data from the private sector, and the private sector in turn has little interest in serving an academic market that is unable to provide a reasonable return on short-term investment. In the UK, data warehouse Experian has signalled some willingness to allow free access to its data and classifications for academics and students in higher education. Such arrangements potentially return enormous long-term value by ensuring that new generations of researchers are trained to be familiar with commercial products.

Conclusions

Geodemographic profiles of the characteristics of individuals and small areas are pivotal to tactical and strategic resource management in many areas of business, and could be similarly central to efficient and effective deployment of resources by public services. Yet existing detailed, locationally disaggregated and frequently updated data infrastructures remain chronically under-used in academic and public service research. This is the more lamentable because the public services themselves *create* data of similar quality, which could provide very valuable context to decision-making, but which are similarly neglected by (or even hidden from) potential users.

Public sector applications suggest new and innovative ways of using geodemographic profiling in very different 'customer' relationships. The policing example described in table 9.1 illustrates that 'customers' may be willing or unwilling recipients of public services: willing to receive reassurance from the police about crime and to contribute towards social capital formation in partnership with them; but unwilling to be brought to book for transgressing the law – the police service is certainly not one in which the 'customer is always right'.

The arguments developed in this chapter echo the concerns of Hartley and Skelcher (chapter 1) that public value perspectives require us to examine the impact of public services not just upon 'customers' and users but also upon citizens. The imperatives of social inclusion and the universality of the stakeholder 'market' makes it unlikely that public services will feel at ease using geodemographic classifications that are black box, commercially sensitive or founded upon data of unknown provenance. Reuse of data collected within the public sector in new bespoke classifications suggests one route beyond this impasse.

The potential of geodemographic modelling remains very under exploited in the delivery of public services, and local service delivery in policing, education and health almost invariably assumes a passive receiving population undifferentiated in attitudes, expectations or even needs. Today's consumer-led public services remain very much less sophisticated in targeting services than their counterparts in the private sector – almost every public-facing part of the retail sector has had geodemographic segmentation systems for years, if not decades. The evidence from thirty years of successful applications is that geodemographic metrics can be used to improve decision-making and improve performance in private sector contexts. However this review has highlighted differences of approach that echo the concerns of Hartley and Skelcher (chapter 1) that public service organizations do not choose their markets, but are obliged to provide services to all taxpayers and citizens that meet agreed eligibility criteria. It remains to be seen whether commercial systems can respond to these challenges, or whether approaches based upon reuse of public sector data in bespoke classifications offer a more promising way forward.

Hitherto, stark differences in working environments and practices have masked the commonalities of interest in geodemographic analysis that exist within and between the public and private sectors. There is an urgent need to develop an improved evidence base for local public service delivery by making geodemographic technologies more transparent, available and acceptable to a wider range of users in public service. There is also an urgent need for research into the relative performance of different approaches to classification in public service applications, and to investigate whether bespoke classifications generated from public sector data offer an alternative to 'off-the-shelf' solutions that have been designed and pitched with private sector applications in mind.

REFERENCES

Ashby, D. I. (2005) Policing neighbourhoods: exploring the geographies of crime, policing and performance assessment. *Policing and Society* **15**(4): 435–69.

Batey, P. W. J. and Brown, P. J. B. (1995) From human ecology to customer targeting: the evolution of geodemographics, in Longley, P. and Clarke, G. (eds.) *GIS for Business and Service Planning*, Cambridge: GeoInformation International, pp. 77–103.

Longley, P. A., Goodchild, M. F., Maguire, D. J. and Rhind, D. W. (2005) *Geographic Information Systems and Science* (Second edn). Chichester: Wiley.

ONS (2006) National Statistics 2001 Area Classification. Office for National Statistics www.statistics.gov.uk/about/methodology_by_theme/area_classification/default.asp accessed 17 October 2006.

Pickles, J. (ed) (1995) *Ground Truth: The Social Implications of GIS*. New York: Guilford.

Vickers, D. W. and Rees, P. H. (2007) Creating the National Statistics 2001 output area classification. *Journal of the Royal Statistical Society, Series A*, **170**(2): 379–403.

Weiss, M. (2000) *The Clustered World*. New York: Little, Brown and Co.

Part III

Managing innovation and change

10 The innovation landscape for public service organizations

Jean Hartley

Introduction and focus

In this chapter I draw on an extensive literature review in order to scope the field of innovation in public service organizations and thereby come to a fuller, better theorized and more contextualized understanding both of innovation and its contribution to improvement in and between public service organizations. Identifying key questions, themes and research evidence will hopefully contribute to theory, policy and practice in this increasingly important area.

It is valuable to examine closely 'the talismans of these years: innovation and its intended, though not always constant relative, improvement' (Gray *et al.* 2005: 7). Innovation is increasingly embedded in the language of governments and public service organizations across the globe. It is sometimes used as a label ('an innovative treatment' or 'an innovative service') without explanation of what is meant by the term, or analysis of what is distinctive. In this sense, innovation may be fashionable rhetoric rather than an analytical term. Albury (2005) notes 'Innovation occurs ever more frequently in rhetorics and discourses of public service improvement. This is not surprising given that it is a term redolent with generally positive resonances – modern, new, change, improvement.' (p. 51). But to avoid the pro-innovation bias which is present in much of the literature (Nicholson *et al.* 1990; Lynn 1997) there is a need to examine rigorously the claims for improvement through innovation and Moran (2003) argues that in fact the British state suffers from hyper-innovation.

To what extent is the commentary on public sector innovation merely 'policy chic' (Altschuler and Behn 1997a) and how far is innovation a valuable feature of governance and public service delivery and a useful concept for analysing organizations? Innovation is seen by policy analysts as a key means to go beyond the quality improvement techniques applied to services and organizations in the 1980s and 1990s into something that could make a substantial improvement in the overall efficiency, effectiveness and responsiveness of government and public service organizations. While some analysts focus primarily on innovation as a contribution to improving the quality of services, others also recognize its potential contribution to recovering the legitimacy of government as a value-creating institution, by being more responsive to the needs and aspirations of citizens and users of services (Moore and Hartley 2008).

In theoretical terms, there is a need to explore the concepts and theories about innovation as they may apply to public governance and public services. The public service sector literature is sparse (Altschuler and Behn 1997b; Albury 2005; Hartley 2005; Moore 2005; Osborne and Brown 2005) and there has perhaps been 'over-adoption' of concepts, models and theories which derive from private sector manufacturing, with insufficient consideration of how the context, goals, processes and stakeholders of public service organizations and services can be different in ways which are significant for the application of innovation theory. I therefore use public sector literature where it is available but also draw on key research in the private sector to examine the extent to which it sheds light on how innovation in the public service sector is developed and sustained, on the basis that there may often be a need to translate findings from the private to the public sphere. Inevitably, given space considerations, in this chapter I do not cover the full range of theory and enquiry about public services innovation but I do provide an overview of the landscape.

First, there is a brief consideration of what constitutes innovation in governance and public services, given that there are a range of perspectives and definitions in the field, each of which encourages the pursuit of certain questions and practices at the expense of others. Second, I examine the different contributors to or catalysts of public services innovation, which provide both constraints and opportunities for innovation at the organizational and inter-organizational level. Third, this consideration of the roles of different actors illuminates aspects of the processes of leading and managing innovation. Fourth, I examine the varied relationships that can exist (or not) between innovation and improvement, and the extent to which innovation can contribute to public value. Fifth, given that diffusion is a key element of public service innovation, I examine some of the main processes of knowledge creation and transfer which underlie this. Finally, I reflect on the similarities and differences in innovation in the public and private sectors, and how these condition the understanding of innovation in public governance and public services.

Defining innovation

There is no well-established analytical terminology either in general (e.g. Wolfe 1994) or in the public service sector (Mulgan and Albury 2003) although it would help research and practice to use explicit and consensual definitions (Wolfe 1994). In addition, given that many public service organizations have not only to commission and/or provide public services but also to achieve this in ways which are fair, accountable and contribute to public value (Moore, 1995), there is a need to consider innovations in governance as well as innovations in public services. In other words, there is a class of innovations which may involve marked changes in the ways that public purposes are defined, resourced and achieved and how decisions are debated, developed and made which have not been analysed in the private sector literature, yet which lie at the heart of considerations of innovations in public service organizations (see also Skelcher, chapter 2, this volume).

Altschuler and Zegans (1997) define innovation as 'novelty in action' and Mulgan and Albury (2003) as 'new ideas that work' (though this latter definition does suggest that the idea has to be successful in order to be defined as an innovation). These emphasize that innovation is not just a new idea but something which has been put into practice. Bessant (2003) also uses such an analysis in distinguishing between invention – having a bright idea – and innovation – which is translating the bright idea into implementation and use.

Some writers have argued for a spectrum of innovation from large-scale dramatic, 'headline-making' innovations to small-scale, incremental changes (e.g. Bessant 2003; Mulgan and Albury 2003) while others argue that there is a need to distinguish innovation from general and incremental change (Lynn 1997; Newman *et al.* 2001; Hartley 2005; Osborne and Brown 2005). There are arguments on both sides but in this chapter I adhere to the latter approach in proposing a definition of innovation as a step change, taking innovation to be more than organizational change, and recognizing that the management challenges and processes may be different compared with incremental development.

Until recently, much of the innovation theory and literature has derived from new product development, where an innovation in technology can be observed and broadly agreed, even if its full implications or its impact are not initially known (Tidd *et al.* 2005). There are important technological developments in public services (Christensen, *et al.* 2000), such as IT, health and highways equipment, but there are limitations in applying concepts about *product* innovation to *service* and *organizational* innovation (Alänge *et al.* 1998). Even technological innovations in the public sector are usually set in the context of services to the public. *Service* innovations and improvements typically have high levels of ambiguity and uncertainty (Lewis and Hartley 2001) since they are affected by the variability of the human characteristics of both service giver and service receiver (the latter, in some cases, as a co-producer). The innovation is often not a physical artefact at all, but a change in service (which implies a change in the relationships between service providers and their users). Alänge *et al.* (1998) suggest that such service and organizational innovations have a number of distinctive features which differentiate such innovations from product innovations. They require greater tacit knowledge; have less well-defined system borders; are less tractable to cost–benefit analysis; rarely have a dedicated development unit (e.g. an R & D unit); are more difficult to trial; concern behaviours and work relations, and are more subjectively assessed.

Because innovations in a service or a governance arrangement involve changes in relationships, judgements have to be made about processes, impacts and outcomes, as well as product. Greenhalgh *et al.* (2004) suggest that innovations have to be 'perceived as new by a proportion of key stakeholders' (p. 40). Innovation may include reinvention or adaptation of an innovation in another context, location or time period (Thompson 1965; Rogers 2003).

Some research only examines successful innovation but a definition based on success may limit analysis both of innovation failure and also of how innovations come to be successful (Moore 2005). An alternative, and perhaps more comprehensive, approach examines innovation and success as separate dimensions. This can be valuable where there is interest in how innovations are developed and sustained, and what barriers and facilitators act to support or weaken innovation activities. This means an interest in how innovations grow, are nurtured, meet problems – and how some of them fail. Van de Ven *et al.* (1999) call this the innovation journey. Learning from innovation failure is a key issue given that a high proportion of innovations in the private sector fail (Tidd *et al.* 2005) and given that we may expect an even higher failure rate in the public sector for a range of reasons (Hartley 2005).

Part of the confusion about the nature of innovation is that it is *both* a process and an outcome. It is a process of creating discontinuities in the organization or service (innovating) and it is also the fruits of those discontinuities (an innovation).

Wolfe (1994) argues cogently for consistency in the ways in which innovations are analysed so that comparisons across context, type and processes can be made. A number of writers have offered typologies or other classifications of innovation. For example, Damanpour (1991) distinguishes between technical and administrative ('organizational') innovations, while a later paper with a colleague (Damanpour and Gopalakrishnan 2001) distinguishes between product and process innovations. They found that there are a number of differences which make technical innovations easier both to recognize and to adopt.

Some writers make distinctions between, for example, product, service and process innovations (e.g. Walker *et al.* 2002; Bessant 2003). Hartley (2005) proposed several dimensions (not a typology) to reflect innovation in public service and governance contexts. These include the dimensions of product innovation (e.g. new instrumentation in hospitals); service innovation – new ways in which services are provided to users (e.g. on-line tax forms); process innovation – new ways in which organizational processes are designed (e.g. administrative reorganization into front- and back-office processes; process mapping leading to new approaches); position innovation – new contexts or 'customers' (e.g. new joined-up services for young people); strategic innovation – new goals or purposes of the organization (e.g. community policing; foundation hospitals); governance innovation – new forms of decision-making to produce public services (e.g. devolved government; public–private partnerships); rhetorical innovation – new language and new concepts which are implemented in political discourse (e.g. the concept of congestion charging for London, or a carbon tax). Any particular innovation may have manifestations across a number of these dimensions and thus the trap of a typology is avoided. Governance and rhetorical innovation have not been analysed in the private sector literature.

Catalysts of innovation

Many texts on innovation start with the assumption that innovation is necessary for competitive reasons and they argue that the *firm* requires innovation in order to maintain competitiveness. However, this can be seen as an analysis of innovation pressures which is context-blind so this deserves some critical reflection. For the private sector, innovation is often seen to be a virtue in itself as well as a means to ensure competitiveness in new markets, or to revive flagging markets (e.g. Utterback 1996; Kim and Mauborgne 1999; Hargadon and Sutton 2000). This is sometimes justified in terms of Schumpeterian logic about competition (Schumpeter 1950). The misguided assumption is sometimes made that because public services (for the most part) are not directly part of the competitive market, then there are either no or insufficient drivers for innovation. However, Mulgan and Albury (2003) and Hartley (2005) both point to a wide range of substantial and sustained innovations in UK society and also argue that innovation is a crucial response to a changing society with changing needs, aspirations and expectations.

In the private sector, the focus is generally on managers and staff as sources of innovation, both working inside the organization to create and action new ideas, and networking outside it to scan for useful ideas, market needs and competitor innovations. However, for the public sector, consideration also needs to be given to the role of policy-makers and policy advisors in the innovation process. In addition, for both the public and private sectors the role of users in contributing to innovation is gaining greater attention.

Both national and local politicians have a central role in innovation, for example, in developing new policy frameworks (Albury 2005), building the support in the organization (Newman *et al.* 2001; Rashman *et al.* 2005) and among citizens and their political parties for the enactment of those innovations in legislation (Moran 2003; Moore and Hartley 2008). Sometimes the policy initiatives can lead to large-scale, universal and radical innovations across a whole nation (Albury 2005; Hartley 2005).

The large scale of some policy-inspired innovations and the legislative, financial and staffing resources deployed means that innovation outcomes are quickly apparent. However, there can be problems with top-down implementation (Cabinet Office 2006) because the capacity for continuous improvement and adaptation is not necessarily embedded. The role of policy-makers in this approach to innovation is to act as commanders – creating legislation and then support for wholesale changes, while assuming that the detailed work of implementation will be carried out by managers and staff.

However, the classic public service model of innovation as designed by policy-makers and implemented by managers is not the sole approach to innovation. Increasingly, innovation is as much a 'bottom-up' and 'sideways-in' process as a 'top-down' process. Research from Borins (2001) suggests that in the USA half of all innovations (51%) come from either middle managers or frontline staff. The figures are higher for developed Commonwealth countries (e.g. UK, Australia) where 82% come from organizational staff (75% from middle managers). Borins notes that:

bottom-up innovations occur more frequently in the public sector than received wisdom would have us believe. The individuals who initiate and drive these innovations are acting as informal leaders . . . Politicians and senior public servants create organizational climates that will either support or stifle innovations from below (p. 475).

Innovation can also be catalyzed through professional and managerial networks, through lateral processes of comparison and sharing good practice. As noted earlier, the sharing of good practice is particularly crucial for public service organizations. A number of writers have examined how networks of professionals can both create innovations (Benington 2001; Hartley and Allison 2002) and also spread the adoption and adaption of good practice (Bate and Robert 2003; Greenhalgh *et al.* 2004; Addicott *et al.* 2006; Hartley and Rashman 2007).

Von Hippel (2005) draws attention to the increasing role of users in creating innovation, both in collaboration with producer organizations but also in networks of their own separate from the organization. This is a phenomenon he investigates in some detail, showing that, in the private sector, customers may bring innovations to a firm for scaling up to mass production or may share and develop innovations in open space. Open source software and surfboard design are two examples of this phenomenon. In the public sector, the public may be not only customers but also citizens and advocates, i.e. with a variety of stakeholder interests in bringing innovations to the attention of public service organizations. They may also co-design services and products (Benington and Moore in press) and part of the argument about creating public value is that co-production is increasingly necessary for many services, particularly where outcomes, such as community safety or education, cannot be provided by the producer alone.

Leading and managing innovation processes

Several authors have identified stages or phases of innovation with some suggesting a clear linear sequence and others that the sequence may be more looped than linear (i.e. that processes may be iterative or overlapping). Stages are nevertheless helpful for conceptualizing processes and the barriers and facilitators at each point, even though in practice some may be blurred or even missed out altogether.

In relation to the public service sector, Mulgan and Albury (2003) have proposed a sequential (though not necessarily linear) model which consists of the generation of possibilities; the trialling and prototyping of promising ideas; replication and scaling up; and analysis and learning. Albury (2005) uses these four components to identify the barriers and facilitators of innovation which managers need to take account of at each stage. However, it may be valuable to modify Albury's framework in that analysing and learning is relevant to all phases and the scaling-up phase has two components – scaling up within an organization and then diffusing the innovation across (or beyond) the sector.

This set of phases has recognizable similarities with the framework of Bessant (2005), who suggests that, regardless of actual sequence, private sector organizations have to grapple with four or even five linked activities if they are to be successful in innovation: searching, selecting, resourcing, implementing and learning. Other stage approaches are available (e.g. Cooper 1988).

Others have critiqued the stages framework, however, arguing that this implies an overly rational model of innovation (e.g. Newell *et al.* 2002). Some writers argue that far from being deliberative or rational, innovation is sometimes emergent (van de Ven 1986), and in fact may be an 'innovation journey' (van de Ven *et al.* 1999).

Alternatively, innovation can be seen as a political as well as a rational process, concerned with building support and resources for new ventures. As noted by Osborne and Brown (2005), this may be politics in terms of the policy context and/or the organizational context of internal politics. To date, there has perhaps been less attention to the role of both formal and informal politics in the processes and outcomes of innovation.

The application of stages/processes derived from the private sector's interest in new product development must be considered with some caution in relation to public services because the sequencing may therefore vary for formal and informal political and stakeholder reasons as well as organizational or managerial reasons. First, phase models were originally developed in the context of the individual firm with the innovation being undertaken either by scientists or managers within the organization. By contrast, innovation in public services may be initiated from 'outside' the organization by policy-makers and policy advisors. Second, the role of policy-makers in innovation means that sometimes the announcement of an adoption of a new innovation may precede the development of the idea (cf. policy announcements made before senior managers have worked out how to implement the idea, or national politicians becoming impatient that their public announcements about innovation have not yet been implemented). Here, there is commitment to adoption prior to trialling. Third, rhetorical innovation may be important in preparing the public or other significant stakeholders for innovative action, yet would not conform to the stages of innovation approach, which is essentially rationalist. For example, the use of rhetorical innovation by the Mayor of London to engage the public in the issue of solving traffic congestion constitutes an innovation but falls outside the stages identified above.

There is a need, therefore, to understand more about the catalysts, promoters and detractors of innovation, recognizing that these may be politicians and policy advisors, lobby groups, the media, etc., not just the managers who are responsible for 'new product development' within the organization.

Innovation and its contribution to improvement

The value produced from innovation has perhaps been under analysed in both the public and private sectors. There is an important difference in innovation between private and public sectors. In the private sector, innovation success can be judged by its impact on profit, wealth creation or market share. This is not the case for public services, where innovation is justifiable to the extent that it increases public value in the quality, efficiency or fitness for purpose of governance or services.

On the other hand, innovation and improvement need to be seen as conceptually distinct and not blurred into one policy phrase. The UK central government currently places a high policy priority on the improvement of public services, so it is easy to see how the concepts of innovation and improvement may become conflated. However, the world is littered with innovations which led either to no or only to short-run improvements, or which had negative unintended consequences. It is therefore useful to consider a number of possible relationships between innovation and improvement. These are shown in figure 10.1. The analysis is based on organizations, but it is applicable also to service areas, business units, or partnerships of organizations.

There are two dimensions in the figure. The first (horizontal axis) concerns whether or not there is innovation in the sense of a step-change in the organization. The second concerns whether or not there is improvement in performance. Improvement does not, *per se*, mean that there is public value but it is a necessary though not sufficient condition.

In the bottom-left quadrant in figure 10.1, marked 1, an organization exhibits neither improvement nor innovation. This may occur where an organization is operating in a highly stable environment, where innovation is not needed because there is a close fit between that environment and the organizational processes, systems and stakeholder needs. Population ecology

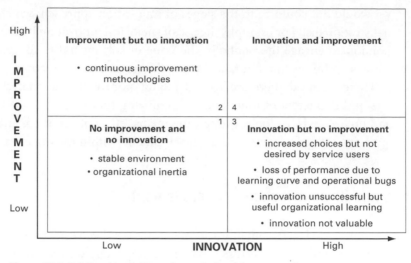

Figure 10.1 Relationships between innovation and improvement

(Hannan and Freeman 1977; Aldrich 1979) suggests that environmental selection processes favour inert organizations which are well adapted to their niche. However, while such a situation is possible, the dynamic nature of change in the economy and society and citizens' changing expectations of public service organizations mean that organizational change is central to the functioning of public service organizations so improvement will be crucial, whether or not that occurs through innovation. Alternatively, in this quadrant, the organization may be in inertia, either because its managers do not recognize a need for innovation or improvement to meet new needs/changing circumstances (Christensen 1997), or else they are paralyzed from taking action to meet the new circumstances (cf. Jas and Skelcher 2005).

In the second quadrant, marked 2, improvement occurs but without innovation. This occurs where an organization focuses on small, incremental changes in order to achieve improvement (e.g. continuous improvement methodology, total quality management, incremental development) but where the changes do not individually constitute innovation in that they are not sufficiently large, general or durable (Moore *et al.* 1997) to constitute the step-change which characterizes innovation. Of course, cumulatively and over an extended period of time, continuous improvement methodologies can lead to substantial and even radical changes in the organization as has been seen in companies such as Toyota (Schroeder and Robinson 1991).

In quadrant 3 the organization implements innovation but there is no resultant improvement. Indeed, there may even be a deterioration of performance. Several situations fit this pattern. First, innovations do not always lead to success – in any sector. Tidd, Bessant and Pavitt (2005) note that product innovation failure rates are high with figures ranging 'from 30% to as high as 95%; an accepted average is 38%' (p. 39).

In considering public sector innovation, there may be several reasons for being even more pessimistic about failure rates. Politicians may be cautious about supporting certain types of innovation, or innovation in particular contexts, since they carry public responsibility for failure. Managers also may be cautious about some situations which require risk taking because of the transparency and accountability expected in public service organizations. The media are often interested in public service innovations and can zero in on failure. Where there is a separation of policy-making from policy implementation there is reduced feedback, which reduces the quality and amount of learning from innovation in its practical application. There are also difficulties in assessing the risk where the boundaries of the service are unclear and ambiguous, due to the intangibility of human services (Lewis and Hartley 2001). A further issue is the complexity and contested nature of success, given that many public service goals are valued differently by different stakeholders and many services are aiming to achieve multiple goals (Hartley, in press). Alternatively, 'over-adoption' may occur, which happens where an innovation is taken up through pressures of policy or management fashion, but where the innovation does not meet local needs, culture or context. Pressures to adopt 'innovative practices' through concerns about being left out or left behind, or for reasons of reputation management or isomorphism, are common in both the private and public sectors (Abrahamson 1991; Powell and DiMaggio 1991).

Second, there is the situation where innovation occurs but is based on a proliferation of choices without the improvement in services needed by service users or other stakeholders. In the private sector, innovations based on increasing choice are valuable in their own right as they may give market advantage (e.g. producing fifty variants of trainer footwear to meet fashion demands). However, in the public services if the extra choices are not wanted or needed, or only give wider but not better services, then innovation exists but has not led to improvement because of the need to consider value for money as an element of public benefit.

In the bottom right-hand quadrant, there is also the situation where the innovation has not led to improvement in the short-term but where the lack of immediate success can either be rectified or can have other benefits. Short-term performance loss is recognized as a feature of organizational change, due to two factors: the need to address operational bugs in the production or service processes (Slack *et al*. 2007) and the learning curve or experience curve which results in part from staff adjusting to new ways of working. This is well recognized in the operations management literature though it has been less acknowledged in the public sector (though see Osborne and Brown 2005).

Innovation without improvement may also occur where the innovation is not, ultimately, successful but where sufficient learning takes place to engage in a later attempt at improvement which benefits from the earlier attempt. There are many examples of this phenomenon in both the private and public sectors (Newman *et al*. 2001; Hartley and Allison 2002; Rashman *et al*. 2005). Again there is insufficient recognition of this phenomenon of learning from 'failure' in the public sector literature (see also Albury 2005; Bessant 2005), though some research suggests that it is beneficial to longer term learning capacity and service and corporate improvement (Rashman and Hartley 2002).

Finally, quadrant 4 in figure 10.1 indicates where an organization engages in innovation which leads to improvement, with noticeable improvements in quality of its outputs and outcomes. However, there are challenges here to move beyond improvement as meeting a set of static performance indicators, to ensuring that the improvements are sustained and that the improvements go beyond service and organizational improvements to ensure public value.

Most studies of firm performance have the firm or the organizational unit as the key 'dependent variable' i.e. whether the innovation leads to benefits for the individual firm (eg Damanpour 1991; Subramanian and Nilakanta 1996) – or at most benefits for a closed network of partners (Powell *et al*. 1996; Powell 1998; Swan *et al*. 2002). However, in the public service sector, the organization is not the primary or necessarily the most useful unit of analysis in many circumstances (Moore 2005) as the primary concern is in improvements across an institutional field. For example, an innovation in treating cancer may be judged successful not only in terms of whether one hospital can maintain a reputational or competitive lead over other services and hospitals, but also in whether the innovation diffuses to other hospitals (and indeed other units of health care) and whether the innovation leads to improved prevention, detection and survival rates in the population. This takes the consideration of the value of innovation well beyond the organization's boundaries.

One element of the context of complexity for public service organizations is that they are embedded in society, producing not only benefits (and obligations) for individuals but also providing public goods and services, establishing collective efficiency, collective rules and purposes (Marquand 2004). Public value (Moore 1995; Benington and Moore in press) is one approach to theorizing about the activities, outputs and outcomes of the public sphere. A key challenge for government is not only to improve the provision of public services but also to create a better society (however society defines this). According to Benington (2005), at its most basic, public value can be thought of as the 'dividends' added to the public realm by activities, services or relationships, or investments of human, financial or technical resources. It encompasses three dimensions: economic value (generation of economic activity and employment); social value (strengthening social capital, social cohesion and constructive social relationships); and political value (stimulating and supporting democratic dialogue and active participation). Analysis of innovation through the lens of public value reveals some substantial differences in the analysis of innovation for the public sector compared with the private sector (Hartley in press).

While studies of performance have largely focused on the desired or intended outcomes of innovation, it is important that we also note that there may well be unintended consequences, both beneficial and detrimental. These may be expected for several reasons. First, complex organizations interacting with their environments will inevitably produce outcomes which are not predicted, according to open systems theory (e.g. Scott 2001). Second, innovations may have longer term consequences that are not initially predicted because the context was not conducive to wider applications at the time (Tidd *et al.* 2005). Third, innovation is not solely a rational process, but includes emergent consequences and political choices, especially in the contested domain of the public sphere, where policy-makers, policy advisors, the public and other key stakeholders such as the media can claim an interest and shape outcomes (van de Ven *et al.* 1999; Osborne and Brown 2005).

The diffusion of innovation

The diffusion of innovation is a critical feature of innovation in the public sector (Rashman and Hartley 2002; Bate and Robert 2003; Mulgan and Albury 2003; Rogers 2003). In the public services, there are pressures not only to develop innovations but also to share them with other organizations in order to enhance public value. Innovations in public services are often spread through open, collaborative networks, and between organizations, services and institutional fields. This contrasts with the deliberate protection of innovations in many parts of the private sector through, for example, patents and property rights or where sharing knowledge is limited either to benchmarking across dissimilar firms/industries or to strategic alliance partners.

Collaborative arrangements to create, share, transfer, adapt and embed innovations have been developed and practised in the UK, for example, through health service collaboratives (Bate and Robert 2003; Addicott *et al.* 2006); Beacons (Hartley and Downe 2007), peer review, pilots and demonstration projects (Newman 2001).

Adoption examines diffusion from the perspective of the recipient individual or organization, as does the concept of assimilation, which also emphasizes that innovations are not taken on board *de novo* but are absorbed into current practices and procedures. Denis *et al.* (2002) point out the fuzziness of boundaries of innovation adoption.

The seminal work on the diffusion of innovation is widely claimed to have come from Everett Rogers in the first imprint of *Diffusion of Innovations* in 1962 and his work has been widely drawn on to explain diffusion, and is still influential (Rogers 2003; Greenhalgh *et al.* 2004), though there are limitations which this chapter explores in the context of diffusion between *organizations*.

A key issue is the level of analysis. The early work on diffusion focused on adoption by *individuals*, and was underpinned theoretically by ideas from psychology, marketing and communication theory. It is a large and unwarranted step from understanding individual adoption decisions to understanding how organizations adopt innovations and how these are assimilated (and sustained or not) by the organization.

There is an increasing recognition that innovations are adopted, to a greater or lesser degree, by new organizations (Denis *et al.* 2002; Rashman and Hartley 2002; Hartley and Rashman 2007). This in part represents the fuzzy boundaries of innovation adoption noted earlier and also the need for new innovations to be assimilated into ongoing practices and systems. For example, in the 2004 national survey of local authority use of learning and diffusion of 'excellent' practice through the Beacon Scheme, 79 per cent of those elected members and managers who had visited a Beacon Council said they had made changes in their own organization as a direct result of the visit. The transfer of learning was an interactive process of knowledge creation and transfer between managers and policy-makers, not a passive copying of 'best practice', and this is shown in survey data from local authority leaders and managers about implementing changes attributable to working with a Beacon organization. Amongst those reporting change implementation, respondents were most likely to report that they had made a change through adopting a Beacon Council idea (63%), then most likely to report that they had accelerated an idea that they had through a Beacon visit (29%) and least likely to say that they had based their improvement closely on the Beacon Council (8%) (Hartley and Rashman 2007).

There is considerable evidence that many innovations are adapted rather than adopted. This occurs even with scientific instruments (von Hippel 1988) and we may anticipate that adaption is even more likely in service contexts (cf. Alänge *et al.* 1998). Hartley and Benington (2006) have argued for the need to move away from mechanistic metaphors (e.g. copy and paste, drag and drop, technology transfer, replication) to more organic metaphors which emphasize the growing of innovations in new 'soil' e.g. they suggest graft and transplant is more accurate as a metaphor of diffusion.

Conclusions

In this chapter I have reviewed a number of key features of the innovation landscape. This is not comprehensive but has focused on some key elements of the context, catalysts, processes and outcomes of innovation in public service organizations. It is clear from this review that there are some similarities in innovation processes and outcomes across the public and private sectors (from which it is important to learn), but also distinctive differences between innovation in *private firms* and in *public organizations* so that theories of public service sector innovation need to reflect the contexts within which the organization is situated. As noted in chapter 1, there are variations within as well as across sectors (e.g. Bozeman and Bretschneider 1994). Also the traditional boundaries between state, market and civil society are now much more dynamic and overlapping (Benington 2000; Newman 2001) so innovation needs to be conceptualized within a dynamic context. These two influences mean that differences (or similarities) can be overdrawn unless there is careful attention to contexts, stakeholders, goals and purposes. This is less an argument for the public sector *per se* but it is an argument for the careful study and conceptualization of context. Tidd (2001) argues that context has a major impact on innovation processes and outcomes, so there is a need to be context-sensitive in innovation studies.

Public service organizations do not exist (primarily) in a market but in a web of relations between levels of government. The policy context noted by Black (2005) is relevant to the functioning of public service organizations. In this sense, the landscape is clearly concerned with public management and organizational functioning in a political and policy setting to a greater extent than is the case for business. Arguably, taking an open systems approach (Scott 2001) or an institutional approach (e.g. Powell and DiMaggio 1991) of the relations between an organization and its environment suggests that some of this wider policy thinking can be relevant for private sector organizations too, though to date this has not been prominent in the innovation literature, which had tended to be focused on the firm as the unit of analysis until the more recent interest in networked innovation (Swan *et al.* 2002) This also means that governance innovations are of considerable interest to public service organizations (and this may become more important for the private sector in the future as well).

The differences are important for conceptualizing and researching innovation. First, the pressures for innovation vary. Market competition is not the primary driving force, as it is in the private sector, though the pressures to innovate also derive from a dynamic and sometimes volatile environment. Second, the unit of analysis for innovation in the private sector is often the individual firm while that of public service organizations is often the institutional field (e.g. hospitals, police services) or even the public service as a whole. Third, the catalysts of innovation in the public sector are multi-level: 'top-down' (through policy); 'bottom-up' (within the organization), or 'lateral' (diffusion/sharing of good practice and engagement with users) and can be overlapping. Managers often have to be able to combine internal innovation processes with policy pressures and transparent and accountable risk management. Fourth, much private sector literature, until recently, has focused on technological innovation. There are limitations in applying concepts about *product* innovation to *service* and *organizational* innovation. Finally, for the private sector, successful innovation is assessed as value creation defined, generally, as profit, wealth creation or market positioning. For public services, innovation is useful where it increases public value in governance or services, in terms of quality, efficiency or fitness for purpose but the values attached to this assessment may also be contested by stakeholders in public debate.

Overall, these features suggest that the transfer of theory and empirical findings from private firms to public services is far from straightforward. Accordingly, there is a need for robust theory and evidence derived directly from the public sector, and the current chapter provides both an overview of the landscape and provides questions for a longer term research agenda.

REFERENCES

Abrahamson, E. (1991) Managerial fads and fashion: the diffusion and rejection of innovations. *Academy of Management Review* **16**: 588–612.

Addicott, R., McGivern, G. and Ferlie, E. (2006) Networks, organizational learning and knowledge management: NHS cancer networks. *Public Money and Management* **26**: 87–94.

Alänge, S., Jacobsson, S. and Jarnehammar, A., (1998) Some aspects of an analytical framework for studying the diffusion of organizational innovations. *Technology Analysis & Strategic Management* **10**(1): 3–21.

Albury, D. (2005) Fostering innovation in public services. *Public Money and Management* **25** (January): 51–6.

Aldrich, H. (1979) *Organizations and Environments*. Englewood Cliffs, NJ: Prentice-Hall.

Altschuler, A. and Behn, R. (1997a) The dilemmas of innovation in American Government, in Altschuler, A. and Behn, R. (eds.) *Innovation in American Government*. Washington, DC: Brookings Institution, pp. 3–37.

Altschuler, A. and Behn, R. (1997b) *Innovation in American Government*. Washington, DC: Brookings Institution.

Altschuler, A. and Zegans, M. (1997) Innovation and public management: notes from the state house and city hall, in Altschuler, A. and Behn, R. (eds.) *Innovation in American Government*. Washington, DC: Brookings Institution, pp. 68–80.

Bate, S. and Robert, G. (2003) Where next for policy evaluation? Insights from researching NHS modernisation. *Policy and politics* **31**: 237–51.

Benington, J. (2000) The modernization and improvement of government and public services. *Public Money and Management* **20**(2): 3–8.

(2001) Partnership as networked governance? Legitimation, innovation, problem-solving and coordination, in Geddes, M. and Benington, J. (eds.) *Local Partnerships and Social Exclusion in the European Union*. London: Routledge, pp. 198–219.

(2005) From private choice to public value. *Public Management and Policy Association Review* May: 6–10.

Benington, J. and Moore, M. (in press) *Debating and Delivering Public Value*. Basingstoke: Palgrave

Bessant, J. (2003) *High-involvement Management: Building and Sustaining Competitive Advantage through Continuous Change*. Chichester: Wiley.

(2005) Enabling continuous and discontinuous innovation: learning from the private sector. *Public Money and Management* **25** (January): 35–42.

Black, J. (2005) Tomorrow's worlds: frameworks for understanding regulatory innovation, in Black, J., Lodge, M. and Thatcher, M. (eds.) *Regulatory Innovation* Cheltenham: Edward Elgar, pp. 16–44.

Borins, S. (2001) Innovation, success and failure in public management research: some methodological reflections. *Public Management Review* **3**: 3–17.

Bozeman, B. and Bretschneider, S. (1994) The publicness puzzle in organizational theory: a test of alternative explanations of differences between public and private organizations. *Journal of Public Administration Theory and Research* **4**: 197–223.

Cabinet Office (2006) *The UK Government's Approach to Public Service Reform* London: Cabinet Office.

Christensen, C. (1997) *The Innovator's Dilemma*. Cambridge, MA: Harvard Business School Press.

Christensen, C., Bohmer, R. and Kenagy, J. (2000) Will disruptive innovations cure health care? *Harvard Business Review*, September, 102–12.

Cooper, R. (1988) The new product process: a decision-making guide for management. *Journal of Marketing Management* **3**(3): 238–25.

Damanpour, F. (1991) Organizational innovation: a meta-analysis of effects of determinants and moderators. *Academy of Management Journal* **34**: 555–90.

Damanpour, F. and Gopalakrishnan, S. (2001) The dynamics of the adoption of product and process innovations in organizations. *Journal of Management Studies* **38**: 45–65.

Denis, J. L., Hebert, Y., Langley, A., Lozeau, D. and Trottier, L. (2002) Explaining diffusion patterns for complex health care innovations. *Health Care Management Review* **27**: 60–73.

Gray, A., Hartley, J. and Broadbent, J. (2005) The state of public management: improvement and innovation. Special issue for 25th anniversary of *Public Money and Management*, January.

Greenhalgh, T., Robert, G., Bate, P., *et al.* (2004) *How to Spread Good Ideas*. Report for the National Co-ordinating Centre for NHS Service Delivery and Organization. London: NHS SDO.

Hargadon, A. and Sutton, R. (2000) Building an innovation factory. *Harvard Business Review* **78**(3): 157–66.

Hartley, J. (2005) Innovation in governance and public services: past and present. *Public Money and Management* **25** (January): 27–34.

(in press) Public value through innovation and improvement, in Benington, J. and Moore, M. (eds.) *Debating and Delivering Public Value*. Basingstoke: Palgrave.

Hartley, J. and Allison, M. (2002) Good, better, best? Inter-organizational learning in a network of local authorities. *Public Management Review* **4**: 101–18.

Hartley, J. and Benington, J. (2006) Copy and paste, or graft and transplant? Knowledge sharing in inter-organizational networks. *Public Money and Management* **26** (April,) 101–8.

Hartley, J. and Downe, J. (2007) The shining lights? Public service awards as an approach to service improvement *Public Administration* **85**(2): 329–53.

Hartley, J. and Rashman, L. (2007) How is knowledge transferred between organizations involved in change? in Wallace, M., Fertig, M. and Schneller, E. (eds.) *Managing Change in the Public Services* Oxford: Blackwell, pp. 171–92.

Hannan, M. and Freeman, J. (1977) The population ecology of organizations. *American Journal of Sociology* **83**: 929–84.

Jas, P. and Skelcher, C. (2005) Performance decline and turnaround in public organizations: a theoretical and empirical analysis. *British Journal of Management* **16**: 195–210.

Kim, W. and Mauborgne, R. (1999) Creating new market space. *Harvard Business Review*, **77**(1): 95–104.

Lewis, M. and Hartley, J. (2001) Evolving forms of quality management in local government: lessons from the Best Value pilot programme. *Policy and Politics* **29**: 477–96.

Lynn, L. (1997) Innovation and the public interest: insights from the private sector, in Altschuler, A. and Behn, R. (eds.) *Innovation in American Government*. Washington, DC: Brookings Institution, pp. 83–103.

Marquand, D. (2004) *The Decline of the Public* Cambridge: Polity Press.

Moore, M. H. (1995) *Creating Public Value* Cambridge, MA: Harvard University Press.

(2005) Break-through innovations and continuous improvement: two different models of innovative processes in the public sector. *Public Money and Management* **25**(January): 43–50.

Moore, M. H. and Hartley, J. (2008) Innovations in governance. *Public Management Review* **10**(1): 3–20.

Moore, M. H., Sparrow, M. and Spelman, W. (1997) Innovation in policing: from production line to jobs shops, in Altschuler, A. and Behn, R. (eds.) *Innovation in American Government*. Washington, DC: Brookings Institution, pp. 274–98.

Moran, M. (2003) *The British Regulatory State: High Modernism and Hyper-innovation* Oxford: Oxford University Press.

Mulgan, G. and Albury, D. (2003) *Innovations in the Public Sector*. London: Cabinet Office.

Newell, S., Robertson, M., Scarbrough, H. and Swan, J. (2002) *Managing Knowledge Work*. Basingstoke: Palgrave.

Newman, J. (2001) *Modernising Governance: New Labour, Policy and Society*. London: Sage.

Newman, J. Raine, J. and Skelcher, C. (2001) Transforming local government: innovation and modernization. *Public Money and Management* April: 61–8.

Nicholson, N., Rees, A. and Brooks-Rooney, A., (1990) Strategy, innovation and performance. *Journal of Management Studies* **27**(5): 511–34.

Osborne, S. and Brown, K. (2005) *Managing Change and Innovation in Public Service Organizations*. London: Routledge.

Powell, W. W. (1998) Learning from collaboration: knowledge and networks in the biotechnology and pharmaceutical industries. *California Management Review* **40**(3): 228–40.

Powell, W. and DiMaggio, P. (1991) *The New Institutionalism in Organizational Theory*. Chicago, IL: University of Chicago Press.

Powell, W., Koput, W. and Smith-Doerr, L. (1996) Interorganizational collaboration and the locus of innovation: networks of learning in biotechnology. *Administrative Science Quarterly* **41**(1): 116–30.

Rashman, L. and Hartley, J. (2002) Leading and learning? Knowledge transfer in the Beacon Scheme. *Public Administration* **80**: 523–42.

Rashman, L., Downe, J. and Hartley, J. (2005) Knowledge creation and transfer in the Beacon Scheme: improving services through sharing good practice. *Local Government Studies* **31** (5): 683–700.

Rogers, E. (2003) *Diffusion of Innovations* 5th edn. New York: Free Press.

Scott, W. R. (2001) *Institutions and Organizations*. 2nd edn. Thousand Oaks, CA: Sage.

Schroeder, D. and Robinson, A. (1991) America's most successful export to Japan – continuous improvement programs. *Sloan Management Review* **32**(3): 67–81.

Schumpeter, J. (1950) *Capitalism, Socialism and Democracy*, New York: Harper and Row.

Slack, N., Chambers, S. and Johnston, R. (2007) *Operations Management*. London: Prentice Hall.

Subramanian, A. and Nilakanta, S. (1996) Organizational innovativeness: exploring the relationship between organizational determinants of innovation, types of innovations, and measures of organizational performance. *Omega-International Journal of Management Science* **24**(6): 631–47.

Swan, J., Scarbrough, H. and Robertson, M. (2002). The construction of 'communities of practice' in the management of innovation. *Management Learning* **33**(4): 477–96.

Thompson, V. (1965) Bureaucracy and innovation. *Administrative Science Quarterly* **10**: 1–20.

Tidd, J. (2001) Innovation management in context: environment, organization and performance. *International Journal of Management Reviews* **3**(3): 169–83.

Tidd, J., Bessant, J. and Pavitt, K. (2005) *Managing Innovation: Integrating Technological, Market and Organizational Change*. 3rd edn. Chichester: Wiley.

Utterback, J. (1996) *Mastering the Dynamics of Innovation*. Boston, MA: Harvard Business School Press.

van de Ven, A. (1986) Central problems in the management of innovation *Management Science* **32**: 590–607.

van de Ven, A., Polley, D., Garud, R. and Venkataraman, S. (1999) *The Innovation Journey.* New York: Oxford University Press.

von Hippel, E. (1988) *The Sources of Innovation* New York: Oxford University Press. (2005) *Democratizing Innovation.* Cambridge, MA: MIT Press.

Walker, R., Jeanes, E. and Rowlands, R. (2002) Measuring innovation: applying the literature-based innovation output indicator to public services. *Public Administration* **80**: 201–14.

Wolfe, R. (1994) Organizational innovation: review, critique, and suggested research directions. *Journal of Management Studies* **31**: 405–31.

11 Innovation type and organizational performance: an empirical exploration

Richard M. Walker and Fariborz Damanpour

Introduction

Innovation is increasingly used as a route to higher levels of organizational performance in public agencies. As technological changes have revolutionized the way organizations are managed and services delivered, governments and public agencies have adopted a plethora of new approaches to management, organization and service delivery to respond to economic crises and demands from the public for more appropriate services (Pollitt and Bouckeart 2000; OECD 2005).

English local government is a prime example of how innovation is used to improve performance. A slate of new management approaches have been introduced over recent years (Newman *et al.* 2001; Walker 2006). These include changes in governance and service delivery, such as the use of contracting, outsourcing and disinvestment, and new management processes, such as strategic planning, target setting, quality regimes and benchmarking. Information and communication technologies have also been increasingly used to improve delivery of existing services and introduce new services to meet emerging service demands. For the majority of local government organizations, these processes and services are novel; hence, their introduction is considered as adopting innovations.

The adoption of these innovations in public organizations has not taken place in a vacuum. While some organizations have acted eagerly to develop new processes and solutions, others have done so more reluctantly. These organizations may indeed have been pressed into action by a policy context that increasingly expects innovation to occur. This is clearly seen in the Labour government's strategy for service improvement (Blair 2002; OPSR 2002). Innovation is seen as a tool to remove professional barriers and demarcations, to drive red tape out of public agencies and to provide the services that the public demands. While public policies and programmes are

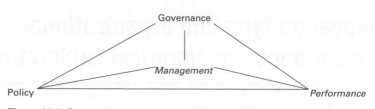

Figure 11.1 Governance, management, policy and performance

politically motivated, the Labour government prides itself on the use of evidence to inform the policy-making process and subsequent service delivery. However, empirical evidence on whether the adoption of innovation contributes to the effectiveness of public organizations is remarkably scarce. A review by Walker (2004) identified only thirty papers that explore the innovation–performance hypothesis, of which only one dataset is in public agencies (Damanpour and Evan 1984; Damanpour *et al.* 1989). The conclusions from Walker's study, while generally supportive of a positive impact of innovation on organizational performance, is circumspect about how this effect might be achieved. The uncertainty regarding the influence of innovation on the quality and effectiveness of services offered by public agencies can be based upon the pro-innovation bias in the literature, lack of empirical evidence, especially from longitudinal studies, and perhaps by deduction in the policies developed by the Labour administration in the early twenty-first century.

In order to begin to fill this void in the literature, in this chapter we empirically explore the relationship between innovation and performance in public organizations. In doing this we focus on two of the four organizing concepts for the book: management and performance; and are interested in the effect management (informed by a policy context which promotes innovation) has on performance (see Figure 11.1). Two questions are examined here. We begin by asking whether innovation affects performance, and if it does what is the lag between the introduction of an innovation and the change in performance? Next, we explore whether the effect of innovation on performance depends upon the type of innovation. The empirical research is conducted on a longitudinal dataset (2001 to 2004 inclusive) of English local government. We examine the innovation–performance relationship in two time periods – *Period 1* (2001–2003) and *Period 2* (2001–2004) – employing two types of innovation (process and service) and two measures of organizational performance (internal and external). Prior to presenting our empirical results, we discuss theory and research findings on the impact of innovation type on organizational performance.

Theory

Definition of innovation

Innovation is a complex construct, has been studied in many disciplines, and has been conceptualized from different perspectives. Broadly, innovation is defined as a process through which a new idea, object or practice is created, developed, implemented or reinvented (Aiken and Hage 1971; Amablie 1988; Rogers 1995) Newness, a common property by definition of innovation in every discipline, is a relative term. An innovation can be considered new to an individual adopter, a group or team, an organization, an industry or the wider society (West and Farr 1990). At the organizational level, the focus of this chapter, *innovation*, is defined as the adoption of a product, service, technology or managerial approach new to the adopting organization (Kimberly and Evanisko 1981; Damanpour *et al.* 1989). The adoption of innovation in organizations can be the direct result of managerial choice or can be imposed by external conditions. Either way, innovation adoption is intended to address internal organizational needs and/or respond to external environmental conditions. Regardless of the impetus, and the internal or external origin, the adoption of innovation is a means of creating change in the organization to ensure adaptive behaviour and contribute to effectiveness of the organization.

Past research on innovation adoption in organizations has primarily examined the determinants of innovation (Aiken and Hage 1971; Subramanian and Nilakanta 1996; Nystrom *et al.* 2002). Reviews of this research, however, suggest that its results are inconsistent (Wolfe 1994; Drazin and Schoonhoven 1996; Tidd 2001). To address the problem of inconsistent results, innovation researchers have distinguished between types of innovation, such as product and process innovations (Tornatzky and Fleischer 1990; Damanpour and Gopalakrishnan 2001), technical and administrative innovations (Kimberly and Evanisko 1981; Damanpour and Evan 1984), and radical and incremental innovations (Ettlie *et al.* 1984; Germain 1996). In this chapter, we distinguish between service and process innovations. This distinction is important because the adoption of each type of innovation requires certain organizational skills and influences expectations and aspirations of different stakeholders.

Service and process innovations

A product is a good or service offered to the customer or client, and a process is the mode of production and delivery of the good or service (Barras 1986). Hence, service innovations in public organizations (as well as organizations in the service industry) are similar to product innovations in manufacturing organizations (as well as organizations in the goods industry). We define *service innovations* as new services offered by local government organizations to meet an external user or client need, and *process innovations* as new elements introduced into an organization's service operations or management systems for rendering those services (Abernathy and Utterback 1978; Damanpour and Gopalakrishnan 2001).[1] According to this definition, service innovations have an external focus and are primarily client driven, whereas process innovations have an internal focus and are primarily efficiency driven. Nevertheless, the adoption of each is intended to change the adopting organization so that it improves, or at least maintains, its level of performance over time.

Innovation and organizational performance

Systems theorists state that performance is the ability of an organization to cope with all systematic processes relative to its goal-seeking behaviour (Evan 1976). Performance is a function of congruency among the organization's internal functions and systems and adaptability of the organization to its external environmental needs and demands. As stated earlier, the adoption of innovation is intended to contribute to the organization's effectiveness by changing the adopting organization so that it can respond to new conditions in its external environment and/or meet new aspirations of its executives or administrators. Therefore, based on the open system model of organizations, the main reason for adopting innovation is to contribute to organizational effectiveness.

The performance gap theory of innovation provides the conceptual underpinning for this rational perspective of the innovation–performance relationship (Damanpour 1990). *Performance gap* is the difference between what the organization is actually doing and what it can potentially do (Down 1966; Zaltman *et al.* 1973). Perceived performance gap creates a need for change in

---

[1] Our definition of process innovation includes both technological process innovations and administrative (also termed organizational and managerial) process innovations (Damanpour *et al.* 1989; Edquist *et al.* 2001).

the organization which would in turn provide motivation to adopt innovations in order to reduce the gap. This logic does not only encompass poorly performing organizations; senior managers of high-performing organizations may also introduce major changes when they perceive that attractive new opportunities can be seized or they foresee impending environmental threats that may compromise their organization's ability to be effective (Wischnevsky and Damanpour 2006). Therefore, we propose that *the adoption of innovation will be positively associated with organizational performance.*

Despite the prominence of the performance gap theory, empirical evidence on the innovation–performance relationship is scarce and not fully consistent (Damanpour 1990; Walker 2004). This chapter contributes by conducting a finer grain examination of effects of innovation on organizational performance than has been conducted previously. We distinguish between service and process innovation, and between internal and external measures of performance, and empirically explore which type of innovation influences which type of performance measure. We offer that the performance gap can be internally and externally produced. It can be filled by introducing innovations in the internal systems of the organization (process innovations) or innovations to meet external users' or clients' needs (service innovations). The performance outcomes of process and service innovations, therefore, could best be understood by associating these innovation types to internal and external measures of performance, respectively. Thus, we expect that *service innovations will more likely affect the external performance measure while process innovations will more likely influence the internal performance measure.*

Methods

Data source

This study is situated in the English local government sector. English local governments are politically elected bodies with a Westminster-style cabinet system of political management. They are multi-purpose authorities delivering education, social services, regulatory services (such as land-use planning and environmental health), housing, libraries, leisure services and welfare benefits in specific geographical areas. In urban areas, authorities deliver all these services; in rural areas a two-tier system prevails with county councils administering education and social services, and district councils providing environmental, welfare and regulatory functions. Though authorities are multi-purpose they do not provide all public services, for example health is provided by health authorities and the police service by police authorities. They employ professional career staff, and receive around two-thirds of their income, and guidance on the implementation of legislation, from central government.

Within each local authority, we collected data from multiple informants at the corporate and service levels; namely, corporate and service officers.[2] These two echelons were used to overcome the sample bias problem faced in surveying large numbers of informants from one organizational level, and address the weakness of prior studies that have adopted elite surveys, which typically collect evidence on organizational leaders' aspirations only and overlook the range of different perceptions within the organization (Bowman and Ambrosini 1997; Walker and Enticott 2004). Past studies suggest that attitudes of managers differ between the corporate and service levels (Aiken and Hage 1968; Walker and Enticott 2004). By calculating an organizational score from a mean of corporate officers and a mean of service officers, variations across organizations are maintained and categorical data are converted to continuous data.

Data are taken from the 'The Long Term Evaluation of Best Value and its Impact' dataset. This is an electronic survey of English local authorities. The survey includes data on informants' perceptions of organization and management, notably culture, structure, strategy making and strategy content, together with drivers of service improvement, background variables and a management reform regime called 'Best Value' (Boyne et al. 2004).[3] In each authority, questionnaires were sent to up to three corporate informants, chief officers in each of seven service areas and three managers in each of these service areas. Seven key services were surveyed: education, social care, land-use planning, waste management, housing, library and leisure, and benefits. All survey questions were in the form of a seven-point Likert scale and informants were asked to rate their authority (for corporate officers) or service (for service officers) on different dimensions of organization and management.

---

[2] *Corporate officers* include the chief executive officer and corporate policy officers with cross-organizational responsibilities for service delivery and improvement. *Service officers* include chief officers, who are the most senior officers with specific service delivery responsibility, and service managers, who are frontline supervisory officers.

[3] A copy of the full questionnaire is available at www.clrgr.cf.ac.uk or on request from the first author.

At the core of the 'Best Value' survey is a representative sample of 100 English local authorities. Representativeness is based upon background variables including deprivation, population and performance (see Martin *et al.* 2003). The survey was conducted annually from 2001 until 2004. When we match aggregated organizational level responses with our measures of performance and the control measures over the four years, a sample size of 94 is achieved. The sample size drops to 72 when we include the external perceptual measure of performance in our analysis, because this measure was not collected for the district councils in the sample. The data were aggregated into the organizational level in our analyses.

Measures

Performance

Two central issues have become clear in the longstanding debate on the best way to measure organizational performance in the public sector (Ostrom 1973; Park 1984; Kelly and Swindell 2002). First, performance is a multi-dimensional construct that covers dimension such as quality, effectiveness, responsiveness, equity and efficiency (Venkatraman and Ramanjum 1986; Carter *et al.* 1992; Boyne 2002). These dimensions are increasingly accepted in the public management literature. Second, perspectives on what constitutes high levels of organizational performance are likely to vary by the stakeholder groups (Andrews *et al.* 2006; Brewer 2006; Walker and Boyne 2006). Key stakeholder groups are 'external' and 'internal'. *External performance* in this study refers to judgements that are made by stakeholders in the external environment of an organization (service consumers, voters, regulators); *internal performance* is based on the views of stakeholders within an organization (senior managers, frontline staff). Our measures of internal and external performance are perceptual. The data for the internal performance measure are collected from organizational members; the data for external performance measure are from the Audit Commission, the main regulatory body of local governments. Both internal and external measures are aggregated measures that capture multiple dimensions of performance.

The Audit Commission (2002) has constructed an external measure of performance for all upper tier or major English local authorities (London boroughs, metropolitan boroughs and unitary authorities and county councils). The Commission acts on behalf of central government, the primary external stakeholder for local authorities in England. Central government creates and abolishes individual local government units, provides around 75 per cent of their funding, and bestows or removes service responsibilities. This measure of performance, the 'Comprehensive Performance Assessment' (CPA), classifies the performance of authorities into five categories (poor, weak, fair, good and excellent). The overall CPA scores are derived from external judgement about a local authority's core service performance (CSP) and its ability to improve. The dependent variable for our empirical analysis is performance, so in this study the discussion is on how the CSP score was derived by the Audit Commission.

The CSP score is an aggregate measure that covers six dimensions of performance (quantity of outputs, quality of outputs, efficiency, effectiveness, value for money and consumer satisfaction). It embraces all the main areas of local government activity. Each service was given a score by the Audit Commission from 1 (lowest) to 4 (highest). These scores were based largely on archival performance indicators, supplemented by the results of inspection of services (which are also strongly influenced by performance indicators) and service plans and standards (see Andrews *et al.* 2005; 2006). While this measure blends archival performance measures with the perceptions of inspectors, all the evaluators are external to the organization. The absolute scores allocated to each authority are converted to continuous data by recalculating the score as a percentage of the possible maximum.

The internal measure of performance was derived from eight items in the survey of local authority managers. It includes quality, value for money, efficiency, effectiveness, equity, staff satisfaction, customer satisfaction and social, economic and environmental sustainability.[4] Respondents to the survey were asked to assess, for each of eight dimensions of performance, the quartile in which their organization was located in relation to other local service providers, with 1 being the bottom and 4 the top. To provide a comparison with the CSP performance measure we used an aggregate measure of internal perceptual performance. The internal performance measures offered acceptable Cronbach alphas: 0.869 in 2003 (for Period 1) and 0.824 in 2004 (for Period 2). Table 11.1 provides descriptive data for the two dependent variables.

Innovation

Measures of innovation were identified in the Best Value survey. The survey provides perceptual information on informants' attitudes to management and organization. To ensure that the measures of innovation operationalize our

---

[4] Promoting the social, economic and environmental well-being of local people is a measure of public sector sustainability that builds upon the triple bottom-line used in the business sector (see Enticott and Walker, in press).

Table 11.1: Descriptive data of measures used in multiple regression models

Variable	Count	Mean	Standard deviation	Minimum	Maximum
Performance					
Performance 2003					
Internal perceptual	94	24.11	2.19	18.52	28.98
External perceptual	72	67.96	7.68	50.00	88.33
Performance 2004					
Internal perceptual	94	24.36	1.89	16.90	29.00
External perceptual	72	72.51	7.53	51.67	90.00
Innovations					
Innovation 2001	94	32.65	3.39	22.46	41.49
Innovation 2002	94	33.13	3.19	19.96	42.25
Innovations 2003	94	34.41	3.47	19.76	43.89
Process 2001	94	25.02	2.53	18.00	30.61
Process 2002	94	24.65	2.64	15.50	30.70
Process 2003	94	25.56	2.62	15.64	32.22
Service 2001	94	7.63	1.41	4.46	10.88
Service 2002	94	8.48	1.07	5.84	11.55
Service 2003	94	8.85	1.37	4.12	11.67
Controls					
Service need	94	25.49	10.90	4.89	58.22
Service diversity	94	2286.73	2107.92	344.84	8296.63
Organizational size	94	295495.80	241189.50	35075.00	1329718.00
Urbanization	94	2167.26	2696.89	40.90	14916.67

definition of innovation, we selected only variables that included the word 'new'.[5] Five indicators of *process innovations* were identified in the survey. They explored informants' attitudes towards information technology and information systems, and approaches to service planning and budgeting, improvement and management processes. These indicators of process innovation reflect key facets of the innovations required by the English Labour government to assist in achieving service improvement (OPSR 2002). *Service innovations* were drawn from Osborne's (1998) categories of total and evolutionary innovations. Overall *organizational innovation* was measured by adding measures of process and service innovations. Table 11.2 lists the measures of innovation together with the descriptive data. The reliability data reported in table 11.2 provides good alphas (between 0.69 and 0.85) for

---

[5] For each variable, informants were asked: Please indicate if the following were a major part of the management [service delivery for service innovations] approach adopted in your service area between April 2001/2002/2003 and April 2002/2003/2004.

Table 11.2: Innovation measures, descriptive data and Cronbach alphas

	Means		
	2001	2002	2003
Process Innovations			
New information technology (e.g. new computer hardware)	5.37	4.97	5.17
New management information systems (e.g. performance management systems)	5.69	5.23	5.39
New approaches to service planning/budgeting (e.g. redirecting resources to priority areas)	4.95	5.00	5.22
New approaches to improvement (e.g. EFQM, re-engineering, charter marks)	4.56	4.64	4.78
New management processes (e.g. new job descriptions, establishing new teams of staff)	4.37	4.77	4.97
Service Innovations			
Providing new services to new users	4.18	3.87	4.02
Providing new services to existing users	4.15	4.64	4.80
All innovation α	0.76	0.77	0.77
Process innovation α	0.69	0.74	0.71
Service innovation α	0.72	0.73	0.85

all measures of innovation. All measures of innovation used in the analysis were standardized as z-scores prior to entry into the statistical models. Table 11.1 lists the descriptive scores for the unstandardized measures of innovation.

Control variables

We included four control variables – service need, service diversity, organizational size, and urbanization – in our analyses. These variables reflect both external and internal controls and have been widely used in past performance studies in public organizations (Andrews *et al.* 2005; 2006; Walker and Boyne 2006).

The degree to which the external environment is demanding is operationalized through a measure of deprivation (*Service need*). This uses the Average Ward Score from the Index of Multiple Deprivation (Department of the Environment, Transport and the Regions 2000), which is the standard population-weighted measure of deprivation in England employed by central government. It provides an overview of the different domains of deprivation (e.g. income, employment and health). As the range of service users becomes more varied, it becomes harder to determine the relative needs of different groups and to provide standardized services that meet their requirements. The complexity of service need (*Service diversity*) uses ethnic diversity to measure variations in the level of service need. A Hehrfindahl index was created by squaring the proportion of each ethnic group (taken from the 2001 census, Office for National Statistics 2003) within a local authority and then subtracting the sum of the squares of these proportions from 10,000. The measure gives a proxy for 'fractionalization' within a local authority area, with a high level of ethnic diversity reflected in a high score on the index.

Organizational size has been long debated in the literatures on both organizational innovation and performance. While its effects are not always consistent on either construct, a recent quantitative review of research findings suggests that larger organizations have higher levels of innovation (Camison-Zornoza *et al.* 2004). To operationalize organizational size we used the size of the population of the local authority. This measure was selected because data on the number of employees, the commonly used measure of organizational size, vary with the level of contracting out and also because larger populations require larger organizations to deliver the requisite level of service. *Urbanization* affects both the level of innovation in an organization and performance (Aiken and Alford 1970). Urban authorities are likely to achieve higher levels of organizational performance because they are not operating across large areas, their citizens and users are more readily accessible and communication is easier. We measured urbanization by the average population density within each local authority. This captures the differences between highly urban city authorities, from those with mixed urban and rural areas to those with predominately rural authorities. Descriptive data for control variables are included in table 11.1.

The effect of innovation on performance

Tables 11.3, 11.4 and 11.5 present the results of ten regression models that explore whether innovation has an effect on organizational performance. Models 1 to 4 (M1 to M4) presented in table 11.3 provide results using the aggregate measure of innovation for both Periods 1 and 2. Models 5 to 8 (M5 to M8) in table 11.4 report the results for process and service innovations for both periods. Models 9 and 10 (M9 to M10) in table 11.5 are autoregressive performance models using 2004 performance as the dependent variable while controlling for 2003 performance. In all models, innovation variables are lagged at least for one year. We focus our attention on the effects of innovation performance and omit discussion about the relationship between external controls and performance, though we include the results for all variables in the tables provided.

Table 11.3: Relationships between organizational innovation and internal and external measures of organizational performance

	Period 1		Period 2	
	Internal M1	External M1	Internal M3	External M4
Intercept	25.99 (0.491)***	72.983 (2.905)***	25.282 (0.450)***	75.066 (2.466)***
Service need	− 0.052 (0.015)***	− 0.189 (0.078)*	− 0.025 (0.014)+	− 0.134 (0.067)*
Service diversity	− 0.001 (0.000)***	− 0.001 (0.000)+	− 0.001 (0.000)***	− 0.002 (0.001)***
Organizational size	0.000 (0.000)	0.000 (0.000)	0.000 (0.000)	0.000 (0.000)
Urbanization	0.001 (0.000)***	0.001 (0.001)+	0.001 (0.000)***	0.002 (0.000)***
Innovation 2001	0.569 0.171**	3.216 (1.008)**	0.806 (0.181)***	1.141 (0.881)
Innovation 2002	0.171 (0.193)	− 0.863 (1.157)	− 0.102 (0.186)	0.583 (1.089)
Innovation 2003	–	–	0.111 (0.165)	1.927 (1.050)+
R^2/Adj R^2	0.467/0.430	0.233/0.166	0.459/0.416	0.312/0.234
F	12.704***	3.485**	10.404***	4.011***

$+ p < 0.10$, $* p < 0.05$, $** p < 0.001$, $*** p < 0.0001$
Note: unstandardized coefficients. Standard errors in parenthesis.

Organizational innovation and performance

In M1 to M4 we use the aggregate measure of innovation (table 11.3). The results suggest that the effect of innovation on performance is not consistent for the internal and external measures of performance across time. In Period 1, a two-year lag exists for the effect of innovation on both internal and external measure of performance. However, in Period 2 the coefficient for Innovation 2001 is significant at the 0.05 level only for the internal measure of performance (M3). For the external performance model in Period 2 (M4), there is only a weak effect for innovation in 2003 ($p < 0.10$) suggesting a one-year lag effect. These results offer limited but not convincing support for a positive effect of an aggregated measure of organizational innovation on two measures of performance.

Innovation types and organizational performance

Table 11.4 distinguishes between process and service innovations to see if these more subtle measures of innovation produce either different results or indicate a unique association between a type of innovation and a measure of performance. Consistent with the analyses in table 11.4, the results offer evidence of effects for both process and service innovations on the internal measure of performance for both time periods (M5 and M7). For the external performance measure,

Table 11.4: Relationships between process and service innovations with internal and external measures of organizational performance

	Period 1		Period 2	
	Internal M5	External M6	Internal M7	External M8
Intercept	25.839 (0.519)***	73.464 (2.936)***	25.444 (0.487)***	75.720 (2.470)***
Service need	− 0.051 (0.016)**	− 0.202 (0.079)**	− 0.026 (0.015)*	− 0.143 (0.066)**
Service diversity	− 0.001 (0.000)***	− 0.001 (0.001)	− 0.001 (0.000)***	− 0.002 (0.001)**
Organizational size	0.000 (0.000)	0.000 (0.000)	0.000 (0.000)	0.000 (0.000)
Urbanization	0.001 (0.000)***	0.001 (0.001)	0.000 (0.000)***	0.002 (0.000)***
Process 2001	0.297 (0.212)+	1.374 (1.106)	0.539 (0.200)**	1.267 (0.859)
Service 2001	0.396 (0.208)+	2.660 (1.056)*	0.373 (0.202)+	− 0.663 (0.914)
Process 2002	0.216 (0.208)	− 1.297 (1.132)	− 0.078 (0.203)	0.411 (1.008)
Service 2002	− 0.084 (0.194)	0.202 (0.974)	0.033 (0.186)	0.727 (0.861)
Process 2003	–	–	− 0.125 (0.198)	− 0.443 (1.073)
Service 2003	–	–	0.254 (0.196)	3.125 (1.031)**
R^2/Adj R^2	0.441/0.388	0.263/0.175	0.441/0.374	0.385/0.281
F	8.384***	2.985**	6.559***	3.692***

$+ p < 0.10$, $* p < 0.05$, $** p < 0.001$, $*** p < 0.0001$
Note: unstandardized coefficients. Standard errors in parenthesis.

however, the findings are less consistent – the two significant effects are for service innovations in 2001 (M6) and in 2003 (M8). The results from M6 suggest that the two-year lag effect of organizational innovation on internal measure of performance seen in M2 is only attributable to service innovation; those from M8 (compared with M4) also suggest a more significant effect for service than for process innovation on the external measure of performance. However, comparing the significant effects for innovation variables for the internal measure of performance in Period 2 (M7 versus M3) suggests an opposite pattern. Results from M7 for process and service innovations in 2001 suggest that the statistical significance of Innovation 2001 recorded in M3 is attributable more to process than to service innovations.

The distinction between service and process innovation, and the influence of each innovation type on internal versus external measure of performance, suggests several preliminary, yet interesting, results for further examination in future research. First, while both process and service innovations are shown to affect internal performance, external performance is only influenced by service innovations. This suggests that internal and external stakeholders have different perceptions about the way in which different types of innovation

Table 11.5: Relationships between process and service innovations with internal and external measures of organizational performance, controlling for prior performance

	Period 2	
	Internal M9	External M10
Intercept	12.089 (1.844)***	19.916 (4.932)***
Service need	− 0.000 (0.001)*	− 0.001 (0.005)*
Service diversity	− 0.000 (0.000)+	− 0.000 (0.000)
Organizational size	0.000 (0.000)	− 0.000 (0.000)
Urbanization	0.000 (0.000)+	− 0.000 (0.000)
Process 2001	0.363 (0.165)*	0.580 (0.608)
Service 2001	0.401 (0.164)*	− 0.259 (0.617)
Process 2002	− 0.235 (0.165)	− 0.188 (0.726)
Service 2002	0.005 (0.150)	− 0.081 (0.578)
Process 2003	0.004 (0.163)	0.464 (0.724)
Service 2003	− 0.104 (0.171)	1.624 (0.731)*
Internal perceptual performance 2003	0.513 (0.007)***	–
External perceptual performance 2003	–	0.769 (0.006)***
R2/Adjusted R2	0.655/0.608	0.790/0.750
F	13.993***	19.525***

$+\,p < 0.10, \quad *\,p < 0.05, \quad **\,p < 0.001, ***\,p < 0.0001$
Note: unstandardized coefficients. Standard errors in parenthesis.

affect organizational outcomes. Second, the effects of process and service innovations are felt with two- and three-year lags in the internal performance models (M5 and M7) suggesting that the lag is not just a single one-off event, but that prior innovations continue to have impact beyond their first introduction.[6] However, when we turn to the external performance models (M6 and M8) a different picture emerges – the lag is limited to either two years (Period 1) or one year (Period 2) and is only for service innovations.[7] Third, the duration of lag influences the results. Prior research on impact of innovation on performance have used five-year time periods (see Damanpour and

---

[6] It is unlikely that the results reported in M5 and M7 can be solely attributed to common source bias – both variations in respondents within each local authority from year to year and staff turnover mean that a large proportion of different people are contained in each year sample.

[7] It is possible to speculate that there is variation in the external perceptual measure resulting from human actions. The process of scoring authorities is relatively political and involves a number of stakeholders, the Audit Commission and other inspectorates who provide information to the Audit Commission and government. Other influences on the score may be attributable to the audit and inspection processes within each authority.

Evan 1984; Roberts and Amit 2003). It is possible that our results are affected by the relatively shorter lag periods in our study. Fourth, our results suggest a relatively longer lag effect on internal performance and a shorter lag effect on external performance. It is possible that the external performance models, relying upon updated annual information, overestimate the impact of recent changes, perhaps changes that inspectors at the Audit Commission are expecting.

Finally, the autoregressive performance models (M9 and M10) are shown in table 11.5. The likely greatest determinant of future performance is past performance. If the effects of innovation dissipate in the face of past performance, innovation would be a weak determinant of organizational performance. The results in table 11.5 confirm the strong impact of past performance, and show that the innovation variables found significant in M7 and M8 are also significant ($p < 0.05$) in M9 and M10. This finding suggests that innovation may likely influence performance, but the power of its impact depends on lag periods and varies by the type of innovation and performance measure used.

Conclusions

Within public organizations the evidence base for arguments about impact of innovation on organizational performance and differential effects of type of innovation on the innovation–performance relationship is limited (Damanpour *et al.* 1989; Borins 1998; Light 1998; Walker 2004). In this chapter we responded to this research need and explored the impact of two types of innovation on two measures of organizational performance in English local government over time.

The results generally support the notion that innovation has a positive effect on organizational performance. However, this effect is not consistent across types of innovation or measures of performance. For instance, for the internal measure of performance taken from staff within the local authority, when past performance is controlled, the evidence suggests that both process and service affect performance with a three-year lag. But for the external measure of performance collated by one of local government's key stakeholders, the Audit Commission, the evidence suggests that only service innovations lagged for one year matter. That is, the presumption that both process and service innovations matter is seen in the internal but not external performance models. These findings leave questions about the relative role of service and process innovations, the length of time lag of innovation type, and the role of internal and external performance measures. Because of their theoretical and practical importance, we recommend research for continued examination of these questions in public organizations.

Service and process innovations are 'what' and 'how' innovations (Light 1998). Past research suggests that there are interactive effects from process and service innovation, both within and between years (Damanpour and Evan 1984; Damanpour *et al.* 1989). In the models we ran to explore these interactive effects, the coefficient for the interaction was not significant (data not shown). However, the results from these models are not reliable because the variance inflation factors exceeded ten, the level at which multi-collinearity is problematic. Therefore, while we found significant effects for both process and service innovation when entered independently into our models, we were unable to tests the possible interactive effects of the two types of innovation on performance due to data limitations. Research in the manufacturing context recommends a combined product–process innovation adoption, and argues that the highest returns to organizations occur when there is complementary adoption of both types of innovation, not each alone (Damanpour and Aravind in press). We recommend further exploration of the possible complementary contribution of service–process innovation adoption to organizational effectiveness in public agencies.

Our partial results may be a product of the limitations of this study. First, while we are fortunate to have longitudinal data, a four-year time period would appear to be insufficient length of time to examine the true impact of innovation on performance. Datasets covering longer time periods are therefore required. Second, our measures of innovation are perceptual. Studies that have been able to tease out relationships between innovation and performance have typically used either secondary data sources or datasets where respondents indicate if a particular type of innovation has been adopted and when. Third, English local government is a highly regulated sector. There is substantial isomorphic pressure to adopt particular practices as programmes of reform are rolled out; hence, it is difficult for local authorities to adopt substantially different innovations. It is possible that the systematic oversight system reduces the variation in our data as organizations seek legitimization through innovation. Therefore, tests of innovation–performance relationships in different public service sectors and in different countries with different policy contexts will be necessary to provide more comprehensive evidence on the impact of innovation types on organizational performance.

REFERENCES

Abernathy, W. J., and Utterback, J. M. (1978) Patterns of industrial innovation. *Technology Review* June/July: 40–7.

Aiken, M and Alford, R. R. (1970) Community structure and innovation: the case of urban renewal. *American Sociological Review* 64(5): 650–65.

Aiken, M. and Hage, J. (1968) Organizational interdependence and intra-organizational structure. *American Sociological Review* 33(6): 912–30.

(1971) The organic organization and innovation. *Sociology* 5(1): 63–82.

Amabile, T. M. (1988) A model of creativity and innovation in organizations, in Cummings, L. L. and Staw, B. M. (eds.) *Research in Organizational Behavior*, 10; pp. 123–67.

Andrews, R., Boyne, G. A. Law, J. and Walker, R. M. (2005) External constraints and public sector performance: the case of comprehensive performance assessment in English local government. *Public Administration* 83(3): 639–56.

Andrews, R., Boyne, G. A. and Walker, R. M. (2006) Strategy content and organizational performance: an empirical analysis. *Public Administration Review* 66(1): 52–63.

Audit Commission (2002) *Comprehensive Performance Assessment*. London: Audit Commission.

Barras, R. (1986) Towards a theory of innovation in services. *Research Policy* 15(2): 161–73.

Blair, T. (2002) *The Courage of Our Convictions: Why Reform of the Public Services is the Route to Social Justice*. Fabian Ideas 603, London: Fabian Society.

Borins, S. (1998) *Innovating with Integrity: How Local Heroes are Transforming American Government*. Washington, DC: Georgetown University Press.

Bowman, C. and Ambrosini, V. (1997) Using single respondents in strategy research. *British Journal of Management* 8: 119–32.

Boyne, G. A. 2002. Concepts and indicators of local authority performance: an evaluation of the statutory framework in England and Wales. *Public Money and Management* 22(2): 17–24.

Boyne, G. A., Martin, S. and Walker, R. (2004) Explicit reforms, implicit theories and public service improvement. *Public Management Review* 6(2): 189–210.

Brewer, G. (2006) All measures of performance are subjective: more evidence on US federal agencies, in Boyne, G. A. Meier, K. J. O'Toole, L. J. Jr. and Walker, R. M. (eds.), *Public Service Performance*. Cambridge: Cambridge University Press, pp. 35–54.

Camison-Zornoza, C., Lapiedra-Alcami, R., Segarra-Cipres, M., and Boronat-Navarro, M. (2004) A meta-analysis of innovation and organizational size. *Organization Studies* 25 (2): 331–61.

Carter, N., Klein, R. and Day, P. (1992) *How Organizations Measure Success: The Use Of Performance Indicators In Government*. London: Routledge.

Damanpour, F. (1990) Innovation effectiveness, adoption and organizational performance, in West, M. and Farr, J. (eds.) *Innovation and Creativity at Work*, London: Wiley, pp. 125–41.

Damanpour, F. and Aravind, D. (in press) Product and process innovations: a review of organizational and environmental determinants, in Hage, J. and Meeus, M. (eds.) *Innovation, Science, and Industrial Change: The Handbook of Research*, New York: Oxford University Press, pp. 38–66.

Damanpour, F. and Evan, W. M. (1984) Organizational innovation and performance: the problem of 'organizational lag'. *Administrative Science Quarterly* **29**(2): 392–409.

Damanpour, F. and Gopalakrishnan, S. (2001) The dynamics of the adoption of product and process innovations in organizations. *Journal of Management Studies* **38**(1): 45–65.

Damanpour, F., Szabat, K. A. and Evan, W. M. (1989) The relationship between types of innovation and organizational performance. *Journal of Management Studies* **26**: 587–601.

Department of Environment, Transport and Regions. (2000) *Indices of Multiple Deprivation*. London: DETR.

Down, A. (1966) *Inside Bureaucracy*. Boston: Little, Brown, and Company.

Drazin, R., and Schoonhoven, C. B. (1996) Community, population, and organization effects on innovation: a multilevel perspective. *Academy of Management Journal* **39**(6): 1065–83.

Enticott, G., and Walker, R. M. (2006) Sustainability, strategy and performance: an empirical analysis of public organizations. *Business Strategy and the Environment* **17**(2): 79–92.

Edquist, C., Hommen, L., and McKelvey, M. (2001) *Innovation and Employment: Process versus Product Innovation*, Cheltenham: Edward Elgar.

Ettlie, J. E., Bridges, W. P., and O'Keefe, R. D. (1984) Organization strategy and structural differences for radical versus incremental innovation. *Management Science* **30**(5): 682–95.

Evan, W. M. (1976) Organization theory and organizational effectiveness: an exploratory analysis. *Organization and Administrative Sciences* **7**(1): 15–28.

Germain, R. (1996). The role of context and structure in radical and incremental logistics innovation adoption. *Journal of Business Research* **35**(1): 117–27.

Kelly, J. M., and Swindell, D. (2002) A multiple-indicator approach to municipal service evaluation: correlating performance measurement and citizen satisfaction across jurisdictions. *Public Administration Review* **62**: 610–20.

Kimberly, J. R., and Evanisko, M. J. (1981) Organizational innovation: the influence of individual, organizational, and contextual factors on hospital adoption of technological and administrative innovation. *Academy of Management Journal* **24**(5): 689–713.

Light, P. C. (1998) *Sustaining Innovation. Creating Nonprofit and Government Organizations that Innovate Naturally*. San Francisco: Jossey-Bass.

Martin, S., Walker, R. M. Ashworth, R. *et al.* (2003). *The Long Term Evaluation of Best Value and Its Impact: Baseline Report*. London: Office of the Deputy Prime Minister.

Newman, J., Raine, J. and Skelcher, C. (2001) Transforming local government: innovation and modernization. *Public Money and Management* **21**(2): 61–8.

Nystrom, P. C., Ramamurthy, K., and Wilson, A. L. (2002) Organizational context, climate and innovativeness: adoption of imaging technology. *Journal of Engineering Technology Management* **19**: 221–47.

OECD (2005) *Modernizing Government. The Way Forward*. Paris: Office for Economic Cooperation and Development.

Office for National Statistics (2003) Census, 2001. *National Report for England and Wales* London: Office for National Statistics.

OPSR, (2002) *Reforming Our Public Services: Principles into Practice*. London: The Prime Minister's Office of Public Service Reform.

Osborne, S. (1998) *Voluntary Organizations and Innovation in Public Services*. London: Routledge.

Ostrom, E. (1973) 'The need for multiple indicators of measuring the output of public agencies', *Policy Studies Journal*, **2**(2): 85–91.

Park, R. (1984) Linking objective and subjective measures of performance. *Public Administration Review* **44**(2): 118–27.

Pollitt C. and Bouckeart G. (2000) *Public Management Reform: A Comparative Analysis* Oxford: Oxford University Press.

Roberts, P. W. and Amit. R. (2003). The dynamics of innovative activity and competitive advantage: the case of Australian retail banking, 1981 to 1995. *Organization Science* **14** (1): 107–22.

Rogers, E. (1995) *Diffusion of Innovation* New York: The Free Press.

Subramanian, A. and Nilakanta, S. (1996) Organizational innovativeness: exploring the relationship between organizational determinants of innovation, types of innovations, and measures of organizational performance. *Omega* **24**(4): 631–47.

Tidd, J. (2001) Innovation management in context: environment, organization and performance. *International Journal of Management Review* **3**(3): 169–83.

Tornatzky, L. G. and Fleisher, M. (1990) *The Process of Technological Innovation*. Lexington, MA: Lexington Books.

Venkatraman, N. and Ramanjum, V. (1986) Measurement of business performance in strategy research: a comparison of approaches. *Academy of Management Review* **11**(5): 801–14.

Walker, R. M. (2004). Innovation and organizational performance: evidence and a research agenda. AIM Research Working Papers Series, London: AIM Research, www.aimresearch.org.

  (2006) Innovation type and diffusion: an empirical analysis of local government *Public Administration* **84**(2): 311–35.

Walker, R. M. and Boyne., G. (2006) Public management reform and organizational performance: an empirical assessment of the UK Labour government's public service improvement strategy. *Journal of Policy Analysis and Management* **25**(2): 371–93.

Walker, R. M. and Enticott, G. (2004) Using multiple-informants in public administration: revisiting the managerial values and actions debate. *Journal of Public Administration Research and Theory* **14**(3): 417–34.

West, M. A. and Farr, J. L. (1990) Innovation at work, in West, M. A. and Farr, J. L. (eds.) *Innovation and Creativity at Work*, New York: Wiley, pp. 3–13.

Wischnevsky, J. D. and Damanpour, F. (2006). Organizational transformation and performance: an examination of three perspectives. *Journal of Managerial Issue* **18**(1): 104–22.

Wolfe, R. A. (1994) Organizational innovation: review, critique, and suggested research directions. *Journal of Management Studies* **31**(2): 405–31.

Zaltman, G., Duncan, R., and Holbek, J. (1973) *Innovations and Organizations*. New York: Wiley.

Public service failure and turnaround: towards a contingency model

George Boyne

Measures of performance have been a central feature of public service reforms across the globe during the last twenty years. Public organizations have been increasingly subject to a proliferation of performance indicators and a variety of external judgement on their achievements (or lack of them). As a result, although performance measures are always open to a variety of interpretations, it has become evident that public service performance varies across organizations, across geographical areas and over time (Boyne 2006). Some client groups and local areas appear to receive effective services that meet their needs, whereas others are offered poor quality and low value for money (Andrews and Boyne 2008). Similarly, some organizations maintain high service standards while others bump along the bottom of the performance table, and yet others waver between adequacy and mediocrity (Jas and Skelcher 2005).

Why does service failure occur in the public sector, and what strategies are likely to lead to a turnaround in performance? In what sense do public organizations 'fail', and which turnaround strategies fit different types of failure? My aims in this chapter are to review theories and evidence on these questions, and to develop a new contingency model which suggests that the effectiveness of different public service turnaround strategies will depend on the nature and causes of failure. This is in contrast to universalistic prescriptions for turnaround, which assume that the same remedies will work in all circumstances. Testable propositions on failure and turnaround in the public sector are also specified.

In the first part of the chapter, the extent of public service failure in England is summarized, and research on types of failure is reviewed. In the second section, two different types of failure are identified, and the circumstances under which they are likely to occur are discussed. In the third section, different turnaround strategies are analysed, and their relative effectiveness is then linked to the types of failure. This section draws upon evidence from the UK and US on the turnaround strategies that have been adopted in public organizations. Finally, the implications of the analysis for the theory and practice of recovery from public service failure are considered.

Failure in the public sector

A historical perspective on the balance between public service success and failure is difficult to establish because information on organizational performance has been scarce until recent years. This did not prevent some commentators, such as public choice theorists, from pronouncing that failure is endemic in the public sector (e.g. Niskanen 1971), usually on the basis of a comparison with an idealized model of perfect competition in the private sector (Boyne *et al.* 2003). The emergence of an emphasis on performance indicators, as part of the global reform programme associated with new public management, has facilitated comparisons of the achievements of different organizations. It is now possible, within the limits of the published indicators, to judge the standing of different schools, hospitals, police forces and a variety of other service providers.

As a result, it is easier to assess whether a service provider is failing in an absolute sense (e.g. children in the care of social services are suffering abuse, hospital patients are dying, homeless households are unable to obtain accommodation). Furthermore, the *relative* performance of different organizations is more visible, often in the form of a 'league table' ranking. Such league tables literally 'create' failure, because even if all organizations are performing well in absolute terms, some are bound to be located in the bottom places. Nowhere has policy-makers' desire for such comparisons advanced further than in the UK, and in England in particular. There is a long tradition of assessing the performance of public service providers in the UK that stretches back to the nineteenth century. For example, central government allocated some of its earliest funding to local school boards on the basis of pupils' achievements on reading, writing and arithmetic (Rhodes 1981). The use of performance indicators did not, however, become widespread until the 1980s and 1990s when they were given a substantial policy boost by the Thatcher and Major governments. For example, under the 1992 Local Government Act, local authorities were required to publish annually over 200 indicators of their expenditure, activities and accomplishments (Boyne 1997). This laid a path that would eventually lead to widespread judgement of failure in local service provision.

The performance indicators industry expanded sharply in the UK with the advent of New Labour in 1997. The first Blair government sought to replace the pressures on public services associated with quasi-markets and

Table 12.1: Failing English public services 2002–4

Type of public service	Number of failures (and % of type of organization)
Health trusts	73 (12%)
Local authorities	25 (7%)
Education authorities	2 (1%)
Social services departments	11 (7%)
Schools	465 (2%)
Other local authority services	178 (12%)
Police services (parts thereof)	12 (9%)
Fire authorities	5 (11%)
Prisons	3 (2%)

Source: Andrews and Boyne 2008.

competitive tendering with the pressures of regulation (Boyne 1998). This regulatory regime had two elements. First, the refinement and expansion of performance indicators to cover almost all public services, accompanied by the publication of league tables on government websites (see, for example, www.dfes.gov.uk/performance for school league tables). Second, the extension of inspection systems from a narrow range of services (e.g. education, social services, policing) to all local government and health services. Thus the 'web' of potential failure spread to cover almost the whole public sector (except, of course, central government itself), and became two dimensional (performance indicators and inspection).

By the start of the twenty-first century, then, the 'technology' was in place to diagnose and expose public service failures that might previously have been missed by central government. The regulatory regime left poor performers in England with few places to hide (the devolved governments in other parts of the UK took a different approach, going so far as to abolish school league tables in Wales and 'naming and faming' high performers in Scotland, in contrast to the policy of 'naming and shaming' the under-achievers in England). The consequence was a sudden surge in the number of public service providers that were publicly labelled as 'failing', following visits by government inspectors. Between 2002 and 2004 the performance of over 1,000 public organizations in England was deemed to be unacceptable, including primary schools, hospitals and whole local authorities (see table 12.1).

The specific criteria and procedures used by inspectorates vary across services (see appendix), but all of them take into account both the substantive results achieved by public organizations and the management arrangements that are used to achieve these results. For example, hospitals are evaluated on the basis of patient well-being, staff development and information management; local authorities are assessed on their service performance and their 'corporate capacity' to improve; schools are ranked not only on the basis of pupils' exam results and behaviour, but also on the quality of leadership and management; and the police service is examined on crime figures and a range of strategies for finance, human resources and leadership.

Thus all of these systems for identifying the extent of public service failure are a blend of judgements on current service performance and the adequacy of managerial strategies and processes for securing improvements in future. These criteria map neatly onto two different theoretical types of failure, which relate to the *results* that are achieved and the *legitimacy* of the characteristics of organizations. The theoretical basis of each of these types of failure is now explored in more detail.

Results, legitimacy and failure

An important axiom in the strategic management literature is that organizations are high performers if they are closely aligned with their environment (Donaldson 1996). The external circumstances faced by organizations can in turn be decomposed into two parts: a 'technical' environment that imposes pressures towards better substantive results (e.g. efficiency, effectiveness), and an 'institutional' environment that constrains organizations to adopt particular internal characteristics. Thus public organizations are likely to be judged as performing well if their stakeholders believe that they are producing the right results in the right way. Similarly, two types of failure can be distinguished. The first occurs when an organization is delivering the wrong results (e.g. low scores on performance indicators). The second type of failure occurs when organizations are delivering services in a way that is regarded as illegitimate by key stakeholders, regardless of the results that are being achieved. It is important to distinguish clearly between these two types of failure, because they have very different implications for the turnaround strategies that are likely to be effective.

Poor results

It has been widely argued that public service performance is a complex and multi-dimensional concept (Boyne 2003). Comparisons of the success or failure of different organizations are problematic for several reasons. First, performance can be interpreted in many different ways which include service quantity, quality, efficiency, equity, effectiveness, consumer satisfaction and value for money. Second, performance is judged by a variety of stakeholders such as service users, producers (professionals and managers), taxpayers and politicians. Different groups are likely to emphasize different dimensions of performance (for example, consumers may give priority to service quality whereas taxpayers are most concerned with value for money). Thus even if different stakeholders include the same performance criteria in their 'decision set', they are likely to attach different weights and so arrive at conflicting judgements on the extent of success or failure. Furthermore, even if the criteria and weights are identical, different measures of performance may be preferred by different stakeholders (for example, doctors may choose a measure of health service quality that is based on professional judgement, whereas patients prefer a measure based on their subjective assessment of their own well-being).

Comprehensive and accurate measures of failure would incorporate these complexities and recognize that any assessment of performance is a fuzzy mosaic rather than a simple picture. Yet, the recent trend towards ranking public organizations in league tables ignores all of this and instead assumes that performance can be compressed and conflated into a single indicator. For example, the Comprehensive Performance Assessment regime in England places each local authority into one of five bands: excellent, good, fair, weak and poor. This is based on two elements: current service provision, as judged by a 'core service performance' score, and 'prospects for improvement' (see appendix). The core service performance score is derived from statutory indicators of service outputs and outcomes that are set by central government, measures of consumer satisfaction, and 'reality checks' made by Audit Commission inspectors. Two local government services (education and social services) are given twice as much weight as the others (e.g. housing, planning) in calculating the overall score.

This measure of failure, and others in the English public sector, is based on a number of questionable assumptions. First, that the perceptions of only three stakeholder groups matter: central government, service consumers and inspectors (who themselves can be regarded as a proxy for their paymaster, central government). The views of some potentially important groups, such as public service professionals, are missing from the mysterious formula that generates the final score. Second, the views of these different stakeholders can somehow be added together, rather than representing separate and legitimately different perceptions of the same phenomenon. Furthermore, the method of combination, and the relative weights accorded to the different stakeholders, remains opaque. Third, the value of different services provided by multi-functional organizations is either '1' or '2'. In the case of the CPA, education and social services are equal to each other and apparently worth about as much as all the other services put together. The methodology that underlies this weighting system remains unclear. A better (or at least more explicit) approach would have been to weight different services by their share of local government spending, their contribution to final outcomes (e.g. economic prosperity) or their valuations in citizen surveys. Finally, a standard valuation of every service at 1 or 2 (or any other combination) implies geographical uniformity in stakeholder preferences. If, however, the ultimate test of public services is their impact on public welfare, then the relative contribution of different services to this objective is likely to vary with local circumstances (e.g. deprivation, demographic composition).

None of this should be taken to imply that public service performance cannot be measured. Rather, failure is to a large extent in the eye of the beholder. If any of the assumptions that underlie the CPA process are altered, then the relative positions of authorities in the 'hall of shame' are likely to change. The boundaries between adjacent categories (e.g. between weak and poor, or good and excellent) are especially likely to be blurred and difficult to delineate precisely. This type of sensitivity analysis has not been a feature of regimes for judging failure in public services.

Despite the limitations of the criteria and procedures for identifying poor performance in the public sector, at least judgement of 'results failure' focuses on the service outputs and outcomes that are actually produced. In other words, this first type of failure suggests, however loosely, that the worst public organizations are making a contribution to public welfare that is weak (or, in extreme cases, negative). By contrast, the second type of failure is concerned not with the value of this contribution but with *how* it is created.

Low legitimacy

Institutional theorists argue that organizations are regarded as legitimate if they conform to the expectations of powerful groups in their environment (Meyer and Rowan 1977). Over time, most organizations adopt legitimate structures and processes as a result of three sets of 'isomorphic pressures' (Powell and DiMaggio 1991). First, coercive pressures imposed by the state through legislation and regulations that constrain their discretion. Most public management reform programmes have a statutory basis and are backed up by a battery of governmental edicts on the characteristics that organizations are expected to adopt. Second, normative pressures that seek to add moral persuasion to legal sanctions. In the contemporary public sector such pressures include the views of professional bodies and 'umbrella' organizations (e.g. the Local Government Association and the Improvement and Development Agency for English local authorities). Third, mimetic pressures that lead organizations to copy each other, and in particular to emulate the management arrangements of those that are believed to be prestigious and successful. The boom in process benchmarking in the public sector in recent years seems likely to have reinforced such mimicry.

Organizations that follow managerial fashion by conforming with these isomorphic pressures are more likely to be viewed as performing well. By contrast, the deviants who stick with 'outmoded' structures and processes are more likely to be judged as failures. These organizations fail not because they are inefficient or ineffective but because they are unattractive to the gaze of their judges.

This perspective on organizational performance is based on the assumption that external stakeholders are interested at least as much in legitimacy as in tangible outcomes. Indeed, the two conceptions of performance are connected because organizations that are isomorphic with prevailing conceptions of legitimacy are believed to be more efficient and effective. In other words, the interpretation of the same set of performance data will be different, depending on whether management arrangements are viewed as legitimate or illegitimate. Furthermore, real connections between the two interpretations of performance are likely to be present. Organizations that are judged as legitimate are more likely to receive support from their political superiors, regulators, external partners in service provision and other stakeholders (Dacin 1997). Such support, which may take the form of political or economic resources, is likely to facilitate the achievement of better results (Oliver 1997; Staw and Epstein 2000). Similarly, low legitimacy can trigger a spiral of decline that leads to poor substantive performance. Eitel (2004: 244) shows how a regional government agency in the US was initially branded a failure because 'official policies were not being properly followed ... [it] was seen as not demonstrating good corporate citizenship, and it was not held in high esteem'. This resulted in difficulties in acquiring good staff and financial resources, internal conflict, weak results and the eventual closure of the agency.

Legitimacy is clearly a core criterion that is used by inspectors when judging the performance of public services in England (see appendix). For example the 'ability to improve' element of the CPA takes into account goal clarity, corporate capacity, performance management and measurement, and the quality of planning. The emphasis on legitimacy is perhaps most explicit in the inspection regime for the fire service which tests whether local fire departments are 'delivering the modernization agenda'. Other procedures that are regarded as 'best practice' in contemporary public service provision include partnership with the private sector (Boyne and Enticott 2004).

The impact of this emphasis on legitimacy in judgement of failure is revealed by a comparative analysis of the performance of local authorities in England and Wales (Andrews *et al.* 2003). Welsh local authorities perform slightly better than their English counterparts on seventy-one statutory indicators of service achievements. Yet, they are significantly more likely to be judged as failing by Audit Commission inspectors. A comparison of inspection reports, and interviews with inspectors, showed that Welsh authorities were viewed as slow to modernize, too reliant on direct provision of services, and lacking corporate capacity. Good service results, then, were not enough: the 'wrong' structures and processes led to a disproportionate number of them being branded as failures.

The relative importance of poor results and low legitimacy

Current inspection regimes for judging public service failure in England are based partly on the results achieved and partly on organizational characteristics. The relative importance of results and legitimacy is not explicit in the inspection guidelines for different services and is not easy to infer, especially in inspection regimes that combine both dimensions of failure in a single measure (e.g. the CPA for district councils in England). It seems likely, however, that the relative influence of results and legitimacy on judgement of failure varies across services. Two variables that seem likely to affect the balance between results and legitimacy are the *measurability of service achievements* and the *structuration of the institutional environment*.

Public services vary in the extent to which their achievements are tangible and measurable. At one end of the scale is a service such as street cleaning which has the objective of removing refuse from public spaces. The effectiveness of this service is fairly easy to track: are public highways clean, has litter been removed, and how do levels of cleanliness compare across geographical areas and over time? These are service outcomes that can be observed and checked (indeed photographic evidence of street scenes is often used alongside numeric indicators of performance). By contrast, some services have remote goals that are difficult to measure. For example, a major responsibility of local authority social services departments is to improve the welfare and happiness of children in their care. The quality of the 'life experience' of their clients is clearly a highly subjective phenomenon, and the results achieved may be spread over many years. Indeed, it might be argued that success can only be judged when the children in care have lived a substantial part of their adult life.

When outcomes are easily measurable it seems likely that service results will be an important element of judgement of failure. By contrast, in the absence of clear and reliable evidence on results, government inspectors and other stakeholders are more likely to rely on assessments of the legitimacy of organization arrangements for service delivery. These arguments lead to the following propositions, all of which are stated *ceteris paribus*:

P1:   The relative importance of results and legitimacy in judgement of failure is influenced by the measurability of service outcomes.

P1a: Public organizations with outcomes that are easy to measure are more likely to fail on results than legitimacy.

P1b: Public organizations with outcomes that are difficult to measure are more likely to fail on legitimacy than results.

A second influence on the balance between results and legitimacy in failure judgement is the strength of the institutional norms that constrain organizational structures and processes. Institutional theorists refer to this as the extent of the structuration of the environment (Powell and DiMaggio 1991). In a highly structured organizational field, the norms for management arrangements have become well established over a long period, and are tightly defined by complementary coercive, normative and mimetic pressures. For example, local education authorities in the UK have existed for over a hundred years and have been subject to successive waves of management reforms that have sought to standardize their behaviour and procedures. Moreover, education managers belong to strong professional bodies, which facilitates both normative and mimetic constraints on their strategies and behaviour. By contrast, institutional constraints are likely to be weaker when structuration has not occurred – for example, when an organizational field is new, or when there are 'competing institutional logics' which blunt or blur isomorphic pressures. Organizations set up to fight the 'war on terror' on the home front largely fit this description: their emergence is recent, and significant debate and conflict exists on the balance between protecting public safety and protecting civil liberties.

When institutional norms are highly structured it is likely that legitimacy will be a strong influence on judgement of failure. In this context, stakeholders will know what a 'good' organization looks like, and take deviance as evidence of failure. If institutional norms have not become sedimented and settled, however, the role of legitimacy in assessments of success and failure is likely to weaken. In this case, attention is likely to focus on results (assuming that such evidence is available). This leads to a second set of linked propositions.

P2:   The relative importance of results and legitimacy in judgement of failure is influenced by the level of structuration in an organizational field.

P2a: Public organizations in a strongly structurated field are more likely to fail on legitimacy than results.

P2b: Public organizations in a weakly structurated field are more likely to fail on results than legitimacy.

An evaluation of the validity of the propositions specified in this section of the chapter would require information on failure in a variety of services with different levels of outcome measurability and structuration. This would involve data on the results/legitimacy balance in failure judgement, the measurability of service achievements and the strength of institutional norms. The continuing attachment of the UK government to performance indicators, public service inspection and a programme of modernization gives public management researchers an excellent opportunity to explore these issues.

Poor results, low legitimacy and turnaround strategies

What actions should be taken to deal with public service failure? How do public organizations that achieve turnaround differ from those which continue to fail? Systematic public sector studies that address these questions have not yet been published. Most of the research that has been undertaken so far comprises 'success stories' of single public organizations in the US that have achieved turnaround (Boyne 2006). These studies provide interesting accounts of strategies that were followed by failing organizations which achieved better performance. However, no comparisons are made with organizations that continued to perform poorly which may, for all we know, have followed the very same strategies.

A small number of case studies of turnaround in the UK have recently appeared, but these display similar methodological problems to their US counterparts. For example, Joyce (2004) analyses the role of a new chief executive in the turnaround of Newham Borough Council in London between 1996 and 1999, but neither explains why previous leadership changes were not accompanied by similarly positive results, nor takes account of other influences on performance improvement (such as more favourable external circumstances – see Andrews *et al.* 2006). Turner and Whiteman track the progress of fifteen English local authorities that were categorized as poor or weak in the 2002 CPA. By 2004 all but three of these had improved by at least one CPA grade. However, the strategic differences between those that continued to fail and those that escaped from this position are unclear.

More systematic evidence on the effectiveness of different turnaround strategies is provided by research on failing firms in the private sector. Many studies have examined the differences between organizations that recover and those that are stuck in failure. These studies typically use large samples of companies in distress and evaluate statistically whether the strategies of the firms that achieve turnaround are significantly different from the strategies of firms that continue to fail. The evidence suggests that three major generic strategies are associated with turnaround (Boyne 2006).

First, *retrenchment* which consists of reductions in the scope or size of an organization. In the private sector, the emphasis is on making cuts in parts of the business that are unproductive and unprofitable. This in turn can release resources for investment in areas that seem likely to deliver higher performance. Retrenchment can include exit from markets where the firm is performing poorly, or contraction of activities in a market by selling assets or reducing the scale of operations, with the aim of increasing efficiency. A second turnaround strategy which appears to be successful is *repositioning*. Whereas retrenchment can be viewed as an 'efficiency' strategy, repositioning is an 'entrepreneurial' strategy that emphasizes growth and innovation (Schendel and Paton 1976). This response to failure involves a new definition of the mission and core activities of an organization, by becoming more dominant in an existing market or by diversifying into new markets and products.

The final turnaround strategy which has been found to be effective is *reorganization*. This term is used in studies of turnaround as a broad description of any change in the internal management of an organization. The purpose of reorganization may be to support strategies of retrenchment or repositioning, or simply to improve the implementation of the current strategy without any alteration in the size or market position of a company. Reorganization can involve changes in planning systems, the extent of decentralization, styles of human resource management or organizational culture. The form of reorganization that is cited most frequently in the literature on private sector turnaround is the replacement of the chief executive or the entire senior management team. It has been widely argued that this is a necessary condition for the reversal of company decline (Mueller and Barker 1997). Furthermore, the appointment of new top managers can be an important signal that a failing organization is 'serious about recovery'.

Translated into a public sector context, these strategies imply cutting back inefficient or ineffective parts of services (retrenchment), perhaps by downsizing or contracting-out; developing new services and extending existing services to neglected client groups (repositioning); and changing the internal characteristics of service providers (reorganization). All of these strategies are feasible in the public sector, and each of them has been attempted by failing organizations (Boyne 2006). For example, the Bureau of Motor Equipment in New York followed a strategy of retrenchment by cutting expenditure on staff overtime and reducing its stocks of materials (Contino and Larossu 1982); the Pennsylvania Department of Transportation pursued repositioning by changing the balance of its activities and altering stakeholders perceptions of its performance (Poister and Larson 1988); and the Houston Police Department reorganized by appointing a new Chief of Police, decentralizing its budgets and reforming its strategic planning system (Moore 1995). Reorganization in the public sector might also involve a whole service *system* rather than a single organization (for example, a local education authority might need to be reorganized to improve the performance of failing schools within its boundaries).

Although the technical and political feasibility of these strategies has been examined, the 'big question' in public service turnaround has not been addressed: do retrenchment, repositioning and reorganization lead to recovery from failure? This question is, in fact, too crude, because it assumes that the impact of organizational strategies is universalistic rather than contingent. In other words, the same strategies are likely to work regardless of the circumstances faced by a failing organization. One important circumstance that is likely to influence the effectiveness of a turnaround strategy is the type of failure that has occurred. Is an organization deemed to be failing because of weak results or low legitimacy?

A public service provider that is suffering from poor scores on indicators of its substantive performance is unlikely to gain much from a strategy of reorganization alone. This may be equivalent to 'rearranging the deck chairs on the Titanic'. In order to improve poor service results it is necessary to change *what* is provided rather than *how* it is provided. This may involve retrenchment in conjunction with repositioning, in order to release resources and redeploy them more productively elsewhere. This leads to the following proposition on turnaround strategies:

P3:   Public organizations that are deemed to be failing because of poor results are more likely to recover if they emphasize strategies of retrenchment and repositioning rather than reorganization.

This is not to argue that reorganization has no role to play in recovery from inadequate service achievements. Indeed, reorganization may support the other two turnaround strategies – for example, the implementation of cuts and reorientation towards a new set of objectives may be easier with a new chief executive and senior management team. Reorganization in this case, however, is a moderating variable rather than the major driving force in securing better results.

The implications for turnaround strategies are different if an organization is judged as failing as a consequence of low legitimacy. In this case, by assumption, the results being achieved are tolerable to external stakeholders (indeed, the service performance of some local authorities judged as 'poor' or 'weak' was in some respects excellent – see Turner and Whiteman 2005). Under these circumstances, little may be gained from strategies of retrenchment and repositioning. Moreover, these strategies may be counterproductive in distracting management attention from the real source of failure: how the organization *looks* in the eyes of powerful groups such as central government and service inspectors. The only practical solution to low legitimacy is to become more legitimate through a strategy of reorganization that leads to structures and processes that fit prevailing institutional norms. Thus,

P4:   Organizations that are deemed to be failing because of low legitimacy are more likely to recover if they pursue a strategy of reorganization rather than retrenchment and repositioning.

The number of discrete reorganization strategies that are available is potentially huge: any internal characteristics can be reformed in an attempt to become more appealing to powerful external groups. However, the menu of options is usually narrowed by the general norms of good management that currently prevail, and by the specific problems highlighted in inspectors' reports. One fashionable prescription in recent years has been 'new leadership', so this is likely to feature prominently in current reorganization strategies that seek to boost legitimacy. This stems in part from research on the impact of executive succession in the private sector, which suggests that new senior managers can significantly boost organizational performance (Boyne and Dahya 2002). Although the replacement of the top manager (or a whole managerial team) may lead to higher legitimacy in the public sector, this may not have the dramatic impact on results that is associated with this strategy in the private sector. The scope for radical strategic change (e.g. exiting an existing product market, moving into new geographical and product markets, replacing labour with capital) is more limited in public than private organizations (Boyne and Walker 2004). This reinforces the argument that turnaround strategies that have strong effects on legitimacy may have weak effects on results, and vice versa.

An evaluation of the empirical validity of P3 and P4 would involve a number of stages. First, the selection of a sample of failing public organizations (probably in the same sub-sector to remove extraneous effects on turnaround that vary between services). Second, qualitative analysis and coding of inspection reports, to establish the relative balance of poor results and low legitimacy in organizations that are judged as failing. Third, tracking turnaround strategies over time, and in particular the extent of retrenchment, repositioning and reorganization. Fourth, a comparison of turnaround and non-turnaround, to evaluate whether the extent of recovery is related to the fit between the type of failure and the strategies that were selected. As table 12.1 shows, the large number of failures, together with the public availability of inspection reports, provides a firm foundation for such an analysis.

Conclusions

Public service failure and turnaround are issues of pressing practical concern in most nations, yet theoretical and empirical research in this field is sparse. In this chapter it has been shown that judgement of failure draws upon two different conceptions of organizational performance: one emphasizes the substantive results of service provision, and the other emphasizes the formal legitimacy of management arrangements. This distinction is the basis of a model of failure and turnaround that is contingent in two respects.

First, the type of failure that befalls a public service provider is contingent upon the measurability of its results and the structuration of its institutional environment. Failure is more likely to be ascribed to poor results when measurability is high and isomorphic pressures and institutional norms are weak; and more likely to be the product of low legitimacy when measurability is low and institutional forces are strong. Second, the effectiveness of turnaround strategies is contingent on the type of failure that has occurred. Reorganization is more likely to lead a failing service provider to be reclassified as 'improving' or 'successful' if its problems are defined by external stakeholders as a lack of legitimacy. Similarly, the impact of retrenchment and repositioning is more likely to be positive if an organization is suffering from poor results.

These are not, by any means, the only contingencies that influence the success of turnaround strategies. For example, their impact may also be moderated by the depth of decline and the external environment of failing organizations. These issues could be explored productively through cross-national research that examines failure and turnaround in the same service in different countries, but in contexts with different levels of performance measurability and institutional structuration. All of this suggests that there are many routes to recovery and that the map that leads from failure to success is complex. The consequence is that models of failure and turnaround need to be explicated clearly, and theorized as comprising contingent links between cause and effect. This chapter has taken a step in that direction.

Appendix: Performance classification schemes for public organizations in England

Health

The Department of Health introduced a system for rating the performance of English National Health Service (NHS) hospitals in 2001, applying this in 2002 to ambulance, mental health and specialist trusts, and to primary care trusts in 2003. The NHS performance ratings range from 0 stars (poor performance) to 3 stars (high performance). Hospitals and ambulance, mental health and specialist trusts are assessed using key targets and performance indicators drawn from three 'focus areas': clinical, patients, and capacity and capability. Assessment criteria, targets and indicators for these types of trust include: hospital cleanliness and infections control for hospitals, call management and transport management for ambulance trusts, and assertive outreach and psychiatric readmissions for mental health trusts. Primary care trusts are assessed using key targets and performance indicators drawn from three different 'focus areas': health improvement, service access and service provision. The assessments of ambulance, mental health and primary care trusts are also based on clinical governance reviews which examine organizational processes such as staff development and information management. A trust's performance rating can be downgraded to zero stars on the basis of its clinical governance review if it reveals significant areas of weakness.

Local authorities

All local authorities in England are subject to Comprehensive Performance Assessment (CPA) which classifies performance into five categories (poor, weak, fair, good and excellent). For upper-tier local authorities (London boroughs, Metropolitan boroughs, unitary and county councils) the CPA scores are obtained from judgement about a local authority's core service performance and its ability to improve. For lower-tier authorities (district councils) CPA scores are based primarily on a 'corporate assessment'.

Six core services (education, social care, environment, housing, libraries and leisure and benefits) together with 'management of resources' are included in the service performance element of the upper-tier CPA. Each service is given a score from 1 (lowest) to 4 (highest), derived from performance indicators, inspection results, and service plans and standards. Ability to improve ratings for upper-tier CPAs concentrate on: 'what the council wants to achieve' (ambition, focus and prioritization), 'how the council sets about what it wants to achieve' (capacity and performance measurement), 'what the council has/has not achieved' (improvements achieved and investment) and 'what the council plans to do next' (learning and future plan). Each council is given a score 1 (lowest) to 4 (highest), derived from a corporate inspection, an assessment of prospects for improvement, and a self-review. Overall CPA judgements are then produced by combining the core performance score with the ability to improve score, with certain provisos about minimum thresholds of performance across all service areas.

Corporate assessments for district council CPAs evaluate ambition, prioritization, focus, capacity, performance management, achievement of service quality, achievement of improvement, investment, learning, and future plans. Each council is given a score of 1 to 4 on these themes, derived from service diagnostics, performance indicators and a self-review.

Social services

The Audit Commission and the Social Services Inspectorate conducted Joint Reviews of social services performance from 1996 until late 2003. In 2004, reviews were replaced by star ratings produced by the Commission for Social Care Inspection, which are released in conjunction with CPAs. Joint Reviews assessed and categorized the performance of social services as 'not serving people well', 'serving some people well', 'serving most people well' or 'overall serving people well', and their prospects for improving as 'poor', 'uncertain', 'promising' or 'excellent'. Performance judgements were based on performance data and 'reality checks', with improvement judgements based on the improvement planning carried out by services.

Inspectors of social services assessed the achievements of social service departments on national indicators and on selected local indicators by comparing them with similar authorities, with councils' own targets and with relevant national standards (Social Services Inspectorate 2002). Departments are also expected to show that they have developed an effective improvement planning processes. To evaluate this, reviews asked four key questions: is performance managed effectively? Are you getting Best Value for money? Are individuals well served? Do you plan well for your communities' needs? (Audit Commission 2001: 6)

Education

Local education authorities

Local education authorities (LEAs) are assessed as part of the CPA process. A council's individual score on education represents the quality of the education service provided by the LEA. A failing LEA is, therefore, one which scores 1 for CPA service performance.

Schools

The Office for Standards in Education (Ofsted) has carried out school inspection since 1993. On completion of inspection, schools are deemed satisfactory or unsatisfactory, with unsatisfactory schools either judged as having serious weaknesses or requiring special measures. An Ofsted evaluation schedule guides the judgement made by inspectors on the effectiveness of all primary, secondary and special schools.

Inspections start with an analysis of available evidence on outcomes, particularly examination results. As they progress, inspectors make judgement on a school's achievements and focus on the reasons for them. To accomplish this, they consider the success of the school, what it should do to improve, the standards of its achievements, pupils' attitudes and values, the effectiveness of teaching and learning, the school's relationship with parents, other schools and the community, and how well the school is led and managed.

Other local authority services

The Audit Commission has assessed the performance of local authority services since 1999. The performance of individual services is assessed and categorized as 'poor', 'fair', 'good' or 'excellent', and prospects for improving as 'poor', 'uncertain', 'promising' or 'excellent'. Judgements are based on performance data and 'reality checks', with improvement judgement based primarily on inspection of an authority's improvement planning.

Inspectors assess the achievements of councils against national indicators and on selected local indicators by comparing them with similar authorities, with councils' own targets and with any relevant national standards. Services are also expected to show that they have developed effective improvement planning processes. To arrive at their final judgement on the quality of local services, inspectors ask three key questions: are the authority's aims clear and challenging? Does the service meet these aims? How does its performance compare? To arrive at their final judgement of the prospects for improvement, inspectors ask: what is the evidence of service improvement? How good are the current improvement plans? Will improvement be delivered? Inspection results are summarized in a scoring chart which plots performance against prospects for improvement. Typically a poor service is in a council with weak 'performance management and planning systems', and is 'unable to secure direction and support from members'. In general, they also 'lack the capacity to achieve the improvement required from their own resources' (Audit Commission 2001: 30).

Fire and criminal justice

Fire service

The Audit Commission began inspecting the Fire Service in 2004. Every fire authority was graded on 'how successfully they are modernizing' using a traffic light system (green – good progress, amber – some progress, red – little or no progress). Inspectors assess: the Integrated Risk Management Plan (IRMP); the extent of change from a rank- to a role-based occupational structure; the Integrated Personal Development System (IPDS); using pre-planned overtime; planning for alternative duty systems; planning for part-time working and other alternatives; and delivering the modernization agenda (Audit Commission 2004).

Inspectors base their conclusions on evidence collected on progress towards the seven aims, using an inspection toolkit document. Inspection criteria were derived from guidance and best practice already issued to fire authorities. Inspectors applied a rule that an authority with a red in any category could not be amber plus or green overall.

Prisons

The Prison Service has been classifying prisons on the basis of their performance since 2003. All prison service establishments in the UK are now rated from 1 (poor) to 4 (exceptionally high) on performance. The Director of Operations makes the assessment for public prisons, in consultation with Prison Service Directors and Area Managers.

The performance ratings are used to inform which of three strands of the improvement programme each prison will follow (performance testing, performance improvement planning, or high performing prisons). The rating is a professional judgement based upon: cost, performance and output data from a Weighted Scorecard, showing performance against key performance targets; compliance with Prison Service Standards; inspection reports; Independent Monitoring Boards; and the views of Prison Service Area Managers and the Prison Service Management Board.

Failing prisons are those which are 'not providing secure, ordered, or decent regimes and/or have significant shortfalls against the majority of key targets' (HMP 2004). Where an establishment has a level 1 rating based on poor performance on a range of factors, it is subject to a performance testing regime assessing its prospects for improvement.

Police Services

HM Inspectorate of Constabulary has been conducting inspections of services within police authorities since 1999. These have followed the same methodology as those for other local authority services. The performance of individual service areas within a police authority is assessed and categorized as 'poor', 'fair', 'good' or 'excellent', and their prospects for improving as 'poor', 'uncertain', 'promising' or 'excellent'.

Inspectors assess service achievements against national and local indicators by comparing them with police authorities' own targets and with top-performing authorities. Services are also expected to show that they have developed effective improvement planning. Inspectors focus on six key areas: leadership; policy and strategy; people; resource management; processes; and results (Home Office 2005: 397–403). Typically, a failing police authority service will be judged to be experiencing similar problems to other failing local authority services – weak performance management and planning, poor leadership and inadequate management of resources.

REFERENCES

Andrews, R. and Boyne, G. (2008) Organizational environments and public service failure. *Government and Policy*, forthcoming.

Andrews, R., Boyne, G., Law, J. and Walker, R. (2003) Myths, measures and modernisation: a comparative analysis of local authority performance in England and Wales. *Local Government Studies* 29(4): 54–75.

Andrews, R., Boyne, G. and Enticott, G. (2006) Performance failure in the public sector: misfortune or mismanagement? *Public Management Review* 8: 273–96.

Audit Commission (2001) *Changing Gear*, London: Audit Commission.

(2004) *Verification of the Progress of Modernisation: Fire and Rescue Service in England and Wales*. London: Audit Commission.

Boyne, G. A. (1997) Comparing the performance of local authorities: an evaluation of the Audit Commission Indicators. *Local Government Studies* 23(4): 17–43.

(1998) Public services under New Labour: back to bureaucracy? *Public Money and Management* 18(3): 43–50.

(2003) What is public service improvement? *Public Administration* 81: 211–28.

(2006) Strategies for public service turnaround: lessons from the private sector. *Administration and Society* 38: 365–88.

Boyne, G. A. and Dahya, J. (2002) Executive succession and organizational performance in the public sector. *Public Administration* 80: 179–200.

Boyne, G. A. and Enticott, G. (2004) Are the 'poor' different? An analysis of the internal characteristics of local authorities in the five CPA groups. *Public Money and Management* 24(1): 11–18.

Boyne, G. A. and Walker, R. (2004) Strategy content and public service organization. *Journal of Public and Administration Research and Theory* 14: 231–52.

Boyne, G. A., Farrell, C., Law, J., Powell, M. and Walker, R. (2003) *Evaluating Public Management Reforms: Principles and Practice*. Buckingham: Open University Press.

Contino, R. and Lorusso, R. (1982) The theory Z turnaround of a public agency. *Public Administration Review* 42: 56–72.

Dacin, T. (1997) Isomorphism in context: the power and prescription of institutional norms. *Academy of Management Journal* 40: 46–81.

Donaldson, L. (1996) *For Positivist Organization Theory*. London: Sage.

Eitel, D. (2004) The dynamic of chronic failure: a longitudinal study. *Public Money and Management* 24(3): 243–50.

HMP (2004) www.hmprisonservice.gov.uk/abouttheservice/performanceratings

Home Office (2005) *Best Value Guidance for Police Authorities and Forces*, London: HMSO.

Joyce, P. (2004) The role of leadership in the turnaround of a local authority. *Public Money and Management* **24**(3): 235–42.

Jas, P and Skelcher, C. (2005) Performance decline and turnaround in public organizations: a theoretical and empirical analysis. *British Journal of Management* **16**: 195–210.

Meyer, J. and Rowan, B. (1977) Institutionalised organizations: formal structures as myth and cermony. *American Journal of Sociology* **83**: 340–63.

Moore, M. (1995) *Creating Public Value*. Cambridge, MA: Harvard University Press.

Mueller, G. and Basher, V. (1997) Upper echelons and board characteristics of turnaround and non-turnaround declining firms. *Journal of Business Research* **39**: 119–34.

Niskanen, W. (1971) *Bureaucracy and Representative Government*. Chicago: Aldine-Atheton.

Oliver, C. (1997) The influence of institutional and task environment relationships on organizational performance: the Canadian construction industry. *Journal of Management Studies* **34**: 99–126.

Poister, T. and Larson, D. (1988) The revitalisation of Penn DOT. *Public Productivity Review* **11**(3): 83–103.

Powell, W. and Dimmagio, P. (eds.) (1991) *The New Institutionalism in Organizational Analysis*. Chicago: University of Chicago Press.

Rhodes, G. (1981) *Inspectorates in British Central Government*. London: Allen and Unwin.

Schendel, D. and Paton, G. (1976) Corporate stagnation and turnaround. *Journal of Economics and Business* **28**: 236–41.

Social Services Inspectorate (2002) *Guiding You Through: A Guide to Preparing for a Joint Review of Social Services*. London: Social Services Inspectorate.

Staw, B. and Epstein, L. (2000) What bandwagons bring: effects of popular management techniques on corporate performance, reputation and CEO pay. *Administrative Science Quarterly* **45**: 523–56.

Turner, D. and Whiteman, P. (2005) Learning from the experience of recovery: the turnaround of poorly performing local authorities. *Local Government Studies* **31**(5): 627–54.

13 Orchestrating complex and programmatic change in the public services

Mike Wallace and Michael Fertig

Successful change: a necessary condition for improvement

This chapter considers how those charged with implementing public service reforms may cope effectively with the complexity and multiplicity of these centrally instigated changes, alongside local and in-house initiatives, unplanned changes and other ongoing work. Improving public services means successfully implementing change for the better (according to the values of stakeholders with the power to define what counts as improvement) while maintaining normal provision. Political pressure for system-wide improvement and the ambition of programmatic policy interventions to bring it about generate multiple, complex changes affecting each public service organization involved. Professionals with formal leadership responsibility shoulder the major burden of supporting and overseeing the implementation of change while sustaining ongoing practice. They operate within the oversight of various stakeholder groups contributing to service governance. Making complex and programmatic change happen is therefore essential for public service improvement.

Our purpose is twofold: first, to explore how public service managers cope with this complexity within the inherent limits of its manageability; and second, to consider the academic and practical implications of our analysis. While our focus is generic, we draw on selected empirical findings from education and health to ground our ideas. As the largest and most complex services, education and health stand to offer the most potent insights into the complexity of change and strategies for coping with it.

Specifically, we address the question: how might an initial conception of complex educational change and an associated practical planning framework, derived inductively from research into a single instance of complex educational change, be refined to extend their applicability to other changes in different public service settings? The intention is to build towards a stronger basis for future research, and thus a stronger basis for practical guidance on developing the generic capacity to manage complex and programmatic change.

The original study was a qualitative investigation of school reorganization in England. It provided an empirical case for exploring what made educational change complex to manage and how it was tackled (Wallace and Pocklington 2002; Wallace 2003). That research entailed 235 interviews, tracking two local education authority initiatives taken under central government pressure to reduce surplus student capacity in the schools under their jurisdiction. The resultant initiatives were introduced in overlapping annual phases. Each involved extensive local consultation and the implementation of school closures, mergers, new building and refurbishment, and support for staff development in the post-reorganization schools. The reorganization initiatives were not conceived as part of the central government reform agenda, but nevertheless had to be undertaken alongside implementing those reforms and maintaining normal service provision.

Activities to explore the wider applicability of ideas emerging from the original investigation included engaging with academics and senior practitioners; a critical review of literature applying chaos and complexity theory to public service practice; and small-scale research on the emergence of the US 'hospitalist movement' (an increasingly complex change where a hospital-based physician coordinates treatment for acutely ill patients), and on the 'Kindergarten–Senior Four Agenda' (K-S4) for improving Manitoban school education.

The remainder of the chapter falls into five sections. First, we justify the need for social-science-informed theoretical development to address the increasing complexity of public service change. Second, we argue that the prevailing relatively deductive approach for doing so has limited potential, either to deepen understanding of this phenomenon or to inform capacity-building for coping effectively with it. Third, we report on our more inductive approach towards conceptualizing the complexity of public service change. We articulate an ironic perspective to address its limited manageability, and identify its characteristics. Fourth, we summarize our practical planning framework and its potential use as an *aide-mémoire*. Finally, we consider the implications of our analysis for managing change to improve the public services, backed by temperate policy making.

The case for engaging with complexity

Public service change is self-evidently becoming more complex, as many western governments engage in reform. Implementation entails learning to put reforms into practice and to operate in new ways once reforms are embedded. The pressure to implement externally initiated innovations has mounted, whether driven by an economic interest in containing the tax demand imposed by service expansion to meet rising user expectations (Foster and Plowden 1996), an ideological interest in increasing service 'consumer' choice while curbing the self-serving power of providers (OPSR 2002), or an altruistic interest in improving service quality.

Alongside service reforms are emergent innovations initiated at different administrative levels. They may be driven by external pressure, the exigencies of local circumstances, or the professional values of service providers and those contributing to their governance. Unplanned and unforeseeable environmental shifts may bring further pressure for a planned response, as with demographic changes affecting service demand. These diverse changes must be implemented in the context of practice that is not undergoing change, but whose maintenance needs managing nonetheless.

Further, an expanding knowledge gap has emerged. Several theoretical approaches have focused on complex aspects of generic organizational change, including the interaction between interdependent parts, as in open systems theory (Scott 1992), and 'requisite variety', positing the need for organizations to match their environment in terms of complexity (Ashby 1960). But such approaches did not emerge from the study of public service settings, nor are they well-grounded in public service research. A contrasting form of theory, derived from social movements including campaigning groups, focuses on building and fostering commitment to a vision (Davis et al. 2005). There is interest in its potential application to health (Bate et al. 2004). But as yet there is little research to support the application of social movement theory to change in the public services.

Indeed, there has been a more general lack of research designed to grasp patterns in the growing complexity and pervasiveness of public service change as a precursor to practical guidance. Older conceptions of the change process applied to the public services, such as re-engineering (Davies 1997), are simplistic. They imply greater managerial control than is feasible, as research on re-engineering suggests (McNulty and Ferlie 2002). The dominant theoretical approach that does tackle complexity head-on tends to leap prematurely from identifying the problem to prescribing the solution, as we shall see.

Chaos and complexity theory: new direction or new diversion?

This approach to public service change forms part of a movement to translate ideas from chaos and complexity theory in the natural sciences to the social world. Early advocates focused generically on organizations, though they often referred primarily to the private sector (Senge 1990; Stacey 1992). Further translation entails applying these ideas to the voluntary sector (Donaldson *et al.* 2005), to the public services overall (Haynes 2003), and to specific services including education (Morrison 2002; McMillan 2004) and health (Anderson and McDaniel 2000; Higginbotham *et al.* 2001).

The main 'intellectual project' or purpose for study (Wallace and Wray 2006) that these authors pursue is to develop 'knowledge-for-action': creating knowledge with practical application from a positive standpoint towards current practice and policy. They aim to inform improvement efforts from within the prevailing ideology framing practice. So for the UK public services, authors are more concerned with implementing changes, including central-government-driven modernization, than with questioning their tenets and unintended consequences. The subsidiary intellectual project is 'instrumentalism': imparting practical knowledge and skills through training and consultancy to improve specific practices, also from inside the prevailing ideology. The result is a dearth of sceptical literature assessing how far chaos and complexity theory actually is applicable to the public services.

Applying chaos and complexity theory to public service improvement has limited potential to narrow the knowledge gap (for a critical review see Wallace and Fertig 2007). It is overly reliant on the strongly deductive application to the human social world of concepts derived from the study of mathematical and natural phenomena. Deduction here implies taking a ready-made theory as the starting point, then seeking to demonstrate its application to a new domain, rather than more tentatively examining the extent and limits of its applicability.

Thus the public services are conceived as 'complex adaptive systems', a network of elements which are corporately capable of 'learning' through 'self-organization' as they interact in myriad ways. The focus is on the fluidity and emergent character of the complex relationships between elements, and on the blurred boundaries between the system and its environment. Small causes produce large effects, multiple causes produce multiple effects, and the latter feed back recursively as new causes. The system is viewed as continually prone to change in ways that are unpredictable in their specifics, inside more predictable parameters. These abstract ideas are elaborated as prescriptions by regarding members of public service and other organizations as agents with the freedom to act in unpredictable though interconnected ways. Their freedom may be harnessed towards improvement (as defined by managers and policy-makers) through creating conditions favouring self-organization amongst spontaneously forming groups, dedicated to improving their contribution to official service goals.

Sociologically oriented public service research suggests that such highly deduction-based prescription is unrealistic (e.g. McNulty and Ferlie 2002; Farrell and Morris 2004; Dopson and Fitzgerald 2005). First, the assumption is questionable that concepts from the natural world may be translated directly to the human social world, when these domains are fundamentally different. The natural world may be governed by observable regularities. But the social world obeys a 'double hermeneutic' (Giddens 1976) where, say, public service professionals come to their own interpretation of their experience. They may be influenced by or react against academics' claims about regularities of behaviour and related prescriptions. They may possess sufficient agency (the capacity to choose between alternative actions) to act according to their own interpretation, which may extend to the intention of confounding academics' claims.

Some chaos and complexity theory advocates posit a direct parallel between the natural and social worlds. Stacey (1992) asserts that human social groups are – literally – complex adaptive systems. This claim maximizes the potential for prescription. But acceptance of its prescriptive force hinges on the scarcely sustainable view that similarities between the two worlds outweigh their differences. Others adopt a more moderate line, as does Haynes (2003) in respect of the public services. He suggests that that chaos and complexity theory applies in an indirect sense: as a metaphor which may inform managers' thinking where it suggests intuitively recognizable patterns in their experience. But a more distant parallel weakens the prescriptive power (Burnes 2005). As Morgan (1986) demonstrated, many metaphors can stimulate managerial thought. As a metaphor, chaos and complexity theory becomes demoted to one of many optional sources for practical reflection.

Second, the deductive approach has channelled attention towards entire systems because it is founded on a holistic theory of relationships. But holism leads here to unhelpful reification, where a public service organization may be referred to as if capable of corporate action independent of the people who constitute its parts. Attention is deflected from incompatible interpretations, conflicting interests, and differential access to power amongst organization members. Berger and Luckmann (1967: 106) define reification as the 'apprehension of the products of human activity *as if* they were something other than human products – such as facts of nature'. Collective nouns – school, health care system – are inescapable. But reification within the conception of organizations as dynamic systems belies the possibility that members' interpretations and actions may be ambiguous, diverse, incompatible and contested.

Third, the intermediate step has been neglected of empirical research into what people actually do, and assessing how far prescriptions bring the results claimed for them (Rosenhead 1998). Accounts of public service change rely on anecdotes (Haynes 2003), illustrative case studies (McMillan 2004) and reinterpreting evidence which was not gathered within the frame of chaos and complexity theory (Morrison 2002). Substantial research projects on management are few, and even there the methodology tends towards action research and co-production of knowledge (ICOSS 2005), rather than more disinterested research.

Fourth, there are intractable logical problems. Advocates 'provide rational arguments against rationality, as well as forecasting with great confidence the impossibility of forecasting, and planning for the absence of planning' (Rosenhead 1998: 21). The emphasis on unpredictability sits uneasily alongside prescriptions (such as promoting self-organization) that are predicted to produce certain outcomes. The emphasis on multiple causes and effects militates against identifying some causes as more salient than others. If everything causes everything, then nothing causes anything.

The need remains to develop a more robust theoretical foundation for empirically grounded guidance on coping with complex and programmatic public service change. Our approach contrasts with the knowledge-for-action orientation of chaos and complexity theory advocates. We aim to develop 'knowledge-for-understanding', asking the relatively impartial question: 'what happens and why?' We see this is a necessary precursor to the normative question: 'how may practice be improved?' We also assume that varying contextual factors contributing to complexity preclude tight prescription. The planning framework we will describe is a tool whose relevance to practitioners' contingent setting is for them alone to decide.

Conceptualizing complex and programmatic change

The theoretical orientation framing our conception of change is itself complex (Wallace and Pocklington 2002: 44–73). It centres on the expression of agency, which includes channelling and delimiting the agency of others, within broad structural economic limits governing what is perceived as feasible, and assumptions about the naturalness of the existing economic order governing what is even thinkable. Multiple conceptual tools integrated into this theoretical orientation are designed to explore the contribution of agency to meaning-making through the flow of interaction that constitutes the change process. They sensitize the analyst to the pluralistic but unequal distribution of power, pursuit of partially incompatible interests, cultural determinants of power and uses of power to shape culture, mediation of interaction amongst a network of stakeholders across public service systems, and elastic linkage between agency and bounding structural conditions (reflected in the choice of policies and instruments for promoting implementation and in the variety of implementers' responses).

Many changes are planned interventions designed to improve service provision, either incrementally or through more extensive reform. Others are planned responses to emerging, unplanned changes. The complexity of change ranges from a simple shift to a multiplicity of radically new interrelated practices. Complex change is two-tiered: an overall entity containing multiple parts. Many such changes are centrally planned as complex innovations. Others emerge. They may evolve from disparate planned changes affecting individual service organizations to complex sets of formalized practices adopted across a public service system.

Programmatic change is three-tiered: a package of mutually reinforcing changes, each of which may comprise multiple parts. Its scope, and therefore its complexity, may range from a single service sector to a unified strategy spanning all public services. Each constituent part is of some complexity and interacts with other changes in the programme. An individual change that becomes complex may be emergent. The case study of the hospitalist movement in US health care (Schneller and Wallace 2007), originating with disparate practices, indicated that our conception applied only as its complexity increased through weak centralization when a hospitalists' professional association became established. This case also suggested that private sector participation in public service provision allowed greater scope for visionary leadership according to individuals' professional values than is feasible in state-funded organizations.

A programmatic change, however, will entail sufficient initial planning for a package of changes to be put forward. Minimally, proposals for a *change agenda* may be articulated which embody scope for emergence through consultation and diverse local development. The second case study, of the K-S4 Agenda initiative in Manitoban education, highlighted how a programmatic change may include user input into centrally proposed priorities. It may foster the local development of new practices that are sensitive to contingent organizational circumstances, rather than centrally pre-specifying the content of constituent innovations. At the other extreme, a centrally specified *profile of innovations* may be proposed, extending to a comprehensive strategy for their phasing and implementation. Even in the latter case, the programme may evolve with implementation experience as problems arise and new ideas surface for further innovations. A programme may entail nested innovations, including those to:

- improve the provision of services directly
- identify whether improvement is taking place
- improve the leadership and management of services, so creating favourable conditions for direct service improvement
- build generic capacity to implement change (not least the innovations in the programme).

Ambiguity and irony in the change process

The tradition of developing knowledge-for-understanding about organizational ambiguity goes back fifty years (March and Simon 1958; March and Olsen 1976; March 1999). Insights largely ignored by complexity theorists still have applicability – organizational life and change were never that simple. An ironic perspective has been developed by Hoyle and Wallace (2005), drawing on this tradition. It is intended as a sensitizing device for focusing on the empirical gap between intention and outcome or between concept and experienced reality, and the conceptual gap between declared and implied meaning, which together contribute to the limited manageability of complex and programmatic public service change (Wallace and Hoyle 2007). Irony has many connotations, from humour about unexpected coincidences, through cynicism where the literal meaning of words used contradicts what was intended, to acknowledgement of things turning out unexpectedly despite one's best efforts. All draw attention to people's limited capacity to make sense of their experiences, to realize their interests, and to control their destiny. The term 'irony' captures the phenomenon of limited human capacity which is central to organizational life and change. In the absence of a canonical definition of this term, the ironic perspective refers to those connotations of most analytic value:

- the *semantic irony* of ambiguity in meaning (as where the can-do language of many public service management job descriptions belies constraints on their incumbents' freedom to manage)
- the *situational irony* of unintended consequences of action (as where UK government public service modernization generates innovation overload, inhibiting the achievement of modernization goals)

The conditions for generating irony in organizational life lie in ambiguity: uncertainty in meaning, where people waver between alternative interpretations or are equivocal about what to do. Ambiguity includes uncertainty over what may happen or what may turn out to be important, as with the outcomes of particular action choices (Hartley 2000). But it also extends to deeper, chronic uncertainty over what actions may mean for the different actors involved. Change increases endemic ambiguity due to the learning required in acting to implement a new or altered practice. Complex and programmatic change implies a substantial shift, creating ambiguity about what this practice means until it is implemented, and therefore uncertainty about how to implement it across public service systems. Sources of ambiguity include:

1. Diverse and diffuse goals – where some are incompatible they cannot all be pursued with equal vigour, or they cannot be operationalized in terms of measured performance
2. Limits to rationality – *cognitive* since all possible outcomes of a change decision cannot be predetermined, *logical* where individuals' choice to pursue a goal prevents it being achieved when others also pursue it, *interpretive* where people come to competing views of the same events or change proposals, and *control* where practitioners use influence to resist or subvert the attainment of change goals
3. Unresolvable dilemmas – where action oriented towards one pole brings negative consequences, building pressure for action towards the opposite pole (as in trying to promote fast-pace change alongside its longer term sustainability)

The bigger the change, the greater the ambiguity, and so the greater the scope for irony. Even ameliorative policy making (such as efforts to reduce unintended innovation overload brought by public service modernization) brings more change and further ambiguity. Change agents and users possess sufficient agency to offer an ironic response by mediating change, possibly underpinned by an ironic orientation, protecting their professional judgements to make change work in the contingent circumstances of local settings.

Characteristics of complexity with management implications

While the content of complex and programmatic change varies enormously, table 13.1 indicates how tentative general patterns or characteristics of complexity with management implications are identifiable for a single change, with parallels for programmatic change reflecting the multiplicity of innovations that constitute it. First, complex change is *large-scale*, affecting a plurality of people with diverse expertise, beliefs and values. With programmatic change different groups may be affected by different innovations, and their cumulative experience affects their response to the later ones in the package.

Second, complex change is *componential*, the various elements affecting different stakeholders at particular times. A single change may contain

Table 13.1: Tentative characteristics of complexity of single and programmatic change

Complexity of a single change	Additional complexity of a programme
1. *Large-scale*	
• a multitude of stakeholders with an extensive range of specialist knowledge and priorities • the allegiance of stakeholders to partially incompatible beliefs and values, within limits	• a continually evolving, differentiated profile of stakeholders involved with different changes in the programme • cumulative experience and collective learning of stakeholders affecting their mediation of the programme
2. *Componential*	
• a diversity of sequential and overlapping components affecting different stakeholders at particular times • a multiplicity of differentiated but interrelated management tasks	• an evolving, hierarchical profile of interrelated innovations, including those to promote programme implementation • tasks may entail managing both parallel and sequential innovations within the programme
3. *Systemic*	
• a multi-directional flow of direct and mediated interaction within and between system levels • an unequal distribution of power between stakeholders within and between system levels who are nevertheless inter-dependent • the centrality of cross-level management tasks	• formal leaders at central and intermediate administrative levels may have cross-level responsibility for orchestrating programme implementation • multiple central and intermediate-level agencies may be responsible for training, disseminating information, monitoring and enforcing the programme
4. *Differentially impacting*	
• a variable shift in practice and learning required • variable congruence with perceived interests and its associated emotive force, altering with time • a variable reciprocal effect on other ongoing activities • variable awareness of the totality beyond those parts of immediate concern	• early innovations in the programme impact cumulatively on the capacity to cope with later innovations • variable learning required to implement one, some or all innovations in the programme within single or across multiple service organizations
5. *Contextually dependent*	
• interaction with an evolving profile of other planned and unplanned changes • impact of the accretion of past changes affecting resource parameters • parameters for local emergence and central direction set by the configuration of political, social and economic institutions	• interaction between the programme and other changes • variable parameters for central direction or invitation, and the capacity to respond to emergent changes stimulated by the programme

multiple components, and a programme will additionally comprise multiple innovations, perhaps targeting service provision, assurance of improvement, service management, and generic change capacity. The variety of components dictates that multiple tasks must be addressed in a coordinated way.

Third, complex change is *systemic*, entailing multiple interactions across a network of stakeholders based at different administrative levels. Modernizing the public services represents a programmatic change entailing liaison within central government about modernization as a whole and modernization in each service sector. Within each service, modernization involves liaison between the centre, any intermediate administrative level, and service organizations.

Many exchanges involve intermediaries, often based in agencies promoting implementation, who interpret the communications of stakeholders based at a more central level seeking to impact on those at a more local level. A service may be closely regulated and fully resourced by central government, partially autonomous from government, or include private sector organizations which are formally independent of government. But the stakeholders on whom all others depend actually implement the change.

Fourth, a key contributor to ambiguity is that complex change is *differentially impacting*. It imposes variable learning demands on different groups according to the novelty of their implementation tasks, suits some perceived interests while compromising others, and affects other work in different ways. Awareness of the change will be hierarchically distributed, depth of local knowledge at the service organization level contrasting with superficial awareness of its entirety. Those with more of an overview at the centre will have more scant local knowledge than their counterparts in service organizations. A programme imposes even greater diversity because the impact of multiple innovations on implementers is cumulative.

Fifth, the *contextually dependent* nature of a complex change or programme relates to its interaction with everything else going on, and to the resource parameters which flow from the history of past service changes. Fundamentally, the potential for emergence (including local initiatives developing within a programme) or for central direction are influenced by structural factors determining the social, political and economic context of any country.

Coping through orchestration

Our investigation suggests that senior leaders cope with ambiguity and consequent irony within complex and programmatic change through what we term 'orchestration', both inside and across different administrative levels (for a detailed account of this metaphor see Wallace 2007). We employ the term figuratively, in line with the dictionary definition 'to organize a situation or event unobtrusively so that a desired effect or outcome is achieved' (Encarta 2001: 1023). This usage captures what senior leaders in complex organizational systems must achieve within their governance arrangements: to make a change or programme happen through allocating tasks to others in their own and other related organizations, typically under conditions which are not entirely of their choosing. Orchestration is defined as 'coordinated activity within set parameters expressed by a network of senior leaders at different administrative levels to instigate, organize, oversee and consolidate complex and programmatic change across part or all of a multi-organizational system'.

Orchestrators steer the change process, those at central or regional levels being distanced from implementation in service organizations. Ambiguity may arise over the disjunction between experiences of orchestrators at different administrative levels. Those at the centre may conceive programmatic change as an entity, with each constituent change forming a part of the whole. But centrally based orchestrators with delegated responsibility for particular changes and those at other system levels responsible for implementing the programme are more likely to perceive each constituent change as discrete (and even divorced) from others in the package. Orchestrating a change entails implementing it alongside other changes and the rest of ongoing work. Orchestrating a programmatic change agenda or profile of innovations additionally entails coping with the implications of each change for other changes in the package.

Together, orchestrators form a loose hierarchical network of mutually dependent senior leaders based at different system levels – who are not necessarily aware of each other's contribution. Their varied knowledge of the change or programme is never comprehensive. They collectively organize and maintain oversight of an array of inter-related tasks as the change process unfolds. Steering change through orchestration is evolutionary, often unobtrusive, and includes attention to detail. Not only does it inherently embody a degree of ambiguity, but it is even possible for orchestrators consciously to promote and sustain ambiguity – as in fostering local mediation of central requirements or the emergence of novel local initiatives.

The visionary and charismatic behaviour of 'transformational' leadership (e.g. Leithwood *et al.* 1999) contrasts with orchestration. Where policy-makers or stakeholders involved in service governance set the direction of change and introduce related accountability mechanisms, service leaders' capacity to choose developmental priorities is increasingly channelled in the instigators' favoured direction. What policy-makers require is *transmissional* leadership faithfully to implement the change they have instigated (Hoyle and Wallace 2005). But service leaders retain some capacity to choose a direction. As indicated earlier, instigators of change depend on implementers' compliance and support. Visionary leadership is more feasible for policy-makers who instigate change, or for service leaders with sufficient leeway to instigate emergent change that expresses their personal service values. Private sector involvement in public service provision allows entrepreneurs to choose whether to offer services within regulations governing the parameters for provision.

Orchestration is also less than transformational in aspiration because, as research suggests (e.g. Moore *et al.* 2002; Weick and Sutcliffe 2003; Farrell and Morris 2004), policy-makers and public service organizational leaders cannot predictably manipulate a service culture by shaping others' shared beliefs, values and subliminal codes of behaviour. They are more likely to be capable of tightening control over others' actions. Orchestration implies coping with external demands and seeking to influence actions first, and beliefs and values second.

While orchestrators may be incapable of cultural manipulation, they cannot afford not to try to shape a service culture. More than minimal compliance is required if others are to implement change fully. So leaders are driven towards attempting to win hearts and minds as well as changing actions. A shift of emphasis away from the visionary side of leadership towards orchestration seems more realistic than clinging to ideas fostering an over-optimistic sense of leaders' ability to choose the direction of change and to control its course through cultural transformation.

A practical planning framework

This framework has three aspects: change management themes, headed by orchestration; the characteristics of complex and programmatic change outlined earlier; and sequential stages in the change process. (For its application to school reorganization, see Wallace 2004.) As a planning tool, reference may be made to one or more aspects to assist coping with an unfolding change or programme. The framework is depicted in figure 13.1.

Aspect 1: orchestration and three subordinate change management themes

While instigators of an emergent change or a programme may express visionary leadership, orchestration comes into play when ideas become firmed up as

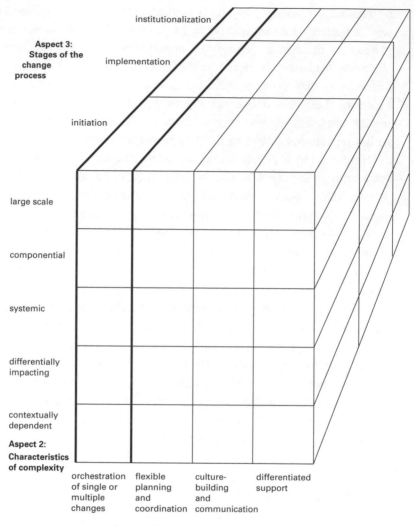

Figure 13.1 Three aspects of complex and programmatic change

a possible change to be implemented. Orchestration entails taking responsibility for task areas to manage a complex change or a programme as a whole:

1. instigating change management activity
2. creating and sustaining favourable conditions for change to happen
3. setting up management structures and delegating responsibilities, including those for other orchestrators

4. monitoring progress with implementing an individual change or the multiple changes in a programme
5. taking corrective or adaptive action, especially in response to unanticipated interaction between changes in a programme, and in the context of other changes and ongoing work that contribute to ambiguity by impacting on changes at hand

Orchestrators frame activities under three subordinate change management themes. They delegate responsibilities connected with these themes while retaining oversight. Many activities require specialist expertise, so may be widely distributed across administrative levels of a public service system.

The first subordinate theme, *flexible planning and coordination*, involves considering everything to be done across different administrative levels. This theme reflects ambiguity flowing from the dilemma over retaining short-term flexibility through step-by-step planning while also retaining coherence through longer term planning cycles. Plans are coordinated for different parts of the individual change or programme. They are updated through continual creation, monitoring and adjustment inside the broad longer term thrust.

The second subordinate theme, *culture building and communication*, relates to orchestrators' dependence on other stakeholders. Orchestrators promote a culture of support for their change or programme goals, whether through publicizing the case for change, consulting about a change agenda, or proclaiming the benefits that a programme will bring. Communication means giving consistent messages and gathering feedback to assist coordination and to pre-empt resistance. For programmes, communication may include highlighting how constituent changes are designed to inter-relate.

The third subordinate theme, *differentiated support*, involves organizing the provision of whatever people need to help them implement an individual change or programme, whenever required. Support extends to backing other orchestrators who are distributed across a service system. Dependent on needs, support includes information, expertise, preparatory training, time, counselling, physical resources, and finance.

Aspect 2: five characteristics of complexity dictating the management themes

The characteristics listed earlier contribute to ambiguity (and so to irony), stimulating orchestration and the subordinate change management themes. Thus Aspect 2 links with Aspect 1. Illustratively, each characteristic of complexity sets imperatives for orchestration. The *large-scale* nature of change implies that orchestrators have to devise means of communicating with, gaining support from, and harnessing the expertise of many other stake-holders. Multi-directional communication channels must be created to establish a robust network with mutual linkages amongst all stakeholder groups, including those contributing to governance. Orchestrators in each public service organization must look to their situation, working closely with their colleagues and possibly sustaining community support. They must also inform themselves about what is happening elsewhere with relevance for their organization.

The *componential* configuration of a change or programme means that orchestrators must plan for all components and the associated management tasks. Those in service organizations may have to plan for just the components and tasks directly affecting them. Where change is *systemic*, cooperation is needed across the network of stakeholders based at different system levels. Gaining support may require compromise to maximize the number of stake-holders who see the change as being in their interest. If change is *differentially impacting* on those affected, orchestrators have to take into account in their planning the possibility that change will make a different impact on different groups. Continual monitoring may be needed to maintain awareness of such impacts and their unintended consequences, which could inform planning to pre-empt or to solve emerging problems. The *contextually dependent* nature of change dictates that orchestrators must take account of the legacy of past changes affecting their responsibility and the availability of resources. They must be alert to the possibility that other policies and associated innovations may help or hinder their management strategies. They have to be ready to adapt day-by-day as circumstances evolve, seeking always to harness the resources available to achieve the best possible outcome.

Aspect 3: sequential stages of the change process

The process of changing is often divided into sequential stages, while recognizing that the boundary between one stage and the next may be blurred. *Initiation* comes first, leading to some decision to proceed with a change or a programme. Who makes any decision and when varies, depending on the degree of emergence or central pre-specification. It may be made by central instigators of planned interventions alone, with or without consulting other stakeholders. For emergent changes, orchestrators in individual service organizations may make the decision, with variable consultation.

The *implementation* stage covers attempting to put a change into practice, often taking some years. Implementation may be phased, whether for an individual change or a programme, implying that orchestrators must juggle with all components or the multiplicity of changes at any time. Unintended consequences arising at this stage may lead to adjustment or more radical rethinking of the change or programme, generating further change to be implemented.

The *institutionalization* stage embraces building the change or programme into what becomes accepted as normal practice. Mediation may result in this practice varying from what instigators envisaged. Other outcomes are possible, as where implementation is abandoned. One stage logically follows another. But the process is not neatly linear, especially where different components of a change or different changes in a programme are at different stages at a particular time. The implementation period for centrally driven programmes is likely to be bounded by the duration of political commitment (often dictated by election cycles). Institutionalization must have happened within the commitment period, unless the latter is renewed.

For an individual change, different components may be at different stages at any point during the evolution of the change process, especially with phased implementation. Similarly for a programme, constituent innovations may be initiated at different times during the programme implementation period. Each component of a change or constituent innovation of a programme may interact with others.

Aspect 3 links with Aspect 1, as in considering orchestration tasks at different stages. Where change is systemic, centrally based orchestrators may have responsibility for implementing it with and through other orchestrators at central and more local levels. The balance of membership of the network of orchestrators based at different system levels may therefore shift stage by stage. From the beginning of the *initiation* stage for a centrally driven programme, government policy-makers and senior civil servants may be orchestrators. During the *implementation* stage, orchestration will be shared across administrative levels with formal leaders in each intermediate administrative organization or service organization. Formal leaders at different levels therefore have to work together. From the time when a new practice becomes perceived as normal, at the *institutionalization* stage, orchestration may become the exclusive province of senior leaders in the organizations where implementation has been completed.

Conversely, for an emergent change which becomes more complex over time, early orchestrators may be the formal leaders of individual service organizations dispersed across the system and unrelated to each other. As information about the change spreads, more centrally based orchestrators may become involved who have a local, regional or national coordinating role.

Applying the framework

Planning could entail considering the link between chosen categories inside any aspect forming a cell of the framework, and between any two or all three aspects. What is or should be happening can be plotted by thinking through:

- for any one aspect, what is entailed in any category or how the contents of two or more categories inter-relate (e.g. among the change management themes, what the tasks of orchestration are, or how the tasks of orchestration link with tasks covered by each of the three subordinate themes)
- for any two aspects, how the content of one or more categories for any aspect relates to the content of categories for the other aspect (e.g. how the componential nature of a change impacts on orchestration and, in turn, the other change management themes)
- for all three aspects, how the content of one or more categories for each aspect relates to the others (e.g. how the componential nature of a change affects the tasks of orchestration during the implementation stage).

Promoting successful change for public service improvement

Developing system-wide capacity to cope effectively with complex and programmatic change is necessary for improving public service provision. No change, no improvement. Theory-building and research have an important part to play in teasing out patterns in this new complexity and suggesting how collective coping capacity may be enhanced. A relatively disinterested, social-science-based, inductive approach to understanding the complexity of change and the way people cope with it offers a sound basis for generating ideas that may realistically inform practice and policy. But the salience of diverse contextual factors contributing to complexity means that the status of these ideas can be only that of empirically backed stimuli for practical reflection.

By contrast, enthusiasm for the deductive and strongly prescriptive application of chaos and complexity theory to the public services seems misplaced. The natural and human social worlds differ too significantly for abstract ideas about natural-world relationships to be convincingly shoehorned to fit public service change without distortion that undermines their prescriptive force.

The conception of complex and programmatic change offered here and the underlying ironic perspective represent a theoretical advance in foregrounding the relative unmanageability of change and coping – rather than controlling – strategies rendering change as manageable as possible. Much conceptual work remains. One priority is to develop a more sophisticated understanding of emergent coping strategies. Another is to elaborate the notion of a system-wide network of orchestrators where much interaction occurs through intermediaries. Yet another is to conceptualize the linkage between orchestrators responsible for managing change and stakeholder representatives who participate in new forms of service governance (Rhodes 1997; Skelcher chapter 2, this volume).

Grounding this theoretical development generates an extensive research agenda. Priorities include investigating how systemic reform and emergent, increasingly complex change are orchestrated within and between public different ent services and sectors. Specific to the ironic perspective is to determine how far public service professionals adopt an 'ironic orientation' underlying their mediatory responses to reforms. One of us (Wallace) is contributing to this agenda through ESRC funded research (Ref. No. R00023 1136): 'Developing Organization Leaders as Change Agents in the Public Services'. The study focuses on how training offered by national leadership development bodies and other agencies to acculturate organization leaders as change agents relates both to UK government programmatic changes to implement public service modernization and personalization, and to fostering independent change and improvement.

Dialogue with senior practitioners suggests that the framework outlined above can offer a useful tool for thinking through the change process. It also suggests that fruitful directions for policy-makers to promote the development of complex and programmatic change capacity include:

- extending systemic awareness to inform decision-making through gathering qualitative information, alongside performance data, about the impact of initiatives on the coping capacity of practitioners
- identifying and supporting the development of those in a position to act as change orchestrators based at different administrative levels
- promoting link roles for boundary-spanning across administrative levels and between public services
- focusing training support on effective coping with ambiguity and the limited manageability of change
- complementary risk-taking through combining any top-down 'low-trust' target and measurement regime with bottom-up 'high-trust' encouragement to experiment and so develop local coping strategies, within broad limits
- fostering emergent change through local innovativeness for incremental improvement amongst service and administrative organizations which is sensitive to locally contingent circumstances

Change capacity building may be necessary for improvement, but it is not sufficient. Not only do political values come into play over what counts as better service provision, but the imperative to cope with change is partly a product of policy making, and is therefore a product of agency. If it is important not to reify complexity, it is equally important not to reify change itself. Policy-makers can make a difference to the complexity and multiplicity of change that orchestrators face, and so to their manageability. Intemperate political haste can make service provision worse.

Temperate policy making would be directed towards realistic improvement. Involving practitioners in agenda-setting could offer a reality-check for politicians' ideas and encourage implementers to cooperate. An incremental improvement strategy that allows for problems to emerge could maximize the capacity for fluent adjustment in the light of any ironic consequences. Building flexibility into reforms could foster the leeway necessary for implementers to make generalized practices work in diverse settings. Promoting the development of coping capacity could help implementers to pre-empt the ironies that striving for impossible certainty can precipitate, and to deploy routine strategies for coping with ironies that slip through. Developing unobtrusive monitoring and mild accountability mechanisms could pre-empt, or otherwise alert policy-makers to, unacceptable extremes of practice. Focusing on surveillance of extremes could minimize unproductively diverting the attention of the conscientious and competent majority of professionals from their core purpose of providing a high-quality service. In sum, our recipe for success in improving the public services is temperate policy making coupled with developing orchestrators' change capacity.

REFERENCES

Anderson, R. and McDaniel, R. (2000) Managing health care organizations: where professionalism meets complexity. *Health Care Management Review* **25**(1): 83–92.

Ashby, R. (1960) *An Introduction to Cybernetics*. London: Chapman and Hall.

Bate, P., Bevan, H. and Róbert, G. (2004) Towards a million change agents: a review of the social movements literature: implications for large-scale change in the NHS. Working paper, NHS Modernization Agency.

Berger, P. and Luckmann, T. (1967) *The Social Construction of Reality*. Harmondsworth: Penguin.

Burnes, B. (2005) Complexity theories and organizational change. *International Journal of Management Reviews* **7**(2): 73–90.

Davies, B. (1997) Re-engineering and its application to education. *School Leadership and Management* **17**(2): 173–85.

Davis, G., Macadam, D., Scott, W. R. and Zald, M. (2005) *Social Movements and Organization Theory*. Cambridge: Cambridge University Press.

Donaldson, A., Lank, E. and Maher, J. (2005) Connecting through communities: how a voluntary organisation is influencing healthcare policy and practice. *Journal of Change Management* 5(1): 71–86.

Dopson, S. and Fitzgerald, L. (eds.) (2005) *Knowledge to Action? Evidence-based Healthcare in Context*. Oxford: Oxford University Press.

Encarta (2001) *Encarta Concise English Dictionary*. London: Bloomsbury.

Farrell, C. and Morris, J. (2004) Resigned compliance: teacher attitudes towards performance-related pay in schools. *Educational Management Administration and Leadership* 32(1): 81–104.

Foster, C. and Plowden, F. (1996) *The State under Stress*. Buckingham: Open University Press.

Giddens, A. (1976) *New Rules of Sociological Method*. London: Hutchinson.

Hartley, J. (2000) Leading and managing the uncertainty of strategic change, in Flood, P., Carroll, S. Gorman, L. and Dromgoole, T. (eds.) *Managing strategic implementation*. Oxford: Blackwell, pp. 109–122.

Haynes, P. (2003) *Managing Complexity in the Public Services*. Maidenhead: Open University Press.

Higginbotham, N., Albrecht, G. and Connor, L. (2001) *Health Social Science: A Transdisciplinary and Complexity Perspective*. Oxford: Oxford University Press.

Hoyle, E. and Wallace, M. (2005) *Educational Leadership: Ambiguity, Professionals and Managerialism*. London: Sage.

ICOSS(2005) ICOSS Project www.psych.lse.ac.uk/complexity/icoss.htm accessed November 2005.

Leithwood, K., Jantzi, D. and Steinbach, R. (1999) *Changing Leadership for Changing Times*. Buckingham: Open University Press.

March, J. (1999) *The Pursuit of Organizational Intelligence*. Oxford: Blackwell.

March, J. and Olsen, P. (1976) *Ambiguity and Choice in Organizations*. Bergen: Universitetsforlaget.

March, J. and Simon, H. (1958) *Organizations*. New York: Wiley.

McMillan, E. (2004) *Complexity, Organizations and Change*. London: Routledge.

McNulty, T. and Ferlie, E. (2002) *Reengineering Health Care: The Complexities of Organizational Transformation*. Oxford: Oxford University Press.

Moore, A., George, R. and Halpin, D. (2002) The developing role of the headteacher in English schools: management, leadership and pragmatism. *Educational Management and Administration* 30(2): 175–88.

Morgan, G. (1986) *Images of Organization*. Newbury Park: Sage.

Morrison, K. (2002) *School Leadership and Complexity Theory*. London: RoutledgeFalmer.

OPSR (2002) *Reforming our Public Services: Principles into Practice*. London: Office of Public Service Reform.

Rhodes, R. (1997) *Understanding Governance: Policy Networks, Governance, Reflexivity and Accountability*. Buckingham: Open University Press.

Rosenhead, J. (1998) Complexity theory and management practice. Operational Research. Working Paper No. 98.25, London School of Economics and Political Science.

Schneller, E. and Wallace, M. (2007) Unsystematic responses to a chaotic service environment: shaping the division of labour in patient care, in Wallace, M., Fertig, M. and Schneller, E. (eds.) *Managing Change in the Public Services*. Oxford: Blackwell, pp. 153–72.

Scott, W. R. (1992) *Organizations: Rational, Natural and Open Systems*. Englewood Cliffs, NJ: Prentice-Hall.

Senge, P. (1990) *The Fifth Discipline: The Art and Practice of the Learning Organization*. New York: Doubleday.

Stacey, R. (1992) *Managing the Unknowable*. San Francisco: Jossey-Bass.

Wallace, M. (2003) Managing the unmanageable? Coping with complex educational change. *Educational Management and Administration* **31**(1): 9–29.

Wallace, M. (2004) Orchestrating complex educational change. *Journal of Educational Change* **5**(1): 57–78.

Wallace, M. (2007) Coping with complex and programmatic public service change, in Wallace, M., Fertig, M. and Schneller, E. (eds.) *Managing Change in the Public Services*. Oxford: Blackwell, pp. 13–35.

Wallace, M. and Fertig, M. (2007) Applying complexity theory to public service change: creating chaos out of order? in Wallace, M., Fertig, M. and Schneller, E. (eds.) *Managing Change in the Public Services*. Oxford: Blackwell, pp. 36–56.

Wallace, M. and Hoyle, E. (2007) An ironic perspective on public service change, in Wallace, M., Fertig, M. and Schneller, E. (eds.) *Managing Change in the Public Services*. Oxford: Blackwell, pp. 75–94.

Wallace, M. and Pocklington, K. (2002) *Managing Complex Educational Change: Large-scale Reorganization of Schools*. London: Routledge.

Wallace, M. and Wray, A. (2006) *Critical Reading and Writing for Postgraduates*. London: Sage.

Weick, K. and Sutcliffe, K. M. (2003) Hospitals as cultures of entrapment: a re-analysis of the Bristol Royal Infirmary. *California Management Review* **45**(2): 73–84.

Postcript

14 Conclusions: current themes and future directions for research

Cam Donaldson, Jean Hartley, Chris Skelcher and Mike Wallace

Introduction

This volume has contributed the work of the AIM Public Service Fellows and their associates to the significant academic and policy agenda of public service improvement. The book has focused on three main questions: how the reform of governance and accountability intertwines with management and may contribute to performance improvement in public services; how performance metrics can be conceptualized, established and utilized as part of an improvement process; and how change and innovation processes can be managed in ways that contribute to public service improvement. Within each theme, the issues and concepts are problematized, in order to ensure that the perspectives on management are set in a wider institutional context of governance and management, of citizens and organizations, and with a plurality of views and values about both 'management' and 'improvement'. We return to these themes now, both to reflect on some key issues arising from the work, and to provide some pointers for the research agenda for the future.

The chapters in this book have shown the difficulties that policy-makers and managers face in negotiating the paradoxes and ambiguities involved in performance management, when both the idea of performance and its measurement are contested. This is the *realpolitik* of public service reform. For whatever the ideological drivers or theoretical imperatives used to express the rationale for reform, the choices made by decision-makers on the ground are strongly influenced by pragmatic considerations. Resource constraints must be reconciled with demands on the service; professional aspirations with political priorities. Reforms come to be seen as either instruments to increase policy-makers' or managers' ability to deliver their goals, or impediments that challenge the negotiated order of a public organization and disrupt established routines and relationships.

This book helps to make sense of this world. Most chapters are based on Mode II research strategies (Gibbons *et al.* 1994) in which the AIM Fellows have worked interactively with policy-makers and managers to generate knowledge that will assist practice. Knowledge creation and transfer has taken place in a variety of ways, including co-research, interactive workshops, conferences, and action-learning, reflecting the broader imperative in the management research community to establish a more engaged approach to research.

Governance and accountability: engaging with the democratic context

The wider democratic context of governance and accountability is never far from the debates in this volume. The public services operate in complex and contested political space. This characteristic places particular demands on managers for transparency, responsiveness and the skilful negotiation of relationships. Changes to the form of governance and pattern of politics are presenting new challenges for research in the field. Until recently, the underlying assumption in the public management literature has been that political principals, legitimized through a system of representative democracy, direct bureaucratic agents located in government organizations. These political principals set goals and priorities, allocate resources, and exercise oversight of managerial performance in policy implementation. Citizens, service users and other stakeholders have an advisory role to play in this policy process, but the primary model is that of representative government. Consequently, the two points at which questions of democratic context intervene in public management research tend to be at the interface of the bureaucracy with politicians and with citizens.

However the generic theory of representative democracy, in which there is presumed to be a principal–agent chain linking citizens, elected representatives, public managers, and government or third-party providers, does not provide an adequate model of the new forms of governance found in the UK and a number of other nations. Skelcher (chapter 2) shows how there has been a significant development of special-purpose governments, in which state, civil society and business interact to shape, determine and execute public policy over a specified policy and spatial jurisdiction. In the UK, these are often called 'partnerships'. The term 'public–private partnership' is used elsewhere in Europe, while US academics talk of 'collaborative public management'.

These special purpose governments operate with a high degree of devolved authority from representative government. They also have multiple organizational principals – many of whom are incorporated into the organization through board positions allocated to them. Indeed, most board members are either managers from public, private or civil society 'partner' organizations, or direct beneficiaries. Elected politicians are rarely found on the boards. There are vertical accountability relationships to higher levels of government, through performance management systems related to key targets and expenditure. But management is also closely integrated into the governance of the body, and the nature of the democratic context is indistinct.

Collier (chapter 3) and Townley (chapter 7) show how contemporary governance arrangements pose new challenges for the accountability of public services. The linear relationships of the representative democracy model have been supplemented by more complex patterns of organizational relationships and intervening principals. Accountability to the profession, to citizens and other stakeholders vies with accountability to elected politicians, and introduces new elements into the design of performance measurement systems (Pidd, chapter 4).

So here we have public management in an ambiguous democratic context. The principal–agent model that we as scholars have often taken for granted does not fit this new political context. Representative democracy is constrained to the traditional core of government at national and local level, while new forms of participative, deliberative and stakeholder democracy are thriving in the devolved spaces created in the aftermath of new public management and (in the UK) 'modernization'. Some public organizations are responding to these imperatives through innovation (Hartley, chapter 10) and the introduction of complex change programmes (Wallace and Fertig, chapter 13). But the challenges are also likely to lead to fluctuations in performance, with some organizations requiring significant support to adjust to the changing governance and accountability environment (Boyne, chapter 12).

Assessing performance

In moving beyond measurement to the wider and legitimate challenges addressed elsewhere in the book, it could be assumed that the measurement challenges have been solved. However, we have wrestled with these for over a hundred years; note Sidney Webb's call in 1901 for a programme of National Efficiency to establish 'statistical excellence in drainage, water supply, paving, cleansing, watching and lighting, housing, and hospital accommodation, and publicly classifying them according to the results of the examination' (Webb 1901). Despite the attentions of recent governments, these challenges still remain. How do we value and measure 'health', 'life', 'a bobby on the beat'? Nevertheless, and partly because of the attentions of recent governments, significant progress has been made; and more is promised via the research outlined in this volume, though the research underlines that many of these values and measures will be contested.

Longley and Goodchild (chapter 9), for example, have shown that the public sector produces data that could more readily be used to provide better targeted and, therefore, more efficient services. Geodemographic profiling by small area is pivotal to the success of private businesses. Yet, such approaches, based on data already available, are less well used in academic analyses and planning of public sector activity. Despite a growing customer focus in the public sector, part of the future challenge still involves us thinking of service users and taxpayers as citizens rather than customers. Also, public services are more limited in the extent to which they can choose their 'markets'. Taking these issues on board and conducting research into this exciting development in geodemographics could help the public services to meet a variety of needs and aspirations more efficiently.

Significant challenges, and again potential, exist as we move from targeting of need to measuring whether it has been met. O'Mahony et al. (chapter 6) and Townley (chapter 7), have shown that private-sector-based measures of productivity are not easily translated to the public sector, and indeed Townley shows that a number of rationalities of performance may co-exist. To give these measures meaning, we need to develop the theoretical underpinnings and put a practical focus on objectives to help to determine what is important. Managers should find such structuring helpful in reflecting carefully on assessments. Exciting developments, working towards such measurement in health and criminal justice have been outlined in these chapters.

One objective is whether met need and productivity can be valued in monetary terms. Baker et al. (chapter 8) outline how this has been achieved in over twenty years of research for the Department for Transport, leading to a value of statistical life which is used in road safety policy making. In the wider public sector, there is still a lot to do. Baker et al. demonstrate the challenges involved in transferring methods in transport to health, thus setting a whole research agenda in that area of public sector activity. What is also shown in this work is that, in many respects, the monetary measurement is incidental; the key is in using this measurement to help ensure that services are provided more in line with public preferences and needs.

Interestingly, despite the conventional association of economics with more quantitative approaches to performance assessment, of which there are good examples in this volume, there is acknowledgement that, for economics-based approaches to be used more in public sector decision-making, economics and other disciplines need to adapt to suit this new environment. Collier, Pidd, and Donaldson *et al.* (chapters 3, 4, and 5) outline the obvious role for quantitative disciplines, such as economics and accountancy, in helping to manage scarcity of resources in the public sector but, to fulfil this role, disciplines such as economics need to take on more 'soft systems' and qualitative research approaches, so as to incorporate a better understanding of the organizations (and especially their objectives). Such innovations can be used alongside, and may even drive, culture change within public sector management, as managers will use more explicit frameworks for managing scarce resources and thus make more visible the tough choices required to meet the needs and aspirations of the public.

Change and innovation

The contributions to this volume suggest that there is no one best way to manage public service improvement but many ways of managing it better, depending on your values. The authors' investigations together highlight just how and why what may seem to be self-evidently laudable and straightforward endeavours to improve public service provision may turn out to be neither. The idea of service improvement is to make bad provision good and good provision better, so is self-evidently value-laden. Yet in pluralistic societies where partially incommensurable values are encouraged to find expression through democratic institutions, what counts as service improvement is inevitably contested. Governance arrangements themselves become subject to improvement efforts. And, as Skelcher (chapter 2) and Collier (chapter 3) demonstrate, judging their success depends on the relative weighting of different values. In assessing the outcomes of new governance arrangements, what balance should be struck between their impact on democratic and service performance when the two do not necessarily coincide?

Values can and do differ over just about any aspect of the ends and means of service provision. How – and how well – service improvement should be managed is as open to challenge and debate as the public value and public goods that services are there to provide. Establishing relative priorities for allocating scarce resources entails forming values not only about which resources merit higher or lower priority, but also about how the decision-making process is informed and managed. Thus Donaldson and his colleagues set out in chapter 5 how health care commissioning choices can be more fully informed through relevant economics-based frameworks. In chapter 9, Longley and Goodchild describe a powerful tool for synthesizing routinely collected local geodemographical information to inform local decisions about directions for improvement. The managerial value assumption that information generally helps decision-making is probably uncontentious, but information about valued public goods cannot be neutral in a context of limited resources and where the values and interests of different groups in society are in tension. So, there are implications for decisions about which of these goods get resourced and which do not.

Making management decisions to improve service provision in the light of whatever information is gathered also brings contestable values about process to the surface. Collier points in chapter 3 to the weakness of governance arrangements for policing, questioning whether some stakeholders who should be contributing to resource allocation decisions are not, whereas others are contributing more than they should. In chapter 12 Boyne challenges the relative importance widely accorded to the legitimacy of management practices against that given to the quality of service provision in judging organizational failure and turnaround. Values relate both to how recovery is managed and perceived, and to the putative outcomes of this effort. The balance of their relative importance is itself a potentially contentious value issue.

It may seem self-evident that managing improvement means finding out and monitoring how well a service is being provided in the first place and then establishing whether changing management practices correlates with a better service. Yet several contributors expose the technical complexities of establishing performance measures worth valuing, as discussed by O'Mahony and colleagues (chapter 6). Townley (chapter 7) and Pidd (chapter 4) reveal how attempts to measure service performance, as a baseline against which to assess the need for and outcomes of improvement efforts, surface contentious values about what should be measured, how, and even whether the act of measuring itself distorts service provision.

Managing improvement efforts is far from straightforward, not solely because they are value-laden. Improvement implies change, hence the imperative for innovation to improve service provision or its management – according to the values of designers. Time for innovation activity is taken from time for other tasks, and yet normal service must be maintained alongside the improvement effort. As Wallace and Fertig show in chapter 13, managers have to cope with the additional ambiguity, or uncertainty about the meaning of service provision, generated by change. Big change brings a big increase in ambiguity, not least because all involved have so much to learn, both to implement the innovation and to make it work sustainably.

Just as the contributors are, arguably, realistic about the complexities of managing improvement, so they are also fundamentally optimistic about its potential. There are many pointers throughout the book towards positive possibilities within the scope of managerial action. Coping with the value pluralism, workload and increased ambiguity of public service improvement efforts promises what, according to a significant majority of stakeholders, does count as solid improvement, so long as it is linked to governance processes.

Innovation, as a particular form, scale and scope of change, is embedded in this volume, both in the chapters which directly address it (Hartley in chapter 10, and Walker and Damanpour in chapter 11) and in those chapters that do not draw on this conceptualization but that are concerned with step-change reform with novel character. For example, the interest in new forms of governance outlined by Skelcher can be considered as an innovation (see also Moore and Hartley in press); and new approaches to defining and measuring value and performance, as suggested in the chapters by Pidd, Longley and Goodchild, and Collier, for example, throw up new governance and management challenges due to new processes, services and organizational forms. Innovation is also widely mentioned in policy circles as a means to achieve improved performance in services, and this is a phenomenon found not only in the UK but also in the USA (e.g. Borins in press) and in other countries across the world (Pollitt and Bouckaert 2004).

Yet, chapter 10 by Hartley and chapter 11 by Walker and Damanpour both show that innovation in the public sector is over-reliant on theory and evidence from the private sector, and there is a considerable need to derive concepts, theory and data from public service settings if innovation and its links to improvement are to be understood. Innovation cannot be considered solely at the organizational level because of the links with governance – both governance innovations themselves, (see also Moore and Hartley in press), and also the ways in which decisions about innovation processes and outcomes are influenced by the governance arrangements. This means that innovations need to be considered at the institutional field level not solely at the organizational level of analysis. As Walker shows, both internal and external judgements/measures of performance may be important in innovation but they do not always correlate.

Research into innovation in governance and public services is still relatively sparse. We hope that this volume has added to the field with both conceptual and empirical contributions, but there is still a large research agenda to be pursued if the understanding and practices of innovation are to yield clear improvements in society and its public services. This volume has only a short section on the diffusion of innovation; this is a crucial issue for public services and more research would be valuable on the contingencies, the actors, the processes and the outcomes for different stakeholders.

End-note

Over recent years there has been a significant renewal of political and societal commitment to public services, whether they are delivered directly by state agencies or through public–private partnerships or other forms of third-party government. But this commitment is contingent on the public services demonstrating that they can improve their capacity to deliver demonstrable benefits for society at large and for specific communities. This places a considerable onus on policy-makers and managers to engage in the debate about public service improvement.

There is a major opportunity here for academic and other researchers to play a role in shaping the ideas and practices deployed for public service improvement. This volume outlines some of these contributions, and provides a foundation for other research initiatives that engage a significant number of scholars in further developing theoretical and applied knowledge on public service performance and improvement.

REFERENCES

Borins, S. (in press) *Innovations in Government: Research, Recognition, and Replication* Washington, DC: Brookings Institution.

Gibbons, M., Limoges, C., Nowotny, H., Schwartzman, S. P. and Trow, M. (1994) *The New Production Of Knowledge: The Dynamics of Science and Research in Contemporary Societies*. London: Sage.

Moore, M. and Hartley, J. (in press) Innovations in governance. *Public Management Review*.

Pollitt, C. and Bouckaert, G. (2004) *Public Management Reform: A Comparative Analysis*. Oxford: Oxford University Press.

Webb, S. (1901) Lord Rosebery's escape from Houndsditch. *Nineteenth Century*, September 1901.

Index

accountability
  and democratic performance 30
  democratic context 282–3
  of police behaviour 49–51
  performance as object of 48–9
  public sector managers 52
  public sector performance 46–7
ageing population, impact on public services 11
altruism and the WTP-based VPF 163
ambiguity in public service provision 80–1, 82–4

Balanced Scorecard initiative 101, 102–3
Balanced Scorecards 70
  use in the public sector 70
Best Value initiative 101, 103–4
  public consultation 74
  virtualism in performance practices 73–4
'big government', perspectives on 6–7
bottom-up innovation in the public sector 202–3
bureaucratic control 77–8

case study approach, public management research
  20, 21
causality, assumptions in governance design 38–41
central control aspect of performance
  measurement 68
change management *see* public service change
chaos and complexity theory, limitations of 259–62
clan, control by 77–8
cluster analysis, geodemographics 179–80
consent, and democratic performance 30
contingent valuation (expressed value) approach to
  valuing safety 164
control by clan 77–8
control mix
  performativity in policing 58
  public sector governance 54–5
control systems
  ambiguity in public service provision 80–1, 82–4
  bureaucratic control 77–8
  control by clan 77–8

cybernetic metaphor of control 76–7
  feedback control 76–7
  grid: group theory of control 78–9
  intrinsic control in professional practice 81–2
  market control 77–8
  political control 76–7
  routine control 76–7
  uncertainty in public service provision 80–1, 82–4
'convergence' view of public and private sectors 6–7
cost-benefit analysis (CBA)
  equivalence with cost-effectiveness analysis
    (CEA) 157–9
  priority setting in public services 91, 93
cost-effectiveness analysis (CEA), priority setting in
  public services 91
cost-weighted output index (CWOI) 129–30
costs of a performance measurement system 72–3
criminal justice system (England), performance
  classification scheme 254–5
criminal justice system (Scotland) 136–8
criminal justice system (Scotland) performance
  boundaries and performance issues 142–4
  communication between agencies 148–9
  complex interactions between agencies 142–4
  mapping the system 146–7
  meaningful measures 144–5
  nature of work organization and work flows
    145–7
  operational and administrative difficulties 136–8
  opposition to setting targets 139, 144–5
  overarching aims and objectives 138–9
  political significance of performance measures
    139–42
  rationalized myths about performance measures
    139–42
  review of the system (Normand report, 2003)
    138–9
  situated rationality of work organization 145–7
customer service provision, public service
  management 7–8
cybernetic metaphor of control 76–7

democratic context of governance and accountability 282–3
democratic performance 29, 30
  and public governance mode (empirical evidence) 34–5
  in hierarchical governance modes 31, 32
  in market governance modes 31, 32
  in network governance modes 31, 32
demographic changes, impact on public services 11

economic competitiveness, contribution of public services 5–6
economic problems in public services
  allocation of scarce resources 89–91
  challenge of competing demands 89–90
  need for a framework to manage scarcity 90–1
  NICE recommendations 90–1, 92
  priority setting 89–90
  sacrifices made to improve performance 89–90
economics in public services
  adoption at national level 90–1
  lack of penetration at local level 90–1
education, performance classification scheme (England) 252
executive agencies 27–8
external environment
  influence on public service management 8–9
  policy context 19–20

factorial ecology method of analysis, geodemographics 178–80
feedback control 76–7
fire service, performance classification scheme (England) 253–4

geodemographic indicator usage limitations 181–3
  choice of defining variables 183
  loss of information in the clustering process 182–3
  spatial heterogeneity 183
  within-cluster variability 182–3
geodemographic indicators
  alternative data sources 183–4
  cluster analysis 179–80
  commercial systems 177
  customer loyalty programmes 184
  definitions 177–80
  derivation from census data 177–8
  factorial ecology method of analysis 178–80
  history and development 177–80
  inclusion of lifestyle data 183–4
  private sector applications 179, 180–1
  public sector applications 179, 181

geodemographic indicators in the public sector
  limitations on usefulness for researchers 189–93
  need for scientific standards in geodemographics 189–93
  new applications 185–8
  public services perspective 186–7, 193–4
  research applications 184–9
  research on clustering methods 188–9
  strategies for increasing research applications 189–93
  stratified sampling and panel selection 188
geographic information systems (GIS), use in public service delivery 176–7
globalization, impact on public services 11
good practice, sharing in the public sector 202–3, 209–11
governance
  avoidance of overlap with other functions 60–1
  concept 28–9
  confusion of policy and governance roles 60–1
  definition 16
  forms of public service governance 16–17
  hierarchical government 16–17
  implications for public management 16–17
  issues in public service management 8
  networked governance 16–17
  relationship to government 28–9
  see also public governance
governance and accountability, democratic context 282–3
governance and performance
  empirical evidence 31
  empirical perspectives 32–3
governance and performance research agenda 38–42
  alternative causalities 38–41
  examination of assumed causality 38–41
  interpretivist approach 42
  reformulating the research design 41–2
governance arrangements
  changes in public service 27–8
  range of forms 27–8
  relationship with public service performance 27–8
governance design
  and system performance 30
  examination of assumed causality 38–41
  interpretivist research approach 42
governance modes 28–9
  and public service performance 28, 30–1, 32
governance of policing 55–6
  chief constable roles and accountability 55–6
  competing power relations 55–6
  diverse demands of stakeholder groups 56

Home Office role 55–6
police authority role and accountability 55–6
The Police Act (1996) 55–6
tripartite governance structure 55–6
governance of public sector performance 54–5
control mix 54–5
influence of new public management 54
multiple publics 54
pluralistic governance model 54
systems of management control 54–5
governance of public services 16–17
governance structures 60
government, relationship to governance 28–9
grid: group theory of control 78–9
gross output (human capital) approach to valuing
safety, 161

health sector characteristics
health care system structure in the EU and US
118–21
historical developments in health provision 116–17
information asymmetries 117–18
national variations in financing and delivery
118–21
nature of the production process 117–18
performance measurement challenges 117–18
health sector performance measures
age-standardized death rates (SDR) for major
diseases 122–5
application of productivity performance
indicators 115–16
cost-weighted output index (CWOI) 129–30
dangers of management by numbers 131–2
disease-specific microeconomic studies 126–8
impact of health status of the population 125
input measures 130–1
lack of a theoretical framework 128–9
life expectancy 122, 123, 124, 125
limitations of quantitative data 131–2
macroeconomic indicators 121–6
outcome measures 129–30
output measures 129
performance relative to resources 121–8
theory of productivity measurement 128–31
total health expenditure 121–6
WHO 'attainment' index 125–6
WHO efficiency of health provision indicator
125–6
health service, performance classification scheme
(England) 250
hierarchical government 16–17
hierarchical modes of governance 28–9
and public service performance 31, 32
Home Office, approach to police performance 56–7

improvement in public services, relationship to
innovation 205–9
innovation
as fashionable rhetoric 197
barriers and facilitators 200
classifications 200–1
definitions 199–201, 219
learning from failures 200
responsiveness to needs of users 197–8
scale of change involved 199
value in public service delivery 197–8
innovation in the public sector
adaption of innovations 210–11
applicability of innovation theory 198
as route to improved performance 217
Beacon Scheme 210–11
bottom-up innovation 202–3
catalysts of innovation 201
comparison with the private sector 201–2
creating public value 203
current themes and future directions 287
diffusion of innovations 202–3, 209–11
dimensions of innovation 200–1
innovations in English local government 217
innovations in governance 199
lack of empirical evidence for effectiveness
217–18
leading and managing innovation processes
203–5
organizational innovation 199–200
perceptions of stakeholders 200
political motivation 217
product innovation 199–200
public value approach 208–9
relationship to improvement 205–9
role of users 203
service innovation 199–200
sharing of good practice 202–3, 209–11
stages of the innovation process 203–5
top-down processes 202
unintended consequences 209
innovation–performance relationship empirical
research 218–19
conclusions 231–2
controls 225, 226–7
data source 221–3
innovation measures 224–6
innovation theory 219–21
innovation types and organizational
performance 228–31
measures 223–7
methods 221–7
organizational innovation and performance
228

innovation–performance relationship (cont.)
    performance measures 223–4, 225
    process innovations and organizational
        performance 228–31
    results 227–31
    service innovations and organizational
        performance 228–31
innovation–performance relationship theory
    220–1
innovation theory
    applicability in the public sector 198
    definition of innovation 219
    innovation and organizational performance
        220–1
    performance gap theory 220–1
    process innovations 220
    service innovations 220
institutional field, policy contexts 20
instrumentalism 260
internal context (policy context) 20
interpretivist research approach 42
interval scales 69

knowledge-for-action concept 259–62

league tables, impact on public service
    failure 237
legitimacy
    and democratic performance 30
    as measure of performance 65–6
lifestyle data, inclusion in geodemographic
    indicators 183–4
Likert scale 69
local authorities, performance classification scheme
    (England) 251

macro-level performance measurement 71–2
management of performance 52
    accountability of public sector managers 52
    application to policing 53–4
    clash with public sector professional values 52
    unintended effects of performance measurement
        72–5
management processes, link with performance
    17–19
management theory, application to public services
    7–10
margin concept 93
marginal analysis, priority setting in public services
    91 see also programme budgeting and
    marginal analysis (PBMA)
market control 77–8
market modes of governance 28–9
    and public service performance 31, 32

markets for public services 7–8
measureability of service outcomes 243–4
multi-organizational collaboratives 27–8

National Intelligence Model (NIM) 51, 53, 58–9
neo-liberal ideologies, influence on public services
    4–5, 6–7
network modes of governance 28–9
    and public service performance 31, 32
networked governance 14–15, 16–17
New Public Management 6–7, 13–14, 32–3
    definition 66–7
    influence on public sector governance 47–8, 54
    performance measurement and control 76–84
    role of performance measurement 66–7
    shifts in corporate governance 54
New Right, influence on public services 6–7
NHS Trusts, virtualism in performance practices 74
    see also health sector
NICE (National Institute for (Health and) Clinical
    Excellence)
    recommendations to PCTs 90–1, 92
    valuing health gain 154–6
    use of QUALYs 154–5
nominal scales 69

open systems theory 259
opportunity costs 93
    priority setting in public services 91
ordinal scales 69
organizational culture and control 77–80
organizational innovation 199–200
organizational performance 29–30
    and public governance mode (empirical
        evidence) 33–4
    in hierarchical governance modes 31, 32
    in market governance modes 31, 32
    in network governance modes 31, 32
    influence of performance indicators 29–30

panel selection, use of geodemographic indicators
    in the public sector 188
partnerships
    implications for public management 16–17
    public–private partnerships 27–8
PBMA see programme budgeting and marginal
    analysis (PBMA)
performance 29–30
    accountability of police behaviour 49–51
    as a continuous process 49
    as a discrete event 48–9
    as object of accountability 48–9
    as results 49
    as theatre 49

link with management processes 17–19
multi-dimensional construct 48–9
problems related to understanding 48–9
process approach 48–9
qualitative assessment 48–9
quantitative assessment 49
performance assessment, current themes and future
    directions 283–5
performance classification schemes (England)
    250–5
    criminal justice 254–5
    education 252
    fire service 253–4
    health 250
    local authorities 251
    police services 254–5
    prison service 254
    social services 251–2
performance gap theory 220–1
performance indicators
    combining baskets of measures 70–1
    correlations between component measures 71
    dangers of oversimplification 82–4
    influence on organizational performance 29–30
    introduction in public services 237–8
    relative weighting of different measures 71
    use of multiple criteria 70–1
performance measurement
    costs of a performance measurement system
        72–3
    effects on people whose performance is being
        measured 72–5
    ossification effect on management 72
    perverse effects and unintended consequences
        72–3
    potential for dysfunctional effects 66
    public consultation 74
    results (outputs and outcomes) 65–6
    star ratings (NHS Trusts) 74
    tunnel vision effect on management 72
    types of performativity 75
    virtualism in Best Value practices 73–4
    why it matters 65–6
performance measurement basics 68–9
    interval scales 69
    Likert scale 69
    nominal scales 69
    ordinal scales 69
    ratio scales 69
    star ratings 69
performance measurement in New Public
    Management 76–84
    ambiguity in public service provision 80–1, 82–4
    approaches to control 76–7

bureaucratic control 77–8
control by clan 77–8
control mechanisms 77–80
cybernetic metaphor of control 76–7
dangers of oversimplified PIs 82–4
feedback control 76–7
grid: group theory of control 78–9
handling statistical uncertainty 82–4
market control 77–8
organizational culture and control 77–80
political control 76–7
professional activity 81–2
routine control 76–7
uncertainty in public service provision 80–1,
    82–4
performance measurement in public services
    provision 66–8
    central control aspect 68
    New Public Management 66–7, 68
    political aspect 68
    reasons for measuring performance 68
    Royal Statistical Society recommendations 68,
        82–4
    symbolic aspect 68
    typical approach (UK example) 67
performance measurement methods
    Balanced Scorecards 70
    basics 68–9
    baskets of measures 70–1
    combining measures into performance
        indicators 70–1
    macro level performance measurement 71–2
performance measurement systems
    aims 134–5
    conventional explanations for failures 135–6
    failure to produce desired effects 134
    multiple and conflicting rationalities 135–6
    negative effects of 134
    rationale for 134–6
performance measures
    and situated rationality of work organization
        145–7
    communicative rationality 148–9
    technical rationale for identifying targets 144–5
    underlying assumptions 239–41
performance measures applied to the health sector
    age-standardized death rates (SDR) for major
        diseases 122–5
    cost-weighted output index (CWOI) 129–30
    dangers of management by numbers 131–2
    disease-specific microeconomic studies 126–8
    impact of health status of the population 125
    input measures 130–1
    lack of a theoretical framework 128–9

performance measures applied (cont.)
  life expectancy 122, 123, 124, 125
  limitations of quantitative data 131–2
  macroeconomic indicators 121–6
  outcome measures 129–30
  output measures 129
  performance relative to resources 121–8
  theory of productivity measurement 128–31
  total health expenditure 121–6
  WHO 'attainment' index 125–6
  WHO efficiency of health provision indicator
    125–6
performance measures in government
  political significance 139–42
  rationalized myths 139–42
performance metrics 17–19
  interpretation of data 18–19
  link to actual service performance 18–19
  reliability and validity 18–19
performativity
  consequences of 46
  definition 46
  effects of performance measurement 75
  historical approach in the public sector 47–8
  limitations in the public sector 47–8
  limitations of quantitative approaches
    61–2
  meanings of the term 75
  performance as multi-dimensional construct
    61–2
performativity in policing 57–9
  accountability of modes of control 58–9
  control mix 58
  information-led approach 58–9
  legitimating principles 58–9
  legitimation of knowledge 58–9
  limitations of quantitative approaches
    61–2
  National Intelligence Model (NIM) 58–9
  performance-driven approach 58–9
  sub-cultures within police forces 58
  tensions between modes of control 58
pluralistic governance model 54, 60–1
police performance 49–51
  accountability of police behaviour 49–51
  intelligence-led approach 51
  National Intelligence Model (NIM) 51
  performance classification scheme (England)
    254–5
  performance-driven regime 50–1
  performance measurement initiatives 50–1
  Police and Criminal Evidence Act (PACE)
    1984 49
  policy issues 56–7

regulation of police powers and responsibilities
    49–50
  tension with ethical responsibilities 50–1
  see also performativity in policing
police performance management 53–4
  chief constable accountability 53
  data collection and reporting 53
  National Intelligence Model process 53
  performance regime 53
  resource allocation issues 53–4
  unique aspects of policing 53
policing governance 55–6
  chief constable roles and accountability 55–6
  competing power relations 55–6
  diverse demands of stakeholder groups 56
  Home Office role 55–6
  police authority role and accountability 55–6
  The Police Act (1996) 55–6
  tripartite governance structure 55–6
  weakness of governance structures 60
policy and governance, confusion of roles 60–1
policy and police performance 56–7
policy contexts for public service management 8,
    19–20
  external environment 19–20
  institutional field 20
  internal context 20
  levels of analysis 19–20
policy issues
  public as consumer 56
  public as taxpayer 56
political aspect of performance measurement 68
political context of public service management 8
political control 76–7
priority setting in public service commissioning
  challenge of competing demands 89–90
  cost-benefit analysis (CBA) 91
  cost-effectiveness analysis (CEA) 91
  lack of capacity to implement guidance 92
  marginal analysis 91
  multi-disciplinary approach 92
  need for a decision-making framework 91–2
  need for qualitative economic research 91–2
  opportunity costs 91
  role for economics 91–2
  see also programme budgeting and marginal
    analysis (PBMA)
priority setting in public services
  Balanced Scorecard 101, 102–3
  Best Value 101, 103–4
prison service, performance classification scheme
    (England) 254
private sector management ideas, application to
    public services 6–7

process innovations 220
    and organizational performance, empirical
        research 228–31
product innovation 199–200
productivity measurement theory 128–31
productivity performance indicators
    application in the public sector 115–16
    private sector 115
    tools for policy analysis 115
professional practice
    intrinsic control 81–2
    performance measurement in public services
        81–2
professional values, clash with performance
    management 52
programme budgeting and marginal analysis
        (PBMA) 60–1, 93
    application of PBMA in organizations 95
    basic principles 93
    concept of 'the margin' 93
    cost-benefit analysis 93
    creation of a management process 95
    lack of uptake by NHS PCTs 95
    opportunity cost concept 93
    questions about resource use 93–5
programme budgeting and marginal analysis
        (PBMA) model 105–8
    evaluation tool for PBMA studies 107–8
    points for future priority-setting exercises 107
programme budgeting and marginal analysis
        (PBMA) process 95–100
    advisory panel 96
    aim and scope of the priority-setting exercise 95–6
    decision-making criteria 96, 97
    identifying options for change 96, 97
    programme budget 95–6
    rating options for change 96, 97–9
    releasing resources 96, 97
    research evaluations 100–1
    results of health care applications 100–1
    supporting evidence and information 96, 99
public
    changing expectations of public services 11
    consultation in Best Value practice 74
    consumer policy issues 56
    taxpayer policy issues 56
public administration, comparison with public
    management 13
public governance, definition 29 see also
    governance
public governance and performance (empirical
    evidence) 32–3
    democratic performance 34–5
    initial conclusions 36–8

organizational performance 33–4
system performance 35–6
public governance forms, embodied assumptions
        32–3
public interest companies 27–8
public management
    accountability for performance 52
    comparison with public administration 13
    definitions 13–15
    governance concept 28–9
    implications of governance 16–17
    importance in public service improvement
        13–16
    link with performance 17–19
    networked governance concept 14–15
    new public management concept 13–14
    policy contexts 19–20
    see also pubic service management
public management research
    case study approach 20, 21
    methodologies 20–1
    qualitative approaches 20, 21
    quantitative approaches 20–1
public–private partnerships 27–8
public sector initiatives
    Balanced Scorecard 101, 102–3
    Best Value 101, 103–4
public sector performance
    accountability issues 46–7
    historical approach to performativity 47–8
    influence of new public management (NPM)
        47–8
    limitations of performativity 47–8
    negative consequences of measuring
        performance 47–8
    separation of policy, governance and
        management 46–7
    see also performativity
public sector performance measurement, use of
    Balanced Scorecards 70
public service change
    differing values and priorities 285–7
    empirical studies 258
    growing complexity and pervasiveness 258–9
    instrumentalism 260
    knowledge-for-action concept 259–62
    limitations of chaos and complexity theory
        259–62
    limitations of older theoretical conceptions 259
    limitations of the deductive approach 260–2
    managing change to improve services 274–6
    open systems theory 259
    re-engineering 259
    social movement theory 259

public service change planning framework 269–74
  applying the framework 274
  change management themes 271
  characteristics of complexity dictating
    management themes 271–2
  componental aspect of change 272
  contextually dependent nature of change 272
  culture building and communication 271
  differentially impacting change 272
  differentiated support 271
  flexible planning and coordination 271
  large-scale nature of change 271–2
  orchestration 269–71, 273
  orchestration imperatives 271–2
  sequential stages of the change process 272–3
  systemic change 272
public service change theoretical conception 262–9
  ambiguity in the change process 264–5
  characteristics of complexity with management
    implications 265–7
  complex change 263
  componental nature of complex change 265–7
  contextual dependence of complex change
    266, 267
  coping through orchestration 267–9
  differentially impacting effects of complex
    change 266, 267
  irony in the change process 264–5
  large-scale nature of complex change 265, 266
  limited manageability of complex and
    programmatic change 264–5
  programmatic change 263–4
  role of visionary (transformational) leadership
    268–9
  systemic nature of complex change 266, 267
  transmissional leadership 268–9
public service failure
  assumptions underlying measures of
    performance 239–41
  evidence for 237–9
  historical perspective 237–9
  impact of league tables 237
  inspection systems 238–9
  introduction of performance indicators 237–8
  legitimacy of service delivery methods 239,
    241–5
  measureability of service outcomes 243–4
  poor results 239–41, 243–5
  relative importance of results and legitimacy
    243–5
  structuration of the institutional environment
    244–5
  types of failure 239–45
  variations in performance of services 236

public service failure turnaround strategies 238, 245–9
  contingent effectiveness of various strategies
    238, 247–9
  evidence from the private sector 246–7
  improving low legitimacy 248–9
  improving poor performance results 247–8
  methodological problems in case studies 245–6
  reorganization 246–7, 248–9
  repositioning 246, 247–8
  retrenchment 246, 247–8
public service improvement
  conformance to a standard 10–11
  definitions 10–12
  differing values and priorities 285–7
  government initiatives 11–12
  range of approaches 10–11
  reasons for emphasis on 11
public service improvement framework 12–21
  governance and accountability 16–17
  management component 13–16
  performance metrics 17–19
  policy contexts 19–20
  research methodologies 20–1
public service management
  aims of public organizations 9
  contextualized application of management
    theory 9–10
  contingent application of management theory
    9–10
  customer service provision 7–8
  distinctive features 7–10
  factors affecting application of management
    theory 7–10
  governance issues 8
  influence of the external environment 8–9
  nature of areas of operation 8–9
  nature of markets for services 7–8
  political and policy context 8
  public value concept 9
  range of stakeholders 8–9
  see also public management
public service performance
  and mode of governance 28, 30–1, 32
  relationship with governance arrangements 27–8
public service reform movement 32–3
public services
  application of private sector management ideas
    6–7
  challenges to their size and influence 6–7
  changing expectations of the public 11
  contribution to well-being of society 5–6
  expenditure as percentage of GDP 5–7
  influence of neo-liberal ideologies 4–5, 6–7
  numbers of employees (direct and indirect) 5

perspectives on 'big government' 6–7
role in economic competitiveness of a nation 5–6
scale and range of functions 4–5
why they matter 4–5
see also New Public Management
public value 9, 70
innovation in the public sector 203, 208–9
public value scorecard 70

qualitative approaches, public management
research 20, 21
quality-adjusted life year (QALY)
definition and purpose 154–5
equivalence of CBA and CEA 157–9
studies on willingness to pay (WTP) 156–60
survey research value of a QALY 168–70
use in evaluation of health gain 154–5
use of VPF to model the value of a QALY 167–8
valuation studies 156–60
quantitative approaches
limitations of performativity 61–2
public management research 20–1
quasi-governmental partnerships 27–8

ratio scales 69
re-engineering 259
relative valuation approach to valuing safety 164–5
reorganization, turnaround strategy 246–7, 248–9
repositioning, turnaround strategy 246, 247–8
research agenda (governance and performance)
38–42
alternative causalities 38–41
examination of assumed causality 38–41
interpretivist approach 42
reformulating the research design 41–2
research methodologies
case study approach 20, 21
public management research 20–1
qualitative approaches 20, 21
quantitative approaches 20–1
results (outputs and outcomes), as measure of
performance 65–6
retrenchment, turnaround strategy 246, 247–8
revealed preference (implied value) approach to
valuing safety 164
routine control 76–7

sampling, use of geodemographic indicators in
the public sector 188
service innovations 199–200, 220
and organizational performance, empirical
research 228–31
social change, impact on public services 11
social movement theory 259

social services, performance classification scheme
(England) 251–2
society, public services contribution to well-being 5–6
stakeholders in public services 8–9
perception of innovations in public services 200
standards, conformance to 10–11
star ratings 69, 74
structuration of the institutional environment 244–5
symbolic aspect of performance measurement 68
system performance 29, 30
and public governance mode (empirical
evidence) 35–6
in hierarchical governance modes 31, 32
in market governance modes 31, 32
in network governance modes 31, 32

top-down innovation in the public sector 202

uncertainty in public service provision 80–1, 82–4

value of preventing one statistical fatality (VPF)
162–3
value of statistical life (VOSL) 162–3 *see also* value
of preventing one statistical fatality (VPF)
valuing health 154–60
combining safety and health valuation 167–70
future research agenda 167–70
learning from safety valuation 160
NICE evaluation methods 154–6
quality-adjusted life years (QALYs) 154–6
survey research value of a QALY 168–70
use of VPF to model the value of a QALY 167–8
valuing a QALY 156–60
willingness-to-pay (WTP) 155–6
willingness-to-pay (WTP) for a QALY 156–60
valuing safety 160–7
altruism and the WTP-based VPF 163
combining safety and health valuation 167–70
contingent valuation (expressed value)
approach 164
economic effects of safety improvements 163
empirical estimation of WTP-based values 164–5
figures applied in various countries 165
gross output (human capital) approach 161
relative valuation approach 164–5
reliability and validity concerns 165–7
revealed preference (implied value)
approach 164
value of preventing one statistical fatality (VPF)
162–3
value of statistical life (VOSL) 162–3
willingness-to-pay (WTP) approach 160–7
WTP-based VPF 162–3
VPF (value of preventing one statistical fatality) 162–3

weighting of different performance measures 71
WHO (World Health Organization)
   'attainment' index 125–6
   efficiency of health provision indicator
      125–6
WTP (willingness to pay), definition and purpose
   155–6
WTP (willingness to pay) for a QALY
   empirical studies 159–60
   equivalence of CBA and CEA 157–9
   health economics studies 156–60
   theoretical perspectives 157–9

WTP-based values of safety
   contingent valuation (expressed value)
      approach 164
   empirical estimation approaches 164–5
   figures applied in various countries 165
   relative valuation approach 164–5
   reliability and validity concerns 165–7
   revealed preference (implied value)
      approach 164
WTP-based VPF 162–3
   economic effects of safety improvements 163
   effects of altruism 163